a Salute to Maine

WHAT SOME PEOPLE THINK OF MAINE.

a Salute to Maine

by DAPHNE WINSLOW MERRILL

VANTAGE PRESS
New York / Washington / Atlanta
Los Angeles / Chicago

FIRST EDITION

Copyright © 1983 by Daphne Winslow Merrill

Published by Vantage Press, Inc.
516 West 34th Street, New York, New York 10001

Manufactured in the United States of America
ISBN: 533-05534-2

Library of Congress Catalog Card No.: 82-90633

table of contents

(in part)

foreword

When the state of Maine adopted as its motto the Latin word *Dirigo*, meaning "I lead," it was a portentous choice based on hope and faith. After more than 160 years of statehood, however, there remains no doubt of its applicability. "I lead" is still its motto; "I lead" is still its policy.

The purpose of this book is to present various instances of that leadership as evidenced in national and international recognition. The information offered has had to be limited. It has come from scrap books, newspapers, books, magazines, interviews, mailings, popular assumptions, and personal knowledge. Any inconsistencies are sincerely regretted. Its main objective is to put between covers, for posterity, some of the outstanding facts about Maine and its people.

Many of the people or their achievements have already been rightfully rewarded by being published in book form. Others included in these pages may never reach that particular distinction, but they have found fame. That is characteristic of Maine people.

Dean Emeritus Ernest Marriner once said, "Maine's best gift to the other states and to the foreign lands has always been her boys and girls, the men and women who carry to the ends of the earth the knack of adjusting to change, of getting along with what you've got."

This book recognizes some of the most outstanding of those people and lauds their ingenuity, their accomplishments, their ability to reach out far and wide. All eliminations of names or deeds have been made with sincere regrets, and with the hope and expectation that some future work will acknowledge their successes.

Primary consideration has been the "firsts," "lasts," and "onlys" as they concern the nation and/or the world, plus events, things, or people unique to Maine and great enough to have had an influential impact, or at least an interesting element.

acknowledgments

My personal gratitude to all who helped in any way in my research and the obtaining of pictures for this book, with special thanks to Elaine C. Barnes, who inspired the idea; to Margaret K. Nickerson, for the use of her extensive reference material; to State Representative Georgette Berube; to John Kelley, Lois Wagner, and Carol Phelps of the Auburn Public Library; and to Edith S. Dolan, Beatrice Harrington, and Albert A. Rowbotham for their unselfish and valuable assistance.

1

Geographical Features and Natural Resources

Clam diggers on the outer bed at Little River

The only galamander in the world, used to haul granite blocks. *(Photo courtesy of* The Courier-Gazette)

Ancient shell heaps at Damariscotta

Atlantic Puffin, found only on the Maine coast and farther north

"Poland Mineral Spring" springhouse

The geographical and physical features of Maine surpass those of any other state in the Union, and they have been an advantage in the growth and prominence of Maine.

Maine terminates the eastern end of a common 3,987-mile border between the United States and Canada, the longest un-patrolled border in the world. Its coastline, stretching 250 miles by road, if straightened to its tide line would be a distance of over 2,500 miles, more than half the width of the continental United States and nearly one half the length of the Atlantic coastline. If one were to add the Alaskan border line of 1,538 miles, the border presents an almost unbelievable continuous frontier. Only two Maine towns are contingent to the border: Calais and Eastport.

Maine is the only state among the forty-eight contiguous states in the nation which is bound by only one other state. It is considered the most easterly land in the Union, barring the argument occasionally raised that the Semisopochnoi Island, off Alaska, has the credit when one considers the "Date Line" as opposed to "180° Meridian."

At East Lubec stands West Quoddy Light, which is actually on the most easterly point of land along the Atlantic seaboard. This light is an interesting 125-foot structure painted barber-pole style with fifteen stripes, eight bands of red and seven alternate bands of white. It is one of the most photographed constructions in the state. Established in the 1800s, the fog bell had to be rung manually by the lighthouse keeper, who was paid overtime for this one duty.

Quoddy Head State Park is 400 acres of land four miles from Lubec. There, rock ledges rise fifty feet out of the ocean and grade upward to a height of more than 190 feet above the sea. The park adjoins the historic West Quoddy Light where tides rise twenty to twenty-eight feet.

Technically speaking, "Sail Rock," a 400-foot headland on Schoodic Point, a dark beak of stone, is the farthest point east in the nation.

Maine has been called the "place where they pry up the sun," because Mt. Katahdin, one of the three highest peaks east of the Rockies, at 5,267 feet, is the first spot in the nation touched by the sun, with the exception of five or six days out of the year when Mt. Cadillac, Mars Hill, or West Quoddy get sun one to three minutes ahead of Katahdin. On a clear day, more land and water may be seen from this mountain than from any other point of land in America, as there are no close mountain ranges to obstruct the view.

Mt. Megunticook, in Camden, and Isle au Haut are the other two Atlantic coast high spots.

Maine mountains were the first American ones seen by Europeans. The ranges were the Schoodic, the Camden Hills, and the Mt. Desert domes. The view from Mt. Battie, in Camden, is classified as the most fascinating one on the Atlantic coast. This ridge was used by the British in Penobscot Bay as a prime lookout point during the Revolutionary War.

Mt. Cadillac, which snatches the early sun from Katahdin for three days out of the year, is the highest point on the Eastern coast, at 1,530 feet. Its location is on Mt. Desert Island, and the road leading to its top has been termed the finest mountain road in the world, as well as the most spectacular and well designed. Henry Van Dyke classified it as the "Most Beautiful in the World."

Mt. Desert is an archipelago of eighteen islands, island-sheltered waterways, and lake-like bays, all within the unique combination of a 1,500-foot mountain, five large lakes, various ponds and streams, rugged ledges, sandy beaches, open water, and sheltered bays. A veritable paradise in wooded terrain, it is often referred to as "the most beautiful island on America's coasts."

Mt. Desert holds several records. The first Indian mission in North America, east of California, was established on the island. The first clash of arms between two nations involving North America occurred here. It is the location of the first national park east of the Mississippi, Acadia National Park, which consists of over 30,000 acres and has an area containing eighteen mountains and twenty-six lakes and ponds. Acadia is the only coastal national park in the East and the only park in the state that has been designated "national." It has the only fjord in North America, one which nearly bisects the island. Nearby, Bar Harbor's "Thunderhole" is especially impressive.

Acadia National Park was established on July 18, 1916, by President Wilson, as a national monument to the *Sieur de Monts*. On February 26, 1919, it became Lafayette National Park; and on January 19, 1929, it received its present name.

As might be expected, the park found favor with naturalist Louis Agassiz, ornithologist John James Audubon, and several artists. It has fifty miles of quiet carriage trails and has furnished some of the best pink granite in the world, a stone which takes an exceedingly fine finish.

At Cutler, on Mt. Desert Island, is the most powerful naval radio station in the world. An amateur radio enthusiast, Alessandro Fabbri, built it; and during World War I it was the first radio to fully intercept the secret code of the German high command.

Fabbri thereupon turned his apparatus over to the U. S. Navy; and in October, 1918, the Kaiser's radio message to President Wilson, seeking negotiation for an armistice, came in on one of the Cutler receivers. Servicemen were able to send word of their safety, to families, through this medium.

When the Naval Airship NC-4, constructed in 1919, became the first airplane to fly the Atlantic from west to east in May of that year, the Bar Harbor Naval Radio established two-way radio contact when the plane was 1,250 miles away, the longest plane-to-ground communication up to that time. It guided both American and English aircraft to safe landings. It was the first to test ship-to-shore radio telephones when the S.S. *George Washington* took President Wilson on his peace mission to Paris in the summer of that year. It was even capable of communicating with a Polaris missile submarine submerged in any ocean on the globe, the only such means in the world.

This valuable instrument has an antenna tower higher than the Eiffel Tower, and is the tallest such structure in the world. Its transmitting system has an output of 2,000,000 watts, twenty times the power of any major commercial radio station.

One unique incident occurred when it received a "Mayday" call from off the shore of Oregon. A Navy tug, which had lost its tow during a gale on Puget Sound, sent a signal that the Puget Sound Naval Radio, thirty miles away, failed to receive. The call for help was immediately relayed across the country, from Mt.

7

Desert, on its $300 console. This incident practically established a later verified fact that the coast of Maine is the best location in the country for receiving and transmitting radio messages.

Northward from Mt. Desert lies the most easterly county in the nation—Washington. Called the "Sunrise County of the U.S.A.," it has multiple natural supplies and lays claim to seven natural wonders. One of these is the greatest rise and fall of tides on any shore of America, tides which, in the Bay of Fundy, vary up to ten to twelve feet on the average. The water levels, which vary twenty-eight feet every six hours at certain times of the year, (the biggest in the world) require the tallest wharves in the world. The tremendous force moves 4 billion tons of water into Passamaquoddy Bay twice daily.

The county has colorful beaches: deep red sand at Perry, black volcanic sand at Bailey's Mistake, blazing white sand at Jonesport. It has also Old Sow Whirlpool, where tidal currents have created one of the largest and most dangerous whirlpools in the world. In addition, there are two thunder holes and a natural rock bridge where surf rolls into 110-foot-deep narrow gashes in the cliffs, creating a roar heard for miles.

At Herring Cove, a two-mile-long ribbon of sand and gravel separates the salt water on one side from good, fresh water on the other side. Nature has also endowed the county with the "reversing falls," caused by the tremendous tides, which create a unique tidal flow where jutting rocks loom in a 300-yard-wide gap.

The most easterly city in the contiguous United States is Eastport, just south of the halfway mark between the equator and the North Pole. The city is situated on Moose Island, in Washington County. For a while the land was claimed by Canada under a post-Revolutionary War treaty because British soldiers had taken over the site in the course of conflict. This claim was later negated.

At the start of the revolution, only one family lived in what is now Eastport; but in 1798, thirty families became incorporated there. Smuggling and adventure were the two greatest public concerns. The Embargo Act was blissfully ignored. Heavy fog, prevalent in the area, provided suitable coverage for such activities. Dark nights and the proximity of Canada contributed to the secretive acts of those in search of goods denied by the posted English officers.

Eastport has long shared with Lubec the title of "Sardine Capital of the World." Lubec is but three miles from Eastport by water. However, its coastal terrain is so irregular that to follow the coastline would be 100 miles.

The first sardines canned in America were produced in the Eastport-Lubec region by Julius Wolff of the Wolff and Blessing Company, New York, during 1874–1875. Maine has retained its sardine-capital-of-the-world title ever since. In fact, no other state cans sardines.

Within a period of four years, a new factory was added each year until by 1886 there were forty-five canneries; and by 1900, seventy sardine plants along the Maine coast were in operation, over half of them in the Eastport-Lubec area. In those days, more than 3,400,000 cases per year were packed, the cans having been made by soldering together three pieces of tin: top, bottom, and sides. However, by 1974, only sixteen canneries existed in Maine, the most prominent ones being in Lubec, Birch Harbor, Rockland, and Stonington. The familiar Underwood Canning Company is credited with having been the first to turn the word *cannister* into the abbreviated word *can*.

Only women are employed as packers, a fact explained by Richard Reed, once executive director of the Maine Sardine Council, because "the men can't stand it. They don't have the patience or the dexterity. It's a hard job and they've never been able to get men to do it."

For several years, Mrs. Rita Willey, of Rockland, was the world champion sardine packer, beginning in 1970 when the contest originated. She could snip heads and tails off herring and pack eighty-five cans, five fish to the can, in ten minutes. Neatness of packing and speed were the requisites. She lost in 1971 because of a "snipped" finger, but reclaimed her status the following year and has retained it through 1982. In 1981, Bertha Rideout, of the Stinson Canning Company, in Bath, was lauded for having packed an average of 2,500–3,000 cans a day for seventeen years.

Rockland is known not only for sardine packing, but as a temporary home for U.S. Navy craft until 1968, as it had the trial course for all government ships on the Eastern seaboard. The seven-mile course was run just out of Owls Head, passing east of Monroe and Sheep Islands. Each island had a so-called "spindle" at its northern end and this structure lined up with a similar one on a high point on the mainland. All of this is now only maritime history; but just a day or two before modern electronic devices were implemented, the course served for the then largest tanker afloat, the *World Glory*.

9

Rockland is also the "Lobster Capital of the World." It has an annual Lobster Day Festival, drawing crowds from many states. Begun in 1946, the event now has its own designated flag and has the largest cooking ovens known.

Martin Pring, as early as 1614, in a written account, referred to Maine lobster as "quite tasty" after he had consumed some during his voyage to the Maine coast. It is difficult to believe that later the now-famed lobster meat was used as bait for fishing for cod, and were sold for one cent each. By 1910, the price had risen to an astounding twenty-five cents per dozen. In 1981, they were listed at $3.79 per pound! Maine lobster has been labeled "the nation's yardstick for gastronomical excellence."

An interesting feature of lobsters is that fifty percent of them are left handed. Or should one say fifty percent are right handed? Maine waters have yielded freak lobsters with shells of such colors as sky-blue, bright red, pseudo-albino, calico, and partly colored. Regardless of shell color, all Maine lobsters are delectable to most people. In 1967, summer tourists to Maine consumed 8,000,000 of them. The leading lobster ports are Jonesport, Portland, Rockland, Southwest Harbor, and Stonington, in alphabetical order. Shipments go to almost all states, especially Hawaii and Alaska, and to many foreign countries.

Another crustacean, the scallop, is found mostly in Casco Bay, Penobscot Bay, and Georges Bank. Their peak year was in 1910, with a catch of 2,000,000 pounds.

Shrimp had a record year's yield in 1966: 3,775,000 pounds. There are four varieties, but the two most popular are *Pandalus borealis* and *Pandalus Montagui*.

Clams are in abundance all along the Maine coast. The soft-shelled ones are particularly valuable. They constitute the second largest industry in fish food, closely following lobster. Fred Snow, of Scarborough, was a pioneer in the commercial canning of clams. Founding his company in 1921, he truly became the "Clam Chowder King." He died in 1970. In 1965, the first "Clam Festival" was held, in Yarmouth, a three-day affair during July.

Although Maine shores abound in mussels, they have never become a major industry in the state. Canning them was prevalent in the late 1800s, but only the Europeans abroad or their kinfolks in the United States recognized them as a delicacy. The first shipment to New York, where they were served in plush hotels, consisted of twelve barrels, each containing three bushels of mussels. A second order came within a week's time. Later, during World

War II, a few canneries used them to replace the loss of deep sea fish, a loss fostered by the proximity of German submarines to our coasts. Since around the 1950s, pollution has all but eradicated the wholesale possibility of a return to the blue-black, iridescent-interior mussel.

Crabs, too, have their place in Maine industry. In 1980, Maine fishermen landed nearly 1.5 million pounds of crabs, having a dockside value of around $300,000. They are usually acquired from lobster traps rather than from direct crab fishing.

Oysters have come chiefly from the Salt Bay of the Damariscotta River, going back 2,000 years in time. Their record size and quantity have diminished during the past 300 years; but the Oyster Heaps, somtimes called "middens," laid claim to oyster popularity even before the white man came to these shores. They are presumably the largest pre-historic Indian "leavings," dating back possibly over 2,000 years and innumerable shore dinners.

The deposits of shells, covering more than 1,000,000 cubic feet, were unearthed by excavation covering three and a half acres of land in addition to piles on private property. They lie in three main layers, some thirty feet deep. Found within the heaps have been shells of such size as one foot to twenty inches long. According to archeologists, this growth was possible many years ago because of Salt Bay on the river; but it has been more than 350 years since oysters of any quantity have been found there.

A layer of soil lies between the bottom and second layer, about six inches thick and mixed with the shells and animal bones. The top layer is now earth, which bears good-sized trees beneath which have been found artifacts, stone fireplaces, and human skeletons. There is a possibility that the prehistoric Red Paint People once dwelt nearby.

It is known that the top layer deposit was made by Wabanaki Indians who came to the region each summer to catch and smoke fish for winter use, and who always enjoyed an annual oyster orgy.

In addition to its wealth of shellfish, Maine leads the nation and the world in quality of its salmon. The first Federal Fish Hatchery was in Bucksport, in 1872, to propagate the Atlantic salmon. Charles Grandison Atkins was the original manager. The hatchery was later permanently established at East Orland.

The Bangor salmon pool, opposite Grotto Cascade Park, with its forty-five foot waterfall, is world famous for its output. Maine is the only state having natural migration of Atlantic salmon in its rivers, according to naturalist Gene Letourneau. He adds that

Edward "Ned" Blakely of Darien, Connecticut, on August 1, 1907, took the second oldest world's record with a Sebago Lake land-locked salmon, twenty-two and a half pounds, one yard long, and fifteen inches around. It was the largest fish ever caught by rod and reel. There is an unconfirmed report that in 1902, Eben Welts of Caribou and Belgrade took a thirty-eight inch long, twenty-three pound landlocked salmon from Square Lake, Maine.

In 1949, Mrs. Earl Small, of Waterville, took a world-record white perch of four pounds, twelve ounces, from Messalonskee Lake. And another world record went to Merton Wyman, of Belgrade, who took a blueback trout of four pounds, four ounces, from Basin Pond, Manchester, in 1973.

There is a special species of trout, the Sunapee, which dwells in Maine's Flood's Pond, the present stronghold of this golden trout. This pond is the only known body of water in North America with a positively pure population of the species. Similar in ways to the togue, the Sunapee spawn on rocky, windswept shores amid small-to-medium-size rocks, usually during their fourth year. They move about in groups and take no parental care of their eggs nor their young. In 1968, a study noted that all Sunapee in Flood's Pond which were over one year old were males; and no Sunapee older than six was in evidence. Sizes range from nine to eighteen inches in length. In the togue family, twenty-one inches is frequent, but such a size would be quite unlikely for a Sunapee.

In 1970, an experiment was begun by stocking other lakes in Maine with the Sunapee. Since their home in Flood's Pond is relatively free from all pollution, as it is the water supply reservoir for Bangor, the experiment was to determine whether or not the fish can live in less pure water; and, in addition, if they can live in water which contains lake trout, which do not exist in Flood's Pond.

Small-mouth bass, found in the Belgrade Region, are nationally famous in both sizes and quantity; and striped bass, found along the coastal areas, are increasing in popularity.

It is a matter of record that the best codfish in the world come from Isles of Shoals, a three-mile group of seven islands, four of which are in Maine territory. Until the middle 1800s, cod were sold as "Isles of Shoals dun fish." The islanders were considered the most rude and uncivilized beings in New England, barring the Indians. They were called "Algerienes" and gave the islands a bad and fearsome reputation.

Portland was once the largest swordfish port on the Atlantic coast. Shad and sturgeon are usually plentiful in the Kennebec River. Tuna are a sportsmen's delight, and a yearly contest is held at Bailey Island for the largest one caught on specific days. Most of the tuna are sent to Japan for consumption and canning.

Alewives, going up Maine's streams for spawning, provide an interesting spectacle. The Ramsdall Packing Company of Rockland was the first to use them in steam canning, in 1942. Damariscotta was the first to use a pickling method, in 1943. Almost yearly there is a big run of alewives at the Warren Falls.

A notable geographical area in Maine is Baxter State Park, which ranks as the most wild, spectacular spot in the United States. It is a 201,000-acre tract, left to the state by ex-Governor Percival Baxter, who ranks as the largest donor of park lands in the nation. These acres of wilderness were specified to "remain forever wild."

Baxter, twice elected Governor (1921 and 1925), showed his appreciation by purchasing, in 1930, Mt. Katahdin, a 6,690-acre tract, and giving it to the state. Within the next thirty-two years, he gave twenty additional pieces of land, all contiguous. He died in June, 1969, leaving over $5,000,000 from which the interest was to be used to operate and protect Baxter State Park, and to acquire additional land.

The park includes Mt. Katahdin, where the gods met for council, according to Indian legend. The idea is enhanced by the fact that there is a natural amphitheater from Chimney Pond, an ideal auditorium. It is the finest "glacial cirque" in the United States, a natural amphitheater carved from rock by glaciers.

Can any state equal the variety of mineral finds in Maine? It has, according to one authority, two geological belts of economic importance from the metal and mineral viewpoints. The southern belt, geologically volcanic, runs along the eastern coast from Pennsylvania Bay to the New Brunswick border and into Canada. Included in this area, Maine has Blue Hill, Pembroke, Castine, Gardner Lake, Franklin and Sullivan townships in Washington County, and the area around Pierce Pond in Hancock County. Near Rumford have been found gold, tungsten, titanium, tantalum, cesium, scandium, and other rare metals, as well as tin, asbestos, and nickel and flourine ores.

In the fall of 1980, Michael Gramby announced the previous existence of a paleo-Indian habitation site in western Maine that archeologists believe to be thousands of years old. This site is unique because it is the highest altitude paleo-Indian site known in the eastern part of the United States. The Vail site, named for

Francis Vail, of East Stoneham, known for his extraordinary mineral collection, is at Aziscohos Lake.

This collection now numbers over 1,500 artifacts such as knives, spear points, wedge-like chisels, stone drills, side scrapers, end scrapers, and other hunting equipment obtained by digging only inches below the sandy bottom of the lake. The fact that thousands of tools have been found within the space of only one acre, yet tracings extend twenty miles north of the site, suggests that the primitive people returned many times to the one spot, hunting at the only place where migratory animals could easily cross the adjoining Magalloway River, which was later dammed to form Aziscohos Lake.

Washington County has several lead-silver prospects in Lubec and Gouldsboro. Alexander Township has produced nickel. Several parts of the county have yielded molybdenum, especially at Catherine Mountain, in the center of the county.

The northern volcanic belt, where base metal occurrence has been reported and prospected, includes the southwestern section from Moosehead Lake to Northern New Hampshire. Copper-zinc prospects exist in Chase Stream Township in northern Somerset County, and metals can be found in northern Oxford and Franklin Counties. There are said to be 30,000,000 tons of high-grade copper-zinc under forest lands near Bald Mountain, west of Ashland.

Asbestos has been located in several places in a fifty-mile-long serpentine belt running from the Woburn, Quebec, area to central Piscataquis County.

In the metamorphic belt in Knox and Lincoln Counties exist possible metallic prospects. One known deposit is that of copper and zinc pods which lie close to nickel deposits at Crawford Pond, in Union.

Currently, there are 184 pegmatite mines and prospects, primarily in seven counties and the lower two-thirds of the state. An additional one of importance in size lies halfway up Penobscot County.

Although Oxford County appears to be the most productive in the field of minerals, it has been acknowledged that some form of the element exists in every Maine county.

Most varieties of the metals and minerals lie beneath the soil, but it is claimed that the first gold ever found in the United States was in the early 1800s at the East Branch of Swift River, in Byron, Oxford County. Small nuggets and flakes of the metal were lying in the narrow, shallow, rocky-bottom mountain stream. This find preceded the California Gold Rush era.

Swift River lies near a much-traveled route and the place still holds fascination for placer mining. Some individuals have benefited from living on the location, becoming hermits, and taking up gold placing as a vocation; but no one has ever been known to amass much wealth from the site as no mother lode is presumed to exist there. The nuggets and flakes most probably were left by the receding glacier of the Pleistocene Epoch.

Perley A. Whitney, a jeweler of Lewiston, did accumulate $12,000 worth of the precious metal in 1906, which in those days was indeed a fortune. Others are reported to have taken from seventy-five cents in a six-week period up to a possible $6,000 in a four-year period of constant mining. Whitney had been fortunate to find a coarse mica schist with gold all through the ledge, and he prospected every stream within a two-mile radius of his home. He had a gold nugget as a stone in a ring and had some coins made.

In 1875, a vein of gold and silver ran through George Oxton's farm in West Camden, and it is alleged that a woman found a sixty-five dollar nugget there sometime between 1950 and 1970.

The gold-panning team of Bilodeau and Vachon named these streams and places as possibilities for finding gold:

> East Branch of Swift River—Byron
> Sandy River—Madrid to New Sharon
> South Branch of Penobscot River—Sandy Bay
> Bald Mountain
> Prentiss
> Gold Brook—Bowman
> Chain of Ponds
> Kibby—Chase Stream tract and T5, R6
> Appleton
> Nile Brook—Dallas
> Rangeley
> Kibby Stream—Kibby
> St. Croix River—Baileyville
> Black Mountain Brook—Rumford

Most of the gold found in Maine came from placer deposits in stream beds. Gold panning is generally allowed on streams that cross state-owned land, but other prospecting or mining on state property requires prior authorization. The team suggests that the best time for panning is in early spring or in early or late winter.

Iron is another mineral beneath the state's surface. The Katahdin Iron Works, a seventeen-acre park nearly hidden by wild growth now, is considered today the most pleasant iron works in the world to visit. Iron was first produced there in 1843. Mining and refining processes ended there in 1890, but more than 7,000 people annually visit the restored stone and brick blast furnace and the huge beehive kiln which once processed hardwood into charcoal to provide heat for the smelting process. Once there were fifteen to twenty charcoal kilns on the lot.

Except for the scar of an old open pit mine, a gash caused by stripping away topsoil and moving thousands of tons of ore, the surrounding forest lands have chiefly returned to their original beauty. The rusty red scar has hardly a blade of grass, however; and only an occasional bush is visible.

Iron was first produced at Katahdin from 1842–43, when 200 men worked to produce 2,000 tons of iron per year. The element came from brown, red, and yellow ore found in layers ten feet deep on Mt. Katahdin. The production from 1843–56 was excellent. Then the rebuilding of the furnace closed the works until sometime between 1874–75. A fire destroyed the plant in 1883; it was rebuilt in 1885, and closed for good in 1890. At the height of production, there were 500 inhabitants in Katahdin. In 1971, a lone survivor and his two dogs lived in one of the houses erected in boom days.

The legendary "mayor" of the Katahdin Iron Works, a Mrs. Sara Green, was brought to live there at the age of six and stayed until her death at eighty-two, in 1969. Her obituary included this comment:

> She was a rural mail carrier, tourist camp operator, lumber camp boss, pulp cutter, and one-woman laundry.

She lived alone at the works for several years, serving as its caretaker.

A higher grade and more easily worked iron ore has been discovered in the western part of the country, so the Katahdin Works will undoubtedly never reopen for production.

Aroostook County has one of the largest proven reserves of low-grade manganese-iron ore in the nation. This grade is valuable in the production of steel.

Nickel has been found in Alexander Township and molybdenum lies in several parts of Washington County and at Cooper Township.

In the early 1970s, the International Paper Company planned to continue exploration of a copper prospect on their lands near Square Lake, in northern Maine.

Slate was discovered in Maine in 1826 by Moses Greenleaf, and a monument to him stands in Williamsburg. The best quarries were in Monson, Blanchard, Brownville, and all of Piscatquis County. At the 1876 Centennial Exposition, Brownville slate won the prize for the best roofing slate in the country. It has been used for roofs in Boston, New York, Washington, South Africa, and China, among other places.

Two Welsh immigrants, Robert Evans and Owen Morris, went up the Kennebec River in the 1830s and unearthed what is now Crocker Quarry. They worked quarries 225 to over 300 feet deep, and the water in the bottom is like a mirror. One gave forth a pea-green water overflow.

Morris went back home to get money, but never returned. However, between 1840 and 1860, many skilled Welsh workers were employed in Brownville. The last attempt to quarry there was in 1952. The quarries are now called "inverted monuments," and only slate piles are visible in the state.

The four outstanding quarries were Merrill, 1846 (Merrill's wife was related to Moses Greenleaf); Highland, 1866; Crocker, 1843; and Barnard and Hughes, 1952.

A natural chasm of slate deposits, with one wall towering 500 feet above the river bed, is Gulf Hagas, the "Grand Canyon of Maine," north of Brownville, in deep wilderness. There are rapids, falls, stone arches, huge bowls, and leaping falls. The major falls are Stair, Buttermilk, and Billings. Trout live in the various pools and rapids between the towering slate walls. An eleven-mile hike keeps the gulf isolated and in its natural state. When the Katahdin Iron Works were in production, there was easier access to the gulf because of various forest paths.

Maine has probably the world's largest storehouse of beryllium, which is used in copper and aluminum alloy and for windows of X-ray tubes. Furthermore, it is quite possible that Maine holds second place for lithium, the lightest of the metals.

Beds of clay are widespread over the state and are used in brick making, manufacturing curtain shades, linoleum, canoes, and other products, many of which are exported world-wide.

17

The first freshwater pearls found in this country were those discovered in Crooked River, Waterford.

Feldspar and quartz constitute a big part of the mineral sources in Maine. Feldspar is found primarily in the Paris-Newry region and has given Maine recognition as having first place in its production: twenty-five percent of all that is used in the United States. It is a substance of importance in porcelain, dishes, and other ceramic products.

Various semi-precious gems are plentiful, particularly in the Paris area, where veins of pegmatite abound. Professor Addison E. Verrill, born in Greenwood, Maine, and later moved to Norway, was the first famous naturalist and geologist to discover Maine's wealth of gem mines. More than 300 varieties of the world's minerals have been identified as existing in Oxford County alone. The list includes amethyst, aquamarine, beryl, chrysoberyl, garnet, jade, and opal. This bonanza was found at Mt. Mica, Paris, in 1820, the year that Maine became a state. The biggest beryl crystal from Mt. Mica weighed fifteen pounds, the largest single mass of gem-quality aquamarine in North America. It is called the Harvey Crystal.

At Bumpus Mine, in Albany, the largest blue-green beryl in the world was extracted. It was eighteen feet long and forty-two inches in diameter. This mine has been said to have yielded over 100 tons of beryl.

According to newsprint, a Maine photographer has a landscape lens an inch and a half in diameter cut from a yellow quartz crystal, a natural color-screen, the only such lens in the world.

Not too long ago, "stone walls" in the Paris region were built entirely of rose quartz, so plentiful was the mineral.

In 1975, at Rangeley, the Industrial Garnet Extractors were taking 42,000 tons a year from the richest garnet discovery in the United States.

During the summer of 1972, possibly the most important, and largest single discovery of its kind in North America since the 1880s find in California, was that of a trove of tourmaline gemstones worth hundreds of thousands of dollars. They were located in the abandoned Nevel Pit feldspar mine on 2,420-foot-high Plumbago Mountain, in Newry. The estimated value of stone extracted up to March 1973 from this pit reached $1,000,000; and the venture was hailed as the most significant find of this century.

The tourmalines were raspberry red, grass green, blue, brown, black, and colorless. Some were several inches long. The

discovery was made by Dale Swett, of Rumford, who stumbled upon the treasure while exploring the old Dunton (Nevel) Pit. It was once quarried in the 1920s by the General Electric Company, for pollucite, on land owned by the International Paper Company.

Three pockets of the gems were located on a Monday, and a fourth on the next day. It took two weeks to empty the fourth pocket, which gave about a ton of the red-pink-green gem called "watermelon." One rare green crystal had twenty-two faces on its pointed end. The Plumbago Mining Company may have hit a six-figure profit from that one strike.

Swett and two associates formed the Plumbago Mining Company to exploit the tourmaline find; and then Frank Perham, considered a foremost gem authority, took over the task of the actual mining. The Winthrop Mineral and Gem Shop, one of the largest such shops in Maine, was selected as sole distributor. Priscilla Stearns Bryant Chavarie managed this shop for over twenty-five years. Before the delivery, the mined stones were placed in a Rumford bank vault and guards were stationed at the mine entrance.

The largest, flawless, blue-green tourmaline in the world came from a pocket in Maine.

Perham's Maine Mineral Store at Trap Corner, West Paris, started its ever-growing prominence in the field of Maine gems with these minerals; feldspar, rose quartz, tourmaline, beryl and mica. The two latter are in big demand for atomic research and radar equipment.

Perham's store, well over fifty years old, attracts visitors from the entire continent and even from abroad. Stanley I. Perham died around 1973, but his wife and daughter have continued the business. The shop is open every day except Thanksgiving and Christmas.

The surrounding area is a mecca for rockhounds. There are six quarries in the region, open to the public for exploration, within a radius of twelve miles from the store. Of these, Perham owns five: Harvard (rare purple apatite), Waisanen (rare Bertrandite and Herderite), Whispering Pines (rose quartz), Nubble (wide assortment of minerals of the pegmatite type), and Eillie Heikkinen (fluorescent minerals in unique arrangement).

In the production of granite, Maine has led all states. Most of it was at first shipped direct from the quarries, thus reducing the cost of transportation. Legend has it that the first man to quarry granite, in 1829, was named Tuck. He sent it from Vin-

alhaven to Fox Island; and from there to Massachusetts, to be used for prison walls. By 1890, Maine was first among the states in granite production, one Vinalhaven firm employing 1,500 men at times.

Granite was once quarried from York to Calais, all along the coast. It centered mostly around Penobscot Bay, as did the lime deposits. Jay quarries have yielded a considerably high amount for Maine buildings and for more than twenty constructions throughout the rest of the nation; and Hallowell had some of the whitest and finest-grain granite in the country. Whereas the lime lay primarily deep inland, the granite was found chiefly on islands.

Granite comes in a wide variety of colors, grains, and textures. Its colors range from light gray to black, light pink to dark red, buff, and pale lavender. Some of the gray and black shades even have a greenish tinge. Black was commonly used for more expensive work because it took a fine polish, split well, came in varied textures, and was coarse enough for mass structures, yet fine enough for monuments and statues.

Joseph R. Bodwell, 1818–1887, established a granite quarry on Vinalhaven with Moses Webster, a quarry which was cited as the leading granite firm in the United States for two decades. It contained stone of every color and texture except the true pink.

The first order for Vinalhaven granite was for a Cincinnati post office. The second was for piers for the Brooklyn Bridge.

A Buffalo post office is one of the best-known structures of Maine granite because of the stone eagles adorning it. According to legend, when one of the workmen was asked how he or anyone could carve such a lovely ornament, he replied, "Well, you just carve away everything that isn't an eagle."

The last stone quarried on Vinalhaven was in 1939, and there was no further sale of granite from the island until 1964 when loose stone was purchased from the Old Sands Quarry. In a park on the island of Vinalhaven there rests today the only galamander in the world.

Daggett, or Big Rock, near Phillips, is the largest mass of porphytitic granite in the East. It is assumed that it was a part of Saddleback Mountain until the Pleistocene Epoch. This world-record glacial boulder is approximately 100 feet long, fifty-five feet wide, thirty-one feet high, and weighs about 8,000 tons. No one knows how much more of the mammoth rock lies underground.

The biggest carving assignment for Maine granite was the

Corinthian columns and the eight races of men depicted on the New York Customs House, which, incidentally, had Maine lime (from Rockland and Rockport) for mortar.

The largest object ever cut from a single piece of granite in the United States was at Crotch Island, off Stonington. The stone was used for the base and pedestal for a fountain commissioned by John D. Rockefeller, in 1913, to be placed in Tarrytown, New York. At last reports, the fountain was still in operation. It was an exact copy of the one at the Royal Palace in Florence, Italy. Maine had the only quarry with adequate equipment and native inborn ingenuity to produce it. A 225-ton slab of flawless Maine granite was required, and the company had to make its own lifting device for the 450,000-pound raw stone slab. The quarry owner, John L. Goss, accomplished the deed. Statues surmounting the granite basin are of Italian Carrara marble.

One of the most recent uses of Maine granite has been for the John F. Kennedy gravesite in Arlington Cemetery. The 1,500 stones from the Deer Isle Granite Corporation weighed over 2,000,000 pounds. This company was selected after examination of granite quarries throughout the United States. The rock used is "Sherwood Pink," mined at the Deer Isle-Crotch Island location, in Penobscot Bay. Its type is called biotite, and people from all walks of life who visit the Kennedy shrine stand on Maine granite.

The largest granite shaft ever quarried up to 1977 and retained in one piece was sixty-feet long and weighed 185 tons. It was shipped on August 16, 1879, to be made into the General Wool Monument in Troy, New York.

It is true that an even larger shaft was produced on August 20, 1899, and it became world famous. It was sixty-three feet long and weighed 310 tons. It was intended to form eight immense, soaring columns for the Cathedral of St. John the Divine in New York City, twice the height of those of the Greek Parthenon. However, although placed on the largest lathe in the world, it could not sustain the enormous weight and the columns each had to be produced in two sections for shipment.

Granite on Somes Sound, the fjord which nearly bisects Mt. Desert Island, has some of the best pink color in the world. The rich, creamy stone takes a spendid high polish. Stone workers were lured from Scotland, Italy, and Sweden, most of them experts in handling this type of stone. Some of this granite is in the Cathedral of St. John the Divine and is also in the 1952 monument called "Four Freedoms," erected in Washington, D.C.

People from all over the world walk in shrines with reverence, listen to taps with heavy heart, or stand in awe before magnificent structures, while beneath their feet or within their sight lies salt-sprayed granite from Maine.

Another resource for bountiful industry in Maine is its limestone. One of the Rockland quarries was the deepest in the world, at 385 feet, when President Taft and his wife viewed it on a visit to the city. At one time, forty-two syndicated kilns existed in Rockland, in addition to some independent ones.

Reputedly, in 1835 the Rockland kilns burned 750,000 casks of lime; and from April, 1851, to April, 1853, over 2,000,000. More than 500 vessels brought firewood for the kilns and carried the finished product to market. The city could supply all the lime the world could use for centuries to come. Progress, in the form of cement, proved to be a cheaper substance, and the lime industry was practically eliminated.

At the height of its popularity, Rockland lime was freighted by two-masted schooners to nearly all the eastern seaboard ports. Oxen and horses hauled heavy carts which rumbled over the dust and cobblestone roads from quarries to kilns, and thence to docks. Around 1890, the Rockland-Rockport Lime Company was established, and a railroad line was built to transport the product from quarry to kiln to dock.

In time, the industry turned to wholesale cement, and the company is now known as the Martin-Marietta Cement Eastern Division, a highly-respected concern in the United States.

The worm industry of Maine, begun in the early 1930s, has progressed so much that Wiscasset is now named "Maine Worm Center of the World." From 1930 to 1950, the Boston, South Portland, and Portland flats were depleted. In 1964, the Maine industry at Wiscasset topped the 1,000,000 mark, making the non-glamorous business fourth in the state. In 1953, there were 400 licensed worm diggers; in 1981, there were 1,100.

The worms come chiefly from the Sheepscot River and flats and are technically known as blood worms (*Glycera dibranchiata*) and sand worms (*Nereis viren sars*), but, oddly, both types never show up on the same tide. An average digger can earn $6,000 to $8,000 a year. Young, fast diggers are known to reach the $15,000 income. Diggers stand in hip boots in the tidal mudflats, flailing the mud with a worm hoe, digging with one hand and snatching up the worms with the other. There are thirteen low tides a week, and a digger usually makes use of at least ten of them in the summer and five in the winter and spring, when the market is lower. A low tide occurring at night requires the worker to wear a flash light attached to his cap or hat.

Pound for pound, Maine worms are the state's highest priced marine product, bringing four to five times as much per pound as does lobster. The worms inhabit only about five percent of the flats, a fact that prompted one digger to call them "pig headed."

Nova Scotia, Ellsworth, and Jonesport were pressing for recognition in the worm field in the 1970s.

Blueberries grow abundantly in Maine, the best ones in the world growing in Washington County. Depending upon the yearly crop and the source of information, seventy-five percent to ninety-five percent of the nation's blueberries come from "Down East." It is thought that when white men came to the New England shores, the Indians sold them dried wild berries in huge wicker baskets, and the white men grew fond of the fruit. Both high and low bush berries are bountiful in the county, the low bush ones providing more than one fourth of the nation's supply.

Maine blueberries have been processed since the Civil War. In 1866, they were harvested by a Mr. Wyman in Cherryfield, and canned for food for the Union Army. Taken to the factories by horse and wagon, they were cooked in large, open, cast-iron kettles. Then the cans were filled and capped by hand. The process provided year-round work as the cans were made during the off season for picking berries. There is a legend that the Declaration of Independence was signed with a formula consisting of Maine blueberries.

As early as 1928, packers sold over half a million pounds of these berries, with a fluctuation in 1941 to only 300,000 pounds because of the country's political and economic situation. However, in 1965 over 17,500 tons were sold from Washington County alone; and a 1975 report listed the previous five-year average crop at 17,000,000 to 18,000,000 pounds. In 1972, of the 16,928,282 pounds, eighty-one percent went to markets, advertised as "fresh" frozen fruit. In 1976, the harvest was 25 million pounds, and the previous year's price of twenty-six-and-a-half cents per pound was raised to thirty-one cents.

The uses of blueberries have gradually increased. In addition to early uses and the frozen product, they are now canned in sugar syrup or in water; dry-packed and frozen for use in packaged cake, muffin, and pie mixes; made into a syrup from the juice; made into preserves; used as flavor for ice cream; and the

23

latest development is blueberry wine. Blueberry pie is a delicacy everyone should experience.

J. Hollis Wyman, of Millbridge, is the state's "Blueberry King" who supplies Pillsbury, Betty Crocker, Duncan Hines, and General Foods from his 20,000 acres of berry fields.

The first Blueberry Festival was held in Union in 1960. That was a long distance from Washington County where the Maine blueberry got its start, but the region around Union is rich in blueberry growth as is the nearby coastline.

A. S. Wells and Son, of Wilton, Maine, is the only known company in the world to can fresh dandelions commercially. The brand name is "Belle of Maine." The business opened in North Anson in 1898; was discontinued in 1906; then moved to Wilton in 1929 to resume production. It has remained almost exclusively a family concern with a hired crew, and has shipped to nearly every state.

At first, one cent a pound was paid for wild dandelions in the Rangeley Region; but a shortage of diggers during World War II forced the company to cultivate the greens, often five crops per season. Three ounces of seed will produce a crop of over eight tons! The growing field in Wilton is three to five acres. Only three weeks are needed for a re-growth after a cutting.

An average of 1,500 pounds can be canned per day. One normal season will provide, canned and sold, over 60,000 cans of Maine dandelions. Eighty percent of these are distributed through eight Maine wholesale houses. The other twenty percent goes to S. S. Pierce of Boston and other commercial houses. Directions for cooking the greens Maine-style are printed on the labels of cans containing spring's "gourmet's delight."

When the first settlers brought the dandelion seed to our shores, it was done for medicinal concern, as the greens were considered a spring tonic as well as being useful in the treatment of "kidney disorders, female complaints, dropsy, fever, constipation, and diabetes."

Popular dandelion wine is not produced nor sold commercially.

Another Maine spring wildgrowth is fiddleheads, first canned by the Wells Company in Wilton and first sold fresh by Donald and Avis Briggs, of Oakfield. The Briggs family harvested the fern tops throughout northern New England each spring. It is claimed that Maine people were the first to eat this tender fern tip, a species that is harvested with only a few days between cuttings. The Wells Company, however, produces the only canned fiddleheads in the world. In 1977, the company added beet greens at their cannery.

A more recently developed industry available from Maine's natural resources is that of skiing facilities. Sugarloaf Ski Slopes provide not only some of the finest skiing conditions in the country, but also have the most dependable snow conditions in the entire East. Maine ranks among the top four states for skiing facilities in general and has some of the best slopes and advantages for the sport in this country.

The slope was first developed in 1955 or 1956 by Amos Winter, of Kingfield, 1901–1981. He was a close friend of F. O. Stanley, the auto magnate.

Another God-given resource peculiar to Maine, one which has resulted in being a commercial business, is the unique Desert of Maine, once known only as the Old Sand Farm. Originally farmed by the William Tuttle family, which moved there in 1797, it now comprises a scientific phenomenon in Freeport. The desert covers hundreds of acres with the finest sand known to man, yet it is completely surrounded by forest growth and green farmland. There are other such accumulations of sand, inland as well as along the coast, but none as large and none which were once tilled with ten to twelve inches of good top soil. It is a small Sahara, surrounded by an ocean and several rivers and ponds.

The sands came from a quirk of winds late in the nineteenth century, and are in over 100 shades and tints, noticeable to the naked eye only when wet. Glints of mica indicate the possibility of the area's having once been a lake bed formed by a glacial deposits. Tops of trees once seventy feet high now seem like low bushes, yet oddly enough still live. An apple tree, of which only two feet remained above ground, bloomed and bore fruit one season.

One reason given for the loss of sod to keep the sand base intact is the possibility of root damage created by grazing sheep. Another reason has been suggested that a destructive fire damaged all roots. No one knows the real answer.

Farther down the coast, an additional sand attraction unique to Maine is Old Orchard Beach, an eight-mile stretch of white sand which forms a beach 400–700 feet wide, the longest and smoothest stretch of sandy beach on the entire Atlantic coast. Its hard-packed sand has been used as a runway for airplanes taking off for Europe. The *Pride of Detroit* was the first transatlantic take-off from Old Orchard Beach, on August 24, 1927. From 1919 to 1938 the public was able to buy tickets for "Thrilling Airplane Rides" at the beach, where the first merry-go-round in the nation was licensed in 1892.

There are several bogs and swamps within the state. The Orono Bog has been designated as a national landmark. But the most significant bog in the entire United States is in Aroostook County. It is an alkaline peat land bog, named Crystal Bog. Its appearance is one of a sea of grass, but it holds a treasure of rarities such as the white fringed orchid and sundews. There are an estimated 300,000 to 700,000 acres of peat bogs in the state, resulting in at least some peat in all sixteen counties, a good reserve for future excavation.

The Oyster River Bog, in Knox County, has around 6,000 acres, lying in parts of four towns. It is a gift from the last Ice Age, about 10,000 years ago. In 1770, Isaiah Tolman, from Massachusetts, took 500 acres of the bog; and that section has remained in the Tolman family for over 200 years. One of the Tolman girls married Samuel Ezra Kellogg, and in their kitchen were toasted the first cornflakes in America. Subsequently, they moved to Battle Creek, Michigan, and established the now well-known Kellogg Products.

Maine is also blessed with Poland Spring water, which was turned into an industry by Hiram Ricker in 1858. It has produced water for sale all over the world for more than 100 years, water which seeps out of granite seams at the spring, between six and fifteen gallons per minute. It is gravity fed through silver-lined pipes to a nearby plant where it is bottled by automatic machinery.

Various cures have been claimed by drinking Poland Spring water since it was first discovered in the 1800s. By 1844, for example, it was believed to have some "medicinal value." Ricker, proprietor of the Poland Spring House, shipped the water to every sizable city in the world by 1897. However, between World War I and World War II, the government prohibited bottled water from being shipped and people got out of the habit of using it. Since 1960, sales have made a steady comeback; and in 1974 it was selling for $1.50 a quart in Las Vegas, where every hotel on the famous "strip" served it. At that time, the cost was seventy-nine cents a gallon in Maine stores.

The Poland Spring Complex has five buildings plus the mineral spring house, where water gushes forth. The closest competitor to this spring water has been that of the French firm of

Perrier Waters, internationally known as bottlers of Vichy and Perrier waters. When the Perrier firm bought the Poland Spring Corporation in 1973, it was the first purchase of that nature in the United States. In 1980, with sales exceeding $5,000,000 the previous year, a new multi-million dollar bottling plant was built to quadruple production. There is currently a possible competitor in the wings—the Coca-Cola Company, which is trying out its "Kristal" in England.

Far to the south end of the state, in Berwick, was the delightful spring water that the judge received in John Greenleaf Whittier's "Maud Muller."

The sun has played an important role in Maine. The first observation of the sun taken in North America was in Islesboro, October 27, 1780, by the Reverend Samuel Williams, professor of mathematics at Harvard College. A small granite marker indicates the exact spot in a field above "The Narrow," land owned by one of the first settlers on the island over 200 years ago.

On August 31, 1932, there was a total solar eclipse at 3:28 P.M. EST. The campus of Fryeburg Academy, in Fryeburg, and the adjoining town of Lovell were chosen as the best locations in the nation from which to observe this phenomenon. Several cameras of professionals were used, including three motion picture company ones. These varied from the forty-foot one for large scale coronal photographs down to a fourteen-inch focus movie camera. Fifteen were used by the staff of the Michigan Eclipse Expedition.

Much powerfully-equipped material was set up in other locations, but most of it met with failure because of cloudy conditions. However, Fryeburg had ideal weather, even to the extent that stars were visible during the eclipse, especially Jupiter, near the sun. Scientists from the United States and from all over the world gathered for this ninety-nine second "black out." It allowed a sufficient period of darkness for the cows to lie down, birds to cease their chatter, and hens to enter their roost houses.

Maine experienced another eclipse on July 20, 1963. It was total in Maine and Alaska only. For that event, 100,000 people came to Maine to cover a fifty-mile strip from the Canadian border to the sea at Bar Harbor. A third eclipse during March, 1970, was the top news story for the year in many surveys, as a series of experiments taken at that time proved beyond doubt that maple tree sap slowed enough drips per minute to cost the New England maple sugar industry $7,800.

27

The next total sun eclipses in Maine are expected to occur in 2079 and 2162.

With so much focus on the sun in Maine, it should come as no surprise that the first national "Sun Day" in May, 1978, was greeted by Maine people gathered on Cadillac Mountain, where the sun first touched the horizon of the American continent at 5:17 A.M.

There are thirty-seven townships in Maine which are situated on the 45th parallel of latitude. One, halfway between the equator and the North Pole, the small town of Perry, marks the exact halfway spot where the 45th degree of north latitude crosses the road. This same parallel crosses through France, Turkey, Mongolia, China, Northern Japan, and Canada.

Jockey Cap, so-called because of its original shape, is located in Fryeburg, and has been confirmed by the National Geographic Society as the largest boulder in the world. The visor fell to the foot of the boulder years ago, and landed in such a way as to form a cave-like structure where, allegedly, Molly Ockett dwelt at one time. The crest of the boulder now has a range finder, especially useful for identifying the various peaks of the White Mountain Range. The boulder's name was first recorded on a 1777 deed. The panorama presented from the top is breathtaking.

Seguin Light, in Casco Bay, holds the country's record for a one-year fog signaling: 2,734 hours. The light was established in 1795.

Casco Bay also holds a United States record by having 366 islands in one body of water, one for each day of the year, including leap year. The largest one is 912-acre Long Island. Most of the names for the other islands are for fowl or birds: Crow, Goose, and Eagle; for animals: Cow, Ram, and Hog; and even for garden produce: Pumpkin, Turnip, and Gooseberry.

Peaks Island, 717 acres, was known during the 1890s as "The Coney Island of the East."

As for reptiles, Maine is the only state in the nation that is free from poisonous snakes.

Birds, too, have had and do have their place in Maine history of the unusual or superlatives. From the auk family, about 2,000 big puffins, called "sea parrots" or "the Charlie Chaplins of Birdland," spend summers on two rocky islands off Maine, Matinicus Rock and Machias Seal Rock, the latter partially Canada owned. A lesser number inhabit Eastern Egg Rock in Muscongus Bay where a new habitation, begun with forty-five birds, seems to have become a success. Mankind drove them from this rock only a few years ago. It is as far south as puffins ever travel from their homes in Greenland, Iceland, the British Isles, and Scandinavia.

Nearly extinct a century ago, they are now a big tourist attraction for the entire nation. They are about one foot long; have the ridiculous shape of a "plump football;" have big, round heads like a "blue-black croquet ball;" and fat cheeks which appear to be patches of white. Their large round eyes have a heartbroken appeal, shining through vermilion lids. A triangular beak conceals much of the face. They might be compared to a small penguin shown in color.

Totally unlike any other bird, the puffin has black and white feathers and a large conical red and yellow striped bill with a touch of blue. The enormous beak is used to crush mollusks and other shell fish. He waddles on red feet, and his small wings require rapid flapping to bear his body weight when in flight.

Another bird which spends summers in Maine is the *Ardea herodias*, or blue heron, one of the largest birds in America. It stands about three feet tall; has a long, thin neck; and catches fish from water and mice on land. Ilesboro has one of the biggest colonies of these birds which inhabit the New England Coast, as far south as they ever go. Their nests resemble bushel baskets when viewed from the air.

Swan Island has long been famous as a haven for the American bald eagle. The island has what is conceded to be the largest bald eagle nest in North America.

There are a few important waterfowl rendezvous places in the nation, and one that deserves great pride is that at Merrymeeting Bay, Maine. It is a 20,000-acre estuary and fresh water bay, into which the Kennebec, Androscoggin, and three lesser rivers empty. Each spring at least 10,000 Canada geese stop at the bay on their northern flight from their southern winter homes, en route to Canada. In the fall, the bay is a mecca for a long list of other fowl, including the fast-flying Black Duck, Blue-winged Teal, Green-winged Teal, American Pintail, Mallard, Greater and Lesser Scaup, Ring-necked Duck, Ruddy Duck, Bufflehead, Barow's Golden-eye, Baldpate, Wood Duck, Shovelers, Redheads, Canvas-backers, and Eiders. Strict game laws protect these and other bird species from disappearing from the earth.

In 1913, the first bird known to have flown entirely around the world was set free from Maine. It was a common tern (*Sterns hirundo*) which was banded at Eastern Egg Rock on July 3, and was found at the mouth of the Niger River, East Africa, in August, 1917.

Arthur Lincoln, of Dennysville, discovered a new species of sparrow in 1833 on a trip to Labrador with the well-known bird lover and artist Audubon, who named the bird "Lincoln Sparrow." It comes south as far as Maine, and is listed in nearly every natural history book.

The shy loon now nests only in Maine and Canada, and winters around the Caribbean. A recording called "Voices of the Loon," prepared by a group of Maine people at a lake in northern Maine, received rave reviews in 1981.

The lakes of Maine hold several outstanding features. Kezar Lake, in Lovell, is listed fifth in Douglas Volk's *The One Hundred Most Beautiful Lakes in the World,* and *National Geographic* calls it "one of the three most beautiful lakes in the world." It has neither treacherous currents nor deep drop-offs.

Cobbosseecontee Lake, in the Winthrop Lake Region, was the first Maine lake to entertain the U.S. Flying Tern Fleet, in 1967. Lake Maranacook, also in the Winthrop Region, was the nation's training waters for oarsmen from all over the country when single sculling was at the height of its popularity.

On the shores of Lake Phillips, or Lucerne, once stood the largest log lodge in the world. The Lucerne area was high in popularity during the 1920s and hosted many dignitaries. The lodge later burned to the ground.

Moosehead Lake has more interesting features than has probably any other single lake on earth. It is the largest lake within the confines of the boundaries of any one state. Various sources say that it surpasses Lake Tahoe, Nevada, in ruggedness of shoreline, 400 miles of it. It has its inlet and its outlet on the same side, which no other lake in the country has. Moreover, the inlet and outlet are not more than one mile apart, a unique fact. Only one body of water in the United States is larger: Lake Okeechobee, in Florida, which has an average depth of only twelve feet, by reason of which many statisticians disqualify it as a *lake.* Moosehead has the largest number of islands within its limits, nearly 500 of them, than has any other lake within one state's boundaries. In *The Lakes of Maine*, their names, both banal and unique, are listed in part.

Androscoggin River, winding through New Hampshire and Maine, has been called the "best harnessed river in the country, if not the world."

As for the woods of Maine, two thirds of the state is forest growth. Maine trees have been outstanding from the early days when they provided the king's masts. For many years, navies from all over the world flew their pennants from "tall sticks" which came from Maine. The first ones were presumably taken by the Royal Navy in 1609, in the vicinity of Penobscot Bay. The last large areas of privately-owned, timber-producing woodlands left in the United States are in Maine.

There have been and are many special trees in the state. For instance, an elm in Mercer reached a thirty-two foot girth, exceeding a Connecticut elm by two inches. A plaque honoring the Maine elm has been placed in the town.

In 1971, the largest Eastern White Pine (*Pinus strobus*) growing in the United States was one with a seventy-three-foot spread, and eighteen-foot-and-two-inch circumference, and a height of 147 feet. This tree was in Blanchard.

Among other record-breaking trees grown in Maine are, or have been: a ninety-five-foot tamarack in Jay; a ninety-foot silver maple in Fryeburg Harbor; a seventy-foot hornbeam in Winthrop; a pitch pine in Poland; a paper birch in Hartford; and the largest red maple tree in the nation, at Leeds. This maple is twenty-six feet around its base, stands eighty-nine feet high, and has a ninety-six-foot crown spread. It is judged to be about 200–300 years old.

Maine grows all types of fir, pine, and spruce trees. In 1973, it won the National Christmas Tree Association competition held in Oregon, by exhibiting an eight-year-old Douglas fir. Thousands of Christmas trees are shipped annually out of the state.

The northernmost growth of the black gum tree is in New Gloucester, Maine, where there is the so-called New Gloucester Blue Gum Stand, a ten-acre tract on the southern side of Little Hill. The area is noted for its virgin, black-gum-dominated, swampy-forest land, where there are trees judged to be over 400 years old.

Weatherwise, the U. S. Department of Commerce Weather Bureau states that "Maine has the most healthful climate in the United States and equals any in the world, not only in the summer but also, contrary to popular belief, in the winter. The sunshine average is close to sixty percent for the year and the monthly averages change very little during the seasons."

Factually, Maine has more clear days per year than does Miami, Florida. One year's ratio was 119 Maine days as opposed to eighty-six Miami days. The only months in which Miami leads, and then by a close score, are January, May, and December.

The state of Maine has one negative statistic which is interesting. About the year 1815, there was a killer frost at some time during every month, and the year became known as "Eighteen-Hundred-and-froze-to-death," or "The Year of No Summer." Kennebec Valley had frost every month and snow in all except July, when it hailed. In mid-August, a man was found frozen to death in snow under a tree.

Occasionally, but rarely, the state leads in low temperature in the nation. 1904 was one of those years, when Rockland Harbor froze over. And on February 13, 1976, Caribou had the lowest temperature reading in the country, a minus 32F.

It is in the autumn of each year that Maine really reaches it peak of colorful glory with its authentically declared beauty of foliage, universally considered unsurpassed in the world.

2

Music, Art, and Literature

The famed "Flying Staircase," an architech-tural wonder found in the Ruggles House, Columbia Falls.

Millie Dunham, world champion fiddler

James Wyeth *(Photo by Jim Moore)*

Birthplace of Henry Wadsworth Longfellow, Portland

Home of *The Pearl of Orr's Island*, Portland

Sculptress Louise Nevelson *(Photo courtesy of* The Courier-Gazette)

In the cultural field, Maine has surpassed all states with its thirteen Pulitzer Prize winners, up to 1977. The fact that there are not more is simply because the coveted award was not in existence in the years of many of Maine's great writers.

As for music, Maine centered its early contribution in singers. The state has nurtured, among other outstanding vocalists, four great prima donnas: Cary, Eames, Nordica, and Scalar.

Anna "Annie" Louise Cary, 1842–1921, was once alluded to in the *Encyclopaedia Britannica* as the most popular singer in America: its greatest contralto. *Time* magazine later referred to her as "The Prima Donna America Forgot."

This forgotten, perhaps, but unforgettable master of voice had a vocal range that spanned three and one half octaves.

Cary was born in Wayne, and at seventeen was teaching school in Scarborough. She sang in Boston to earn additional finances. Her professional singing debut, however, was on December 26, 1862, in Italy, where she had been studying voice. Her New York debut came in September, 1870; and in November of that year, she appeared for the first time in Portland, a city which she loved.

In spite of her fame and many engagements, she managed to return to Portland every year after that. Her summer home was at Prout's Neck, near the city of her love.

She was very informal in her habits, often spurning any wrapping for carrying a fresh fish from the market, an old European custom.

Cary seemed destined to become the focus of many "firsts." She was the first American woman to sing a Wagnerian role, as Ortrud, in *Lohengrin*. She was soloist at the first performance given

37

by the Boston Symphony Orchestra. She sang in the first United States performance of *Aida* ever given in Russia, and received jewels and silver from the czar for her success. She appeared once with Madame Nordica at a commencement concert at Bates College, in Lewiston, Maine.

When she married, in 1882, she retired. Even though her death occurred in New York, her love for Maine included a request in her will that the state flag be buried with her, which was done. The newspapers of her day proclaimed that she "had the whole world at her feet."

A second great vocalist was Emma Eames, 1867–1952. Eames was called the "Girl of the Golden Voice," and had her early education in Boston. Later she came to Bath with her parents and attended Bath High School. In 1891, she sang at the first performance at the Metropolitan, in Mascagni's *Cavalleria Rusticana*, and in the first performance there of Mozart's *The Magic Flute.*

Her career parallels that of Anna Louise Cary and a third great opera singer, Madame Nordica; however, Eames was frequently termed the best of the three. Her musical training in Paris led to her professional debut at the Grand Opera in Paris on March 13, 1889, in *Juliette*. She became the rage of the city and was decorated by the French Academy of Music as an honorary officer.

Following her career in Paris, she appeared regularly in both New York and London, in roles which were sung in French, Italian, Spanish, German, and English. In London, she was given the Golden Jubilee Medal by Queen Victoria herself.

After her marriage to Emilio de Gogorza, whom she met in a railroad station, she returned to Bath and there had a true showplace built, which they eventually sold to return to Paris. Together, Eames and her husband inaugurated the Temple of Music at Bar Harbor, by giving an outstanding concert performance.

As did Cary, Eames sang once with Nordica, in 1894, in *The Marriage of Figaro.*

She was so impressed by a bookplate executed for her by Ernest Kaskell, of Bath, that the design is reportedly on her marble tombstone in that city. Symbolic of her life, in her opinion, it represents a Maine scrub pine clinging to a rock, with musical notes surrounding the motif.

Lillian Nordica, the third famous operatic singer from Maine, was the youngest of four daughters, born on a farm in Sandy

38

River Valley, Farmington, on December 12, 1857. She died in Indonesia while on a world tour, on May 10, 1914. As did Eames, she studied first in Boston and then went to Milan, Italy, where she made her operatic debut and became, in the opinion of her contemporaries, the best soprano opera singer of her time. She was the first American to sing Wagnerian roles with the Metropolitan Opera Company and thus became America's first prima donna by achieving world acclaim in *The Ring*, in the early 1900s.

Nordica worked hard for her success. She borrowed money and lived frugally. She once said that "without work there is no success." *Work* was her byword and philosophy, and it led her to success with all the royalty and crowned heads of Europe, resulting in a gift of a valuable bracelet from the czar of Russia. After her success with *La Traviata* and *Tristan and Isolde*, she worked almost exclusively in Wagnerian roles, in which she reached stardom; and it is doubtful that anyone ever has surpassed or shall surpass her in these roles.

Nordica was married three times. Her first husband, from Farmington, set out to cross the English Channel in a balloon and was never heard from. She and her second husband, a Hungarian Army officer, were divorced after a brief marriage. Her third, a New York banker, consented to spend their honeymoon in Farmington, where she gave her final Maine concert, in 1911. It was an hour-long program, reportedly closing with a beautiful rendition of "Home, Sweet Home."

In Italy, she was known as *Giglis Nordica* as it was more of a drawing name than was her own. It meant "Lily of the North," and eventually she became known worldwide as simply "Madame Nordica."

Her first concert, in Boston, was in Bumstead Hall, 1876. From then on, she was never surpassed as Marguerite, Brunhilde, or Elsa in the Wagnerian cycle. In 1897, she was the star at the first Maine Music Festival, with a chorus of 1,000 voices.

Her entire family, parents and four sisters, were musical. Lillian tried the hardest to take over the torch from the next eldest daughter, who died when she was just reaching recognition. They were a close, happy family in Norton Woods. Lillian had beauty, charm, voice, and a deep sense of the dramatic: all requirements for an opera star.

Nordica was a pure soprano whose voice won her a respectable fortune in gems. In addition to the previously mentioned bracelet, she was given jewels by the czar and by Queen Victoria.

Her collection of pearls was valued at over one half a million dollars, one single strand of black pearls being appraised at $75,000. One of her tiaras contained 233 nonpareil diamonds.

Her death was the result of a shipwreck off the Australian coast, from which she contracted pneumonia, returned to the concert stage too soon, and died in Batavia, Java, on May 10, 1914.

The fourth world-famous opera singer from Maine was Mlle. Minne Scalar, credited with over thirty operas, who performed with such notables as Caruso and Van Dyke.

She was born Minnie Anne Plummer, in West Paris, on April 15, 1869. At seventeen, she went to live in South Paris. Minnie studied in several European capitals and took her stage name, Minne Scalar, from some French friends. The meaning is "climbing the stairs," an appropriate title for her at that time.

Scalar sang in all of the major opera houses of Europe, the United States, and Canada. In France, she was the first American prima donna of the French Opera Company. In Italy, she fulfilled a request performance for Italian Queen Margarhita. In Holland, her debut was made in 1903, without a rehearsal or a meeting with the orchestra. In London, she once filled in for Madame Nordica, who was ill.

The London press reviews, after this substitution performance, gave her a rating above Nordica, Eames, and Cary. She mastered to perfection the Wagnerian operas, just as Nordica had done, but never reached the same pinnacle.

Scalar was on the faculty at Hebron Academy from 1887 to 1889, and her last public concert was given there in June, 1912. Her husband, C. A. Stephens, author, and editor of the *Youths' Companion*, was a Norway man. They lived there until her death in 1944. Not known for her compassion nor gentleness, she once presumably commanded her husband to return to a store during a raging blizzard, because he had forgotten to buy her a pencil when he had gone earlier in the day. Accustomed to her humors, he quietly obeyed.

In addition to the four great operatic stars of Maine, there were and are several other singers who have been recognized nationally and internationally. A list of some of them follows in alphabetical order:

Mlle. Giovana Avigliana, of Gardiner.
Flora Berry, of Durham, sister-in-law of Anne Cary.
Phoebe Pendleton Crosby, of Islesboro, who became an

aid to film stars Irene Dunne and Jeanette MacDonald.

Sarah Robinson Duff, a Bangor soprano.

Mabel Bates Fessenden, of Waterville.

Charlie Gilliam, of Orr's Island, known as "Coastline Charlie." A sardine fisherman in summer and a country-wide
popular western singer, he tours the United States with
his band during the winter months.

Garry Grice, of Falmouth, who played with the Bavarian
State Opera in Munich and carried the lead tenor in
the New York Opera in 1981.

Laurel Hardy, a part-time Maine resident, affiliated with
the Metropolitan Opera in 1977.

Jeannie King, of Monson, who toured the entire country.

Elizabeth Kriger, of Portland.

Caroline Lazzari, once a student at Bucksport Conference
and later a Metro star.

Marion Witham McAlister, of Bangor, winner of the first
prize at a Paris Conservatory of Music contest.

Clara B. Nickels, who sang with Anne Cary in Russia, and
whose career was checked only by her untimely death.

Evelyn Fogg Olcott, a Portland contralto.

Marie Powers, who summered in Fryeburg for many years
and whose concerts included several in La Scala, Italy.
Her recorded rendition of *The Medium* was very popular.
She gave her last operatic work in Japanese, in Tokyo.

Buffy Sainte-Marie, of "Sesame Street," a popular children's
television program. She was born in Harrison. Her voice
has been termed "unusual" and "unique."

Ethelynde Smith, of Portland.

Wynifred Smith, of Carthage.

Rudy Vallee, of Westbrook, whose voice has been recognized on the stage, the screen, and television.

As an offbeat, one might state that Elizabeth Arnold, the
mother of Edgar Allen Poe, once sang in a Portland theater.

It seems incredible that any other one state can surpass Maine
in contributing to the music world, with such an aggregate of fine
voices.

As for band music, there is little doubt that the marches of
R. B. Hall, of Richmond, directly follow the popularity of those
of John Phillip Sousa. The U. S. Navy Band played Hall's "March
Funebre" for the procession from the Capitol to Arlington Cemetery at President's Kennedy's burial, as it has for all full-honor

41

ceremonies for naval officers for years. Other Hall marches include "New Colonial," "American Cadet," and "Independentia." Sousa himself found nothing but praise for the musical compositions of Robert Hall.

Robert Brown Hall was born in 1858 at Bowdoinham's Abbagadasset Point, and died in 1907. He worked in a shoe factory for years, and then studied the cornet and formed his own band. He soon had too many engagements to fulfill. On one occasion, a one-day trip, he was held up by fog and the band played a three-day concert for the price of one. He had an international reputation, yet he never left Maine. Appropriately, he was called "Maine's Sousa."

Another anecdote is that his band started to play, through error, during a speech of U. S. Senator James Blaine, who roared, "I can talk against any other man, but not against a brass band."

Hall composed, arranged, conducted, and played. His works were in demand all over the country. Later, he added an orchestra. His favorite composition was "The Tenth Regiment March." His best seller, however, was "Officer of the Day," which sold 300,000 copies to one European firm alone. During his lifetime he composed over 100 marches, in addition to waltzes, serenades, polkas, schottisches, and cornet specialty numbers. Still available is the "R. B. H. Band Book of 15 World Famous Marches."

Hall lived in Waterville and was often engaged by Colby College for commencement activities. Married at forty-four, he suffered a stroke shortly afterward, affecting the right side of his body and mouth. He never returned to his best playing and was only forty-seven when he died. The Waterville Military Band played his lovely "March Funebre" at his funeral.

Today there is an R. B. Hall Memorial Band in Waterville, which is actively engaged in promoting a commemorative stamp honoring Hall on the 125th anniversary of his birth.

From brass band to fiddle is from R. B. Hall to Mellie Dunham, of Norway, Maine, who became World Champion of Old Time Fiddlers in 1925, at age seventy-two. He earned his title by winning a state fiddlers' contest in Lewiston, from a field of thirty-nine contestants. The selection that he played was one of his own compositions, "Rippling Waves." He was sponsored by automobile magnate Henry Ford who, after Mellie's national triumph, sent him on the theater and nightclub circuit. Neither Mellie nor "Gram," his wife, was fond of these entertainment centers, and they did not continue the circuit work very long.

Mellie's favorite expression when he was ready to play, was to advise his accompanist, "Let 'er rip!" He was extremely particular as to who accompanied him, yet Mellie could not read one note of music.

Mellie Dunham's vocation was working in a family-owned snowshoe factory, and he personally made the snowshoes worn by Admiral Peary when Peary planted the American flag at the North Pole. Those shoes are now the property of the Smithsonian Institution. Mellie was at Peary's home around 1908, and suggested that Peary let him fashion the snowshoes for his trip rather than leaving them to be factory made. Mellie promised to return the money if Peary was not satisfied with the product. Needless' to say, Peary was.

George Ward Nichols, of Mt. Desert, 1831–1885, although a writer to some extent, should be remembered for his founding of the College of Music of Cincinnati, which through his efforts made the city a reputable music center.

He was also one of the founders for a School of Design.

His best literary work was *The Story of the Great March*, 1865, which sold over 60,000 copies in one year and was translated into several languages.

Yet another type of Maine's musical contribution lies in a college song. Rarely has one person been responsible for the universal acceptance and knowledge of his alma mater song, but Rudy Vallee was.

Rudy grew up in Westbrook and entered the University of Maine in 1921. He had worked in his father's drugstore, but his heart was in the music world. He would spend every available minute away from studies at the university, practicing at the Orono Town Hall, where he would not disturb his fraternity brothers' studying.

As he went up the ladder from the Hi-Ho Club and entered radio, stage, screen, TV, and movie stardom, he carried the U. of M. "Stein Song" right along with him. Even today there are state officials who, regretfully, are unaware that the state has its own "State of Maine Song" as an official composition, and that the "Stein Song" is popular merely through Rudy's association with the University. In 1977, he described himself as the "Pat Boone of the Stone Age."

In addition to music and acting, Rudy Vallee has had several books published.

Randolph "Randy" Brooks, of Sanford, 1920–1967, was a

foremost trumpeter during the 1940s.

Concerning the official state song, down through the years, the first one was the DeMoss composition, 1895, a song with lyrics sprinkled with specifics. They included the 1846 Prohibition Law which brought to Maine "temperance and righteousness," and pointed out that the law of right of Maine's "sober" people was upheld.

Later, the State Grange was instrumental in promoting "State of Maine, My State of Maine," words and music by George Thornton Edwards, copyrighted in 1913. This song was issued in all possible forms, even on lantern slides for use as an illustrated melody. The text is purely laudatory.

In 1922, Mary Thompson-Green produced "Dear Old Maine." This became the choice of the State Federation of Business and Professional Women, who contributed to its popularity. The song alludes to the business women and to three prominent state figures: Neal Dow, instrumental in Maine's being the first state to adopt the prohibition law of 1846; Tom Reed, a senator and speaker of the House; and James G. Blaine, senator and secretary of state, who nearly won his candidacy for the presidency in 1884. The author of this song, an operatic vocalist, died in January, 1924.

Finally, on November 8, 1931, the Maine Publicity Bureau promoted a contest for a state song, which drew 115 entries. Nine judges narrowed the number to four songs which they considered the most suitable; and these four were broadcast from Portland, Maine, over the radio station WCSH. The same vocalist was used to assure uniformity in the songs' renditions.

The Boston *Sunday Globe* heralded Maine's idea by an article headlined MAINE SINGS FOR PUBLICITY, and in large print stated that RADIO FANS WILL CHOOSE—AND THE OFFICIAL (State) SONG WILL BE BORN. And so it was. The only state song arbitrarily selected was retained from that time on. The listening public was the selection committee.

The winning song was *State of Maine Song,* by Roger Vinton Snow. It eulogizes the state and its natural resources in a steady 6/8 time, lively and stirring. Snow, a Portland lawyer, wrote both words and music, and this was his only contribution of major import to the arts. He died April 1, 1952.

The Maine Federation of Business and Professional Women's Clubs later took out the copyright on the song and controlled its publication.

Other Maine composers include Walter Piston, of Rockland, who won the Pulitzer Prize twice, in 1948 and 1961: Effie Canning, of Rockland, composer of "Rock-a-Bye-Baby"; F. N. W. Crouch, of Portland, who wrote "Kathleen Mavourneen"; William B. Bradbury, of York, composer of "Jesus Loves Me"; the Reverend Edward S. Ufford, of Appleton, who authored among other hymns the well-known "Throw Out the Lifeline"; Elizabeth Chase Edwards (Florence Percy), of Strong, who in 1850 contributed "Rock Me to Sleep"; and Frank E. Churchill, of Rumford, responsible for the scores of the Walt Disney films *Snow White and the Seven Dwarfs, Dumbo,* and *The Three Little Pigs.*

Additional hymn composers and writers who should not be omitted include James Lyon, who, at the age of twenty-six, was the first native-American composer, in cooperation with Francis Hopkinson. Lyon resided in Machias, and his *Urania* was the first collection of psalm tunes published in the colonies, containing music written by an American. Furthermore, he published several religious books and was the first minister of the Parish of Machias. He lived from 1735 to 1794.

Then there is Supply Belcher, of Farmington, 1751–1836. He composed psalms and anthems, and was called "the Handel of Maine." His book titled *The Harmony of Maine* was the country's popular music collection of his day.

Samuel Longfellow, brother of Henry Wadsworth Longfellow, composed many favorite and still popular hymns.

The first oratorio by an American was written by a Maine man in 1873—John Knowles Paine. It was a symphonic *Oratorio of St. Peter*, which received world acclaim and made him the first great American composer.

Paine was born in Portland in 1839 and died in 1906. In 1867, he performed his "Mass in D" in Berlin, Germany, conducting it himself. His famed oratorio was given in Portland City Hall by the Haydn Society of Portland, on June 3, 1873, assisted by the forty-one-member Harvard orchestra from Boston and by eminent artists from abroad.

He also composed the "Harvard Hymn" to indicate his loyalty to an institution where he was full professor of music for forty years. He first became known as "The Father of American Music" and later as "Dean of American Composers." Even today one may hear a Paine overture on TV, but greater renown came through *Azara*, an opera based on an old French tale, the first entire opera composed by an American, 1901.

An organist at sixteen, he was the nation's first recognized organist because of his work on the *Messiah,* which he accompanied without orchestration on Christmas night, 1851. Moreover, he was the first American symphony composer to write a commissioned work to commemorate the nation's centennial, and the first to occupy a chair of music at an American college or university.

The founder of the American Guild of Organists was William C. MacFarlane, a Maine-born musician who was also the first municipal organist in the country.

Another composer, Arthur Flagg Roundy, of Fairfield, 1882–1978, was the author of several universally popular marches, and was in demand to conduct bands. Perhaps his most famous composition is the "103rd Infantry March." His "I Guide" has legally been adopted as the State of Maine Anthem. The highly gifted pianist was affectionately known as "Mr. Music."

The enduring "sea chanty" is quite possibly a descendant of the Maine lumberjacks' "shanty," so called because it was sung in the shanties of the lumber camps of Maine. According to Joanna Colcord, an authority on music origins in the state, many lumbermen went to sea during the milder months when it was impossible to sled logs or to work in deep woods. In due course, their songs became "chantys" from the French *chanter* as many Maine lumberjacks were of French-Canadian origin and had crossed directly into the northern Maine woods.

It was Luther Whiting Mason, of Turner, born in 1818, who won international fame for his original method of teaching music in the schools. He was later honored by the emperor of Japan, the country in which Mason introduced the eight-note scale. He was the first foreigner to be received by the empress of Japan.

Mason, proficient in several instruments, died in 1896.

World-famous Pierre Claude Monteux, who established a master class in flute for musicians all over the United States, and later settled in Portland, founded the Hudson Valley Philharmonic which counted ninety-six musicians at the time. He also established the famed Domaine School of Orchestral Conducting and Training. He left Maine to appear annually in Europe as both conductor and soloist.

The New England Music Camp, nationally attended and highly respected for its work, was developed in 1937 under Dr. Paul Wiggin. It is located on one of the Belgrade Lakes and has a wide clientele. Sunday concerts, held in the Bowl-in-the-Pines, draw crowds from great distances.

The camp started with sixty campers, eighteen buildings with leaky roofs, and a staff of twenty. Dr. Wiggin, of Winthrop, insisted on having only the best on his staff. When the Maine State Legislature commended the Camp for its one-third of a century, in 1970, there were ninety buildings, a staff of twenty-five, and a faculty of thirty, with a student enrollment of about 200.

The Rossini Club, of Portland, organized in 1869, is said to be the oldest still-active musical club in America and possibly in the world. Its concerts and recitals use only its members.

Maine was the first state in the nation to have a school music project. Young Audiences, Inc., in 1966, joined with the Music of Maine, Inc., a non-profit organization, to provide free live music programs for school students.

Maine has so many of the most splendid pipe organs remaining in America from the 1800s, that in 1981 the National Convention of the Organ Historical Society met in the state for the first time. The majority of these organs are located in the Downeast section of Maine: Bangor, Belfast, Blue Hill, Bucksport, Calais, East Machias, Machias, Orono, Orrington, Searsport, Stockton Springs, and Woodland.

Turning from music to another form of art, Franklin Simmons, of Portland, was the first American to win national fame in the art of sculpture. He was born on January 11, 1839, in Webster, later lived in Bath, and finally came to Lewiston. He started painting lessons at age eleven, oil instruction at age fifteen, but the clay along the Androscoggin River caught his eye and he went to Boston to study sculpture. His first studio was in Lewiston. However, he continued with his formal learning, even to the study of Latin, presumably to familiarize himself with ancient art.

He soon began to receive commissions for busts, and his future was assured by his memorial for the gravesite of Major General Hiram Gregory Berry, of Rockland, in 1865. He then went to Washington, D.C., where he fashioned heads of men in Lincoln's cabinet, including Hamlin and Secretary of the Treasury William P. Fessenden, both Maine men. Generals became his favorite subjects: Grant, Meade, Sherman, Sheridan, and Wright, followed by Farragut and Porter.

Simmons was the first American sculptor to incorporate so-called "accessories," meaning figures, at the base of the pedestal. His only equestrian statue was that of General Jonathan Logan, a commander at Vicksburg. After eight years of labor, Simmons had this work dedicated by President McKinley.

Maine still has much of the art of Simmons open to the public, such as the Edward Little statue in Auburn and the Longfellow statue at Longfellow Square, in Portland. The latter statue was a world-wide effort, with donations coming from readers of Longfellow's poetry all over the world, plus $8,000 in dimes earned, saved, and given by school children in New England. Simmons died suddenly on December 6, 1913.

The "Life and Death" sculpture by Charles Eugene Tefft, a 19th century artist, covered one complete side of a room and established him as one of the important sculptors of the day. The design was reproduced in three-foot bas-relief at the annual exhibition of the American Art League. After that, he took several honors, and his works are currently in many states.

Tefft's first living model was General Joshua L. Chamberlain, a former governor of Maine. Other Maine subjects were Hiram Ricker, of Poland Spring fame, and Hannibal Hamlin, Lincoln's vice president. It is generally believed that the only portrayal of President Lincoln in a praying posture came from a creation by Tefft.

A third Maine sculptor achieved success by depicting the Maine Indian. Using four mammoth pine logs to construct the body, Bernard "Blackie" Langlais constructed the largest Indian monument in the world at the time. It was approximately sixty feet high and was placed in Skowhegan. It took two years to carve the wood, which had been treated for twenty years.

Langlais had the hands of the Indian holding not a bow and arrow, as is usual, but a fishing net and spear. The headdress consisted of two feathers rather than the conventional war bonnet. This was to indicate his trust in the non-belligerent Maine Indian.

Langlais was born in Old Town, July 23, 1926. He later moved to Cushing. He began his art by using odd pieces of wood. His works are extremely innovative: a deer, hung after slaughter; a giraffe, designed for children to climb. His "Wild Lion" is one of his most popular pieces. Huge, gigantic, and chaotic are adjectives which describe his work. He died on December 26, 1977.

The fourth outstanding Maine sculptor is Louise Berliawsky Nevelson, of Rockland, who, in 1974, held the title of the "greatest sculptor of the times." In 1980, she was referred to as "the dowager of the Manhattan art establishment" because of her long residence in that area, over thirty years. Her work is now in all major museums and collections in the country.

Nevelson's sculpture is of wood, and depicts walls of all slate-black, all white, or all gold. Her "Silent Music" has an eighty-three-foot base, which indicates the size of her customary artistic pieces. Legend has it that she started with pieces of wood from her father's lumber yard, but it is no legend that she reached recognition in 1967, when the Whitney Museum held the first major retrospective of her sculpture.

Her creations sometimes consist of an "assemblage" of chair arms, crate staves, toilet seats, newel posts, and practically anything else imaginable. Everything that she makes is big, enormous, immense, along the lines of Langlais.

She also does lithograph work, oils, and etchings, and has been influential in the International Congress of Painters, Sculptors, and Graphic Artists. She held her first exhibit in New York in 1933, and her first one-woman show there nearly ten years later.

Nevelson is distinctly individualistic. She has scores of what are termed "outrageous" dresses of such a type that she may wear them day and night to save time in repeated dressing. In February, 1977, at age seventy-seven, she was included among the world's best-dressed women. Her brother was amazed, as were many other people. Her sister said, "I'd say that Louise is one of the twelve most unusual women, but I didn't know that included the category of dress."

The judges proclaimed her to be an artist with "immense personal style who applies her own strong principles of art to her dress."

To give one example of her idiosyncrasy in clothing, one report stated that she sometimes wears a leather belt as a necklace, a coat made from a paisley shawl and lined with chinchilla, or perhaps a 16th century mandarin Chinese robe over a blue denim shirt. She considers facial makeup an important issue. Three-inch eyelashes, for instance, are worn by combining two or three sets of them. This, she says, is for personal glamor. A heavy substance to darken her eyelids produces a more distinctive facial impact.

Her short-term marriage produced a son, who is also a sculptor. However, she admits to preferring art to man, and prefers to be the master in her own home, which she finds preferable to any social life, saying, "Leave the world to the world."

Another Maine sculptor of distinction is Robert Laurent, of Ogunquit, whose work in alabaster, wood, and bronze is internationally recognized, with the highest regard going to his bronze pieces.

Paul Akers's first piece of art, a bust of Milton, called "Milton," is now in Colby College, Maine. This is the one referred to and described in Hawthorne's *The Marble Fawn*.

Marian Dwyer, of Damariscotta Mills, is a rapidly rising sculptor who began carving in 1962 without previous experience or training. She won an award at the Louis Tiffany Annual International Arts Competition, and has shown great skill in stone carving. To date, she has had shows in Maine, New Jersey, and New York.

The ducks that Gus Wilson, keeper at Spring Point Light, in Portland Harbor, used to carve for less than one dollar, now bring up to $4,000 each.

A different type of art may be found in architecture. Maine still has several standing examples of the finest-built houses in the nation. The Victorian Mansion, in Portland, is considered the outstanding Victorian design and Italianate architecture in the country. Built from 1859 to 1863, it was the dream home of Ruggles Sylvester Morse, of Leeds, who made his fortune in the hotel business.

The mansion was modeled after the Osborne House, the favorite residence of Queen Victoria, on the Isle of Wight. It has elaborate interior walls and ceilings, a flying staircase with 300 carved bannisters, etched pier glass mirrors, ten French gold-leaf mirrors, carved marble mantels and fireplaces, and gilded dragons "drowned with baroque angels." The woodcarving was done by an English woodcarver who took three years to complete the delicate work, using only a pen knife. A minimal price for such a dwelling in the 1980s would be around $3,000,000. Morse indulged in the elaborate structure to show the girl who jilted him what she had missed by not becoming Mrs. Morse.

Montpelier, in Thomaston, is an authentic replica of the home of Major General Henry Knox. The original was built in 1794, but burned many years ago. The contents are supposed to be authentic, and include the general's traveling case, a gift of Lafayette, and a bookcase said to have belonged to Marie Antoinette and purchased after her execution.

The Wedding Cake House, in Kennebunkport, is decorated outside by elaborate and intricate scroll-saw work which makes the house resemble a huge valentine. It is quite possible that no other house in the nation can equal its marvelous, carved scrollwork.

The Hamilton House, in South Berwick, built in the 1770s,

is one of the greatest Georgian homes in America. Curving drive-ways, fancy doorways, elaborate cornices, four black-topped white chimneys, expansive lawns and terraces, were what John Paul Jones saw when he was entertained there by Colonel Jonathan Hamilton on the eve of Jones's departure for France, in the fall of 1777, to tell of Burgoyne's surrender.

The Tate House, built in 1755 by Englishman George Tate, is now owned by the Colonial Dames of America.

The Black House, in Ellsworth, 1802, is an authentic piece of Georgian-design architectural beauty in red brick. Its spiral staircase is especially intriguing. It was the home of Colonel John Black.

In Columbia Falls, the Judge Ruggles house, built in 1818, has been preserved in its natural state by the local Ruggles House Committee. It, too, has delicate penknife wood carving; and at the time of its construction, the villagers swore that the carver's knife "was guided by the hand of an angel." The judge was a wealthy lumber dealer, store owner, postmaster, prominent citizen-at-large, captain of the militia, and justice of the court of sessions.

The Nickels-Sortwell Mansion, built during 1807–1808, in Wiscasset, is another example of exquisite architecture in Maine. There are many more examples of real architectural beauty throughout the state.

Among the art museums in Maine, two stand out as perhaps the major ones. A unique one at Ogunquit displays entirely American art executed after 1910. There is no abstract nor extreme form of contemporary expression. Special effort is made each year to show the works of some Maine artist. The museum was established as a gift to the public by painter Henry Strater, of Ogunquit, and was built in 1952 with a permanent collection, principally the gifts of Strater. It contains primarily the works of early modernists whose works were touched by their exposure to Maine.

The Farnsworth Museum, in Rockland, is considered to be the finest of all small city museums in the country. It is the cultural center of the entire mid-coastal region of the state.

The museum is a memorial to a recluse, Lucy Farnsworth, who left $1,500,000 for the project. Ignored during her life, in contrast to her much more beautiful sister Jenny, Lucy hoped to bring beauty and pleasure to those who followed her lifetime. This was achieved by frugal living, practically a hermit's existence, and a cruel "pay or get out" attitude toward her tenants. Her stipulation was that the museum, adjoining her homestead, should have free admission and that it bear the name of her father. It provides for a year-round workshop for arts and crafts plus studies for educational and cultural pursuits.

The contents of the museum almost surpass belief. Its library on art is outstanding; its rooms are open to all kinds of classes and meetings; and the extensive art collection represents both American and European artists who have expressed Maine in their own way.

Its major pride is in the fact that it owns Andrew Wyeth's original painting of "Her Room," purchased at a cost of $65,000 in 1964, the largest sum ever paid for the work of a living American painter up to then. In conjunction with this is the fact that the museum owns the world's largest treasures of Wyeth paintings, approximately fifteen pieces, which are displayed individually.

The Wyeth family history of painting began with Newell Convers Wyeth, or "N. C.," 1882–1945, who was a famous illustrator of magazines and children's books. He summered at Port Clyde, Maine. Some of his oils are at the Farnsworth Museum.

His son Andrew, known today as America's favorite painter, was honored by having the first and only one-man American artist show in the White House. This took place in 1970, when twenty-one of his paintings hung on especially designed soft, gold, velvet-covered panels. Among his most popular works are "Christina's World," "Her Room," "Distant Thunder," and "Young Fisherman and His Dory." All of these portray Maine backgrounds, mostly around the Cushing area where the Wyeths had a summer home. His "Christina's World" has been rated second only to "Washington Crossing the Delaware" in familiarity throughout the country. A painting of Christina's home, called "Weatherside," took Andrew twenty-five years to finish, so particular was he to become totally familiar with every detail of its history before undertaking each section.

His shows set new attendance records. In December, 1981, his "March Hawk," done in 1964, sold for $420,000, a record price for a work sold at auction during any artist's lifetime.

His works are correct as to every detail. He was the second American artist to be honored with membership in the Institute of France. John Sargent preceded him. To receive the sword of the Institute, Andrew wore the traditional eighteenth century costume. One final note of interest is that he paints portraits as near as six inches away, "to see the pores and act of breathing."

Andrew's sister Henriette became a well-known portrait painter, and his sister Carolyn studied with her father and was the only teacher of her nephew Jamie.

Jamie, Andrew's son, has duplicated his father's fame. When only twenty, his paintings brought a five-figure price, and the majority of his exhibits have been highly successful. He deals primarily with animals, portraits, or coastal scenery. One unique coastal painting depicts an abandoned bell at Manana Island. One of his most popular animal paintings is that of "Den-Den," his tame, enormous pig, for which he has said that he has strong vibrations. His best-known portrait was an oil of the late President Kennedy, done in 1967. It had its original showing in America at the Farnsworth Museum.

Christmas always held a deep significance and enjoyment for generations of Wyeths, so what could have been more appropriate than that Jamie was commissioned, in 1971, to design one of the two Christmas eight-cent U. S. Postage stamps. He chose "Partridge in a Pear Tree" in soft gray, brown, green, and yellow, with a bright red contrast in the words "On the first day of Christmas my true love sent to me."

Another Maine artist, George Bellows, as a small boy, called himself an artist, but trained to be an athlete. When he finally turned to art, he became known as the most vigorous of American painters of his time, the most brillant, the most highly intelligent, and the most "born artist." Many of Bellows's works are focused on New York as he saw it: squalor, fighting, parks, and the city as an entity. All this is most vividly expressed in his "New York–1911."

Rockwell Kent once showed Bellows some cold, dark, primite, gray and black sea coast pictures of Monhegan Island, off the Maine coast. Bellows came to see the place and eventually spent his summers in Maine, fascinated by the shipyards, the sea, and the tiny island off Sherman's Point.

At the time of his death, in 1925, at age forty-two, he was considered the "Painter of America." One universally recognized painting of his was that of "The Dempsey-Firpo Fight," but his Maine scenes abound in popularity: "Criehaven" (1917), "The Dreamer" (1913), "Cleaning Fish," "Boat Landing" (1913), "Matinicus" (1916), "Evening Swell" (1911), "The Big Dory" (1916), and "Romance of Autumn at Sherman's Point," which is in the Farnsworth Museum.

Harry Cochrane, of Monmouth, painted the murals in the Kora Temple Shrine in Lewiston, considered one of the most unique edifices in the nation. His murals at Cumston Hall, Monmouth, are equally famous. He was also a writer, with a two-volume history of Monmouth and a pageant composition depicting the history of the Shrine organization.

The works of Jonathan Adams Bartlett, an American folk artist of Rumford Center, 1817–1902, have recently brought high prices. His attention to detail is especially pronounced, particularly in his portraits. He was one of the early itinerate painters, and he did attractive wall frescoes in the Rumford area. He had many other facets: furniture maker, vocalist, instrumentalist, master penman, and elocutionist.

Mardsen Hartley, a foremost expressionist, has been internationally acclaimed as one of the finest American artists of the more modern era. He was born in Lewiston, 1877, and died in 1943. He worked in a shoe shop in Auburn, remained in Lewiston to open his first studio when his family moved West, then went out of state to study. He painted and sketched the sea, rocks, mountains, and especially seagulls. Mt. Katahdin was a favorite subject. He published three books of poetry: a small general edition in 1925; *Androscoggin*; and *Sea Burial*. During the 1930s, he exhibited in Berlin, London, Paris, Dresden, and Vienna, as well as in large American cities.

John Marin, 1870–1953, has been called the best watercolor master of his era. He lived in Stonington and at Cape Split. As did Hartley, he captured new idioms leading to modern art, with his "broken planes and a dancing vitality."

Beverly Hallam, of York, has received international fame. Her paintings and monotypes are in some of the country's most exclusive museums. She developed and modified polyvinyl acetate so that it could be used as an artist's medium, and is given credit for the development of what is now termed "acrylic" as a paint for artists.

Harrison Bird Brown, of Portland, 1831–1915, was both prolific and popular. He exhibited in the New York National Academy of Designs. His favorite subject was the Casco Bay Islands. Within the latter part of the twentieth century, his paintings have returned to popularity.

Stephen Etnier, of Harpswell, born in 1903, has produced fifty to sixty paintings a year. He was among the forerunners of today's magic realism. His works hang in colleges, in libraries, in the Farnsworth Museum, and in museums in Boston, New York, Hartford, and Washington, D.C. His wife Elizabeth (he has had four) wrote the best seller *On Gilbert Head*.

Winslow Homer, 1836–1910, had a home in Scarborough. Even today he is often referred to as the greatest painter in American history. His were mostly sea pictures, many painted from his favorite spot off Prout's Neck. He had a vigorous, naturalistic style. His animal pictures have been praised, especially "Fox Hunt," which one authority termed "one of the country's 100 best paintings."

Marine painter Frederick J. Waugh, 1861–1940, began his career along the Maine coast, at Bailey Island, in 1905. His first painting was "Coast of Maine," and he continued to use the word *Maine* in the titles of many subsequent works.

He had lived in England for thirteen years when at age forty-four he made his first visit back to the United States, and from then on he used his native country in his works. In England, however, he had three paintings accepted for show at the Royal Academy and was a regular illustrator for the weekly "Graphic," in London. The showings in the States have mostly leaned toward his Monhegan Island themes, and have been shown at the National Academy of Art.

Ruth "Perky" Safford, of Blue Hill, and Washington, D. C., is credited by several museum directors as the only American artist who makes a speciality of portraits of the interiors of buildings. Her interior of the Black House is in the permanent collection of the Farnsworth Museum. Other interiors include those of the Old North Church, Mt. Vernon, summer homes of distinguished Americans, and the National Gallery of Art.

At an early age she came with her family to Little John's Island, in Casco Bay. Later, the family established a waterfront home called "Tranquility," which was designed by Mrs. Safford, an architect in her own right.

Ruth Safford's most keen interest is in beautiful stairways. She uses watercolors and gouache for her interiors and is one of the ten women who are represented in the very exclusive Guild of Boston Artists, whose membership is limited to sixty.

The symbolic paintings of George Ortman, of Castine, are often difficult for the layman to interpret.

Charles Codman, of Portland, was a well-known pioneer artist in the early 1800s.

Charles Dana Gibson created those epitomes of female pulchritude around the turn of the century. They were the pin-ups of the world for at least fifty years. Gibson lived in luxury on a twenty-five acre estate, Indian Landing, on Seven-Hundred Acre Island, near Islesboro. He entertained lavishly and once took over *Life* magazine, which dropped in sales and then folded within five years, to be later reborn under Henry R. Luce.

Gibson started his career by winning a one dollar prize in a contest open to all messenger boys. His drawing, a sketch of President Garfield after his assassination, was the winner. Later in life, he painted Maine fishermen and Maine scenes, in oil. He was the best known artist of his time. His death came in 1944, at age seventy-seven.

In 1981, Clint Magoon, of Rumford, placed first in a national painting contest of 1,500 entries. Magoon was but nineteen years old. He depicted a family in a field, watching an approaching storm. The painting was later put on display in the Metropolitan Museum of Art in New York City.

Can there possibly be another church in a settlement as small as South Solon, population unlisted in some resource books, which has its interior walls and ceiling done in glowing frescoes executed by mid-century artists? The use of fresco is the oldest known method of wall painting. Michelangelo used it in the ceiling of the Sistine Chapel, in Rome. Matisse used it in France. And Mrs. Margaret Blake, a trustee of the Chicago Art Institute, had the idea, when passing a small, white, 1841 country church, of using frescoes on the badly peeling interior walls. For five years a group of competing artists worked singly or in groups, and the result was one of beauty for the South Solon Free Meeting House.

Bruce O. Nett, of Kents Hill, took a color picture showing a Coast Guard cutter entering Portland Harbor, off the rocks at Portland Head Light. In October, 1970, an eighteen-by-sixty-foot Kodak Colorama, the world's largest transparency up to then, was made from Kent's picture and was hung in Grand Central Railroad Station in New York, in observance of Maine's 150th year of statehood.

Maurice "Jake" Day, former illustrator for the Walt Disney pictures in Hollywood, now lives in Damariscotta. He is the first notable illustrator to retire in Maine; and his exterior Christmas decorations, before the energy crisis in the 1970s, were magnificent.

John "Jack" Muench, of Freeport, is a master printmaker and a powerful abstract painter. He has had over thirty one-man shows, including one at the Smithsonian Institution and one at the National Collection of Fine Arts. In addition, he has shown his works at over 200 group shows.

Reuben Tam, Hawaiian by birth, has depicted Maine sea and sky. His paintings are owned by the foremost museums in the country and are in many private collections. He is a student of geology and poetry.

Mildred Burrage, of Wiscasset, left the impressionists to work with Maine mica, with excellent results.

William Baldwin, of Swanville, is a realist painter with an impressive eye for detail.

Other painters of note include: Bacon, Brown, Coombs, Dodd, Fisher, Fitzpatrick, Hardy, Hartgen, Helikerh, Kienbusch, Montgomery, Schroe, Thon, Welliver, Winters, and of course the talented Ipcar who, in addition to her painting, is an illustrator and writer of children's books. She is the daughter of William and Marguerite Zorach, a family of three generations of contributors to the arts and letters. William won several awards, medals, and citations for his sculpture.

Berenice Abbott is Maine's outstanding artist in photography. Born on July 17, 1898, she has been a Rockland resident since the 1950s. One of her publications is *A Portrait of Maine*.

Maine has been depicted in one way or another on U.S. postage stamps several times. Portland Head Light has twice been pictured on postage stamps; the *Virginia*, the first ship built in America, has been on a stamp; and in 1969, an authentic 1870 scene of Norway, Maine, showed a cluster of homes, a sleigh drawn by a pair of horses, and a man and woman walking arm in arm through a gate, on their way to church; and then Liberty's post office was pictured, in 1974. Later, the poet Millay was honored.

In 1981, the Hallmark Greeting Card Company filmed Bethel, Maine, for a pre-Christmas TV commercial. The town was chosen because of "its picturesque surroundings, old homes, tall steeples" and available snow. During the same week, Alka-Seltzer commercials were filmed there.

The Annual Sidewalk Art Festival in Portland offers more prize money than any other such exhibition in the United States. It is held during August and is unique in both quality and quantity of exhibits.

In the field of theatricals, Maine had, in 1976, the only museum in the country which housed a theater collection within an actual theater, the Boothbay Theater Museum. It contained more than 300 letters written by Edwin Booth and some of his props in various roles. It also had a prompt book that belonged to John Wilkes Booth, brother of Edwin and assassin of President Lincoln.

Other items of interest included a headdress worn by the "Divine Sarah" Bernhardt in *Cleopatra*, and a fan used by Eva le Gallienne in *Camille*. There were also theatrical figurines depicting such scenes as one from *King Lear*, in which Edwin Booth appeared, playbills, tickets, and other items of theatrical history.

The "Divine Sarah" came to Portland twice. On her 1906 visit, as she strolled down Congress Street, window-shopping, her pet collie was killed by a trolley car. She returned to Portland once more, in 1911.

During her 1906 visit, she presented *La Sorciere* at City Hall. In 1911, she played *La Dame aux Camelias* at the Jefferson Theater. This last presentation entailed forty persons, three maids, a valet, sixty-five trunks, and boxcar loads of scenery. She always demanded payment in gold.

Bernhardt's Portland business manager was Edward J. Sullivan, for whom the actress acted as matron of honor at his wedding in 1912, and who hosted the newlyweds aboard her private railway car for a wedding trip to the West Coast. Sullivan was the only man to have managed two great theater celebrities, Bernhardt and her closest rival, the famous Italian genius Eleonora Duse.

Sullivan was a real "dandy" in pink silk shirts, vanilla ice-cream-colored trousers, and a straw hat. He was born in Portland around 1878 and was involved in both theatricals and vaudeville. The Edward Sullivan Tolan collection of photos and letters of the great Bernhardt, which are housed in Philadelphia, is considered one of the most valuable ones to be in private hands. It even includes Sarah's rosary, given to her by the Pope, and a small brass clock that she carried on her American tours.

One of Bernhardt's leading men was Lou Tellegen, well known in Maine summer theaters where he often appeared with Adelyn Bushnell, an actress born in Thomaston, and her actor husband, Marshall Bradford.

A Maine idol of millions during the 1890s, one whom some called "Queen of the Stage," was Maxine Elliot, of Rockland. She shared her renown with her sister Gertrude, also an actress famed for her beauty.

Maxine was born Jessica Dermott and was extremely beautiful. A theater in Times Square, New York, was given her name. In at least equal proportion to her stage name was her title of "International Society Leader." She knew all the great and famous people of her times. Her house guests included the late Duke of Windsor, Edward, and his duchess; Winston Churchill; and David Lloyd George. In 1936, she rented her villa, the *Chateau de L'Horizon*, at Cannes, France, to King Edward VII of England.

Her home on Pleasant Street, Rockland, was moved to Hall Street to make way for the new railroad station, and a plaque was placed on the house, which later burned. Another plaque, placed at the original site, on the lawn of the railroad station, succumbed to vandalism.

Another theatrical star from Maine was Adelyn Bushnell, 1889–1953. Among her successes were the play *I Myself*, 1934, which she both authored and played in on Broadway, and her last performance as a star of *Phantom Cargo*. She was the lead of various stock companies from coast to coast, writer and director for vaudeville headliners and radio stars, then later for TV stars, many of the latter in collaboration with her husband. The strain on her voice from her stage appearances took its toll and she retired to direct and write, turning out several novels and selling many television scripts.

One of her most popular dramas among her local audiences in Maine was written in memory of her mother and was based on a supposedly successful remedy for cancer, which her mother actually had attempted. "Addie" was a down-to-earth individual with a big heart and a total absence of self-esteem.

A third versatile actress was Reta Shaw, of South Paris, Maine. While waiting for an acting career in New York, she used her musical talents, which had begun in her father's "Snappy Syncopaters" band of the "Roaring Twenties." She also did monologues, some of which were self-accompanied musical ones, in cocktail lounges and nightclubs, or for organizations. To supplement her income, she gave piano lessons.

When recreational workers were needed during World War II, Reta enrolled in the Red Cross and spent twenty-nine months entertaining troops in Iceland, England, France, Belgium, and Germany. Using her guitar and her portable organ, she played in bombed-out barns, muddy fields, and other undesirable places; but she loved the work. Her voice was strong and sure; her talent was well received. If she had ever had doubts of becoming an actress, this experience quelled those doubts.

Her first important role on the legitimate stage came in the 1940s in *Annie Get Your Gun* with the Mary Martin Touring Company. Then came in succession *Gentlemen Prefer Blondes*, with Carol Channing; *Picnic*, with such notables as Rosalind Russell, Kim Novak, and William Holden; and *The Pajama Game*, a long-running Broadway musical.

Turning then to Hollywood, she appeared in the films *Mary Poppins, Global Affair, Pollyanna, Bachelor in Paradise*, and others.

In television, she was highly rated as a comedienne in such shows as "Bob Hope Presents," "The Red Skelton Show," "The Lucy Show," "The Andy Griffith Show," "The Ann Southern Show," and others. Her last role was in *The Ghost and Mrs. Muir*, which ran for several seasons, plus reruns.

Praised by her co-workers and treated "as a queen" on the movie lot, she never let it turn her head. She was active in the PTA and the Girl Scouts when her daughter was in school. Semi-retired, she did commercials and, more important to her, some summer stock which recalled her true love—the stage.

Her Hollywood home was unpretentious. Once intending to be a missionary of the church, she had turned that intent into being a missionary of laughter. She referred to her comedy work with this comment: "If you can help one soul along, that's enough." Reta helped many "souls" by her cheerful, comedy missionary work. Her death came on January 8, 1982, at age sixty-nine.

Linda Lavin, the star of the TV program "Alice," grew up in Portland and graduated from the Waynflete School there.

Myrna Fahey, of Carmel, 1933–1973, at age twenty-two was playing opposite such well-known actors as John Barrymore, Jr., and Bob Hope. She later appeared in *Zorro* and *Gunsmoke* and the series *Father of the Bride*. Her early death from cancer cut short her Hollywood stardom on TV. She bore a remarkable likeness to Elizabeth Taylor.

Connie Roussin Spann, of Lewiston, is a radio and television personality. She currently owns TV station WPVI, on which she first appeared in 1964.

She was hostess for several years for the popular TV show *Romper Room,* and in 1973 received a Photoplay Gold Medal Award.

An entirely different form of acting is that of mime, first popular in the United States during the 1950s, when the acknowledged master of the art, France's Marcel Marceau, became known during his tour of the States. A pupil of his, Tony Montanaro, became famous in his turn and around 1972 settled in South Paris, where he gives lessons in his art at Celebration Theater.

By 1976, he had three separate units of his company on tour.

He first knew Maine through summerstock acting which brought him to the Camden Hills Theater. Maine abounds in excellent summer playhouses. There is scarcely a popular actor or actress who has not yet played at one of them. Victoria Crandall's Brunswick Music Theater, which opened its first summer season in 1959, is rated the finest such theater in the nation.

Ogunquit Playhouse, in southern Maine, has been termed "America's Foremost Summer Theater," possibly because of its fine repertoires and because of the outstanding quality of the performers. Among the famous names are: Bette Davis, Ethel Barrymore, Ethel Waters, Cornelia Otis Skinner, Anthony Quinn, Myrna Loy, and Douglas Fairbanks. The company's byline is "You can see the performers near enough to shake hands," and that is true. There is excellent performer-audience rapport. This theater opened in 1932.

Lakewood Theater, in Madison, was legally proclaimed the "state theater" by the Maine legislature in 1967. Its first performance was *Life with Father*. In *Ceiling Zero*, with guest performer Mary Rogers, daughter of Will Rogers, the play concluded with a plane crash. Coincidentally, it coincided with the real-life crash of her father, Will, and Wiley Post, in Alaska, when both lost their lives. Mary's mother was in the audience at Lakewood at the time. Immediate sympathy calls included one from Charles "Lindy" Lindbergh.

Lakewood is a resort property of 110 acres with prime lakeside frontage and a nine-hole golf course. It is the only so-called "theatrical resort" left in the United States. The compound includes a 1,000-seat theater, a country club, and thirty-four motel units, plus other buildings.

A growing theater is the Theater at Monmouth, in Cumston Hall. It is steadily advancing in quality as it heads into its thirteenth season in 1982.

The complete list of successful stage, screen, radio, and TV artists from Maine would indeed be lengthy.

One who was a "first" and an "only" at the time was the Algonquin Chieftain Henry "Red Eagle" Parly, of Greenville, Maine. He appeared in over fifty silent films, in Broadway dramas, and in musical comedies. He lectured, wrote over 500 short stories, and performed with "Buffalo Bill" in Wild West shows on the Barnum and Bailey circuit. He died in 1972, at age eighty-seven, at his home in Greenville. He may have had the most varied theatrical career of any American Indian.

Other Maine people with wide-reaching success in the above media are Nicholas Wyman, of Portland, in musicals; Phyliss Thaxter, of Cumberland Foreside, in movies, stage and TV, especially commended for her role in *The Longest Night*; Jean Arthur, of Portland; Jacques D'Amboise, of Portland, a ballet dancer in *Carousel*; Justin "Jud" Strunk, Jr., of Eustis, comedian and author, 1936–1981, who died in a crash of his own airplane; and Marshall Dodge III, a Portland humorist, recordist, and author of the radio series in the 1950s and '60s, *Bert and I*. He was killed in the early 1980s by a hit-and-run driver in Hawaii at age forty-five. He was the father of the Maine Festival.

A radio personality of dubious fame is Mildred Elizabeth Gillars, who once shocked people by being the first coed at Ohio Wesleyan University to wear knickers. Born in Portland, on November 29, 1900, she lived also in Greenwich Village, New York, Paris, and North Africa. Her goal was public recognition. Therefore, when she was in Germany at the opening of the World War II, she went on radio for the entire duration of the war as "Midge at the Mike," known by the GIs as "Axis Sally," a counterpart to Japan's "Tokyo Rose," a notorious propagandist.

John Ford, of Portland, 1895–1973, was one of the greatest movie directors of the big screen. His brother, Francis, was an actor. John directed numerous westerns, became president of the Motion Picture Directors' Association of America, won a gold medal for his "Four Seasons" in 1928, plus Academy Awards in 1940 (*The Grapes of Wrath*), 1941 (*How Green was My Valley*), and 1952 (*The Quiet Man*).

In *Stagecoach*, he selected an unknown to play the lead, and thus started the career of the popular John Wayne. His customary habit while directing was to chew his handkerchief. Active service in World Wars I and II, plus the Korean conflict, was an additional attribute.

Actors Gary Merrill and Bette Davis spent some of their married life in Cape Elizabeth, Maine, where Gary still resides, doing, as he says, "Nothing."

Camden received national recognition when the town was

used as a setting for the movie based on the TV series "Peyton Place." Some scenes were filmed in Rockland. Other Maine locations favored with the theatrical arts include *On Golden Pond*, starring Katherine Hepburn and Henry Fonda, which was originally planned to be on Great Pond, in Belgrade; *Emmeline*, by Judith Rossner, in which the original filming was done at Fayette; and the TV movie of *Captains Courageous,* starring Freddie Bartholomew and Karl Malden, which was shot off Camden, Maine.

In the area of newspaper and magazine success, which is truly an art, the first publication in this country evolved on St. Croix Island. It was a sort of brochure of events put out by members of the De Monts' expedition, and was distributed primarily among the local colonists. Champlain served as chronicler.

The first Maine individual to achieve success in newspaper work was Edward Winslow, 1595–1655. He was a highly-educated colonist and historian who established the first trading posts in Maine, Massachusetts, and Connecticut for the prosperity of the colonists. His journals contained the first account of the exploration and settling of Plymouth Colony and are rated as highly valuable historical documents.

Charles Francis Richardson, of Hallowell, 1851–1913, founded the New York *Good Literature* and was its editor for a while. He held a commendable reputation in the United States as professor of Anglo-Saxon and English language and literature. His *The Choice of Books* was re-issued in both English and Russian, and his two-volume *American Literature, 1607–1885,* was used throughout the nation for over ten years.

Maine had a pioneer and the first martyr in freedom of both press and speech—the Reverend Elijah Parish Lovejoy, of Waterville, 1802–1837. He was killed in Illinois, in 1837, the victim of five well-aimed shots fired from a mob, while he was protecting his press from damage caused by a fire started by a fanatic. But he left a heritage about which President Hoover once said, "Since his martyrdom, no man has openly challenged free speech and free press in America." He was an editor who openly pronounced his opposition to slavery. One line accredited to him turned out to be true. He said, "I can die by my post, but I can never leave it."

Lovejoy was born in Albion, Maine, and was buried in Alton, Illinois, on his thirty-fifth birthday. His name is revered in the Elijah Parish Lovejoy Award given annually at Colby College,

Maine, his alma mater. Among the credits for writing and reporting indicated on the award are the words "a heritage of fearlessness and freedom."

Erwin D. Canham, long-time editor-in-chief of the *Christian Science Monitor*, was one of the best-known and best-respected editors that Maine ever produced. He was born in Auburn, in February, 1904, and died in Guam, in January, 1982. Canham was the first newspaperman to head the nation's Chamber of Commerce. He was also named as an alternate U.S. delegate to the United Nations, in 1949. However, he was first and foremost a newsman who defended the people's right to know, and he had the knack to present and disseminate the news both capably and fairly.

John Neal, of Falmouth, 1793–1876, was the first American to contribute regularly, in 1823, to English periodicals. He wrote on American subjects and reviewed American authors, including himself. In 1828, he became editor of *Yankee* and held that position until his death.

Neal taught fencing and established the first American gymnasium. In addition, he practiced law, owned granite quarries, and was involved in several business pursuits. He was a genuine Yankee character, was the first editor to encourage Poe and Whittier by printing their works, and was the nation's first major art critic. He wrote constantly, but left little of worth.

Cartoonist George Danby, of Bangor, had his cartoons published in such papers as the *Philadelphia Inquirer* and the New York *Daily News* in 1981, when he was but twenty-four years old. Danby began as an editorial cartoonist in Maine, had his first out-of-state position with the New Haven *Register*, and then came his employment under the McNaught Syndicate.

C. A. Stephens, of Norway, was long associated with the *Youths' Companion*, from 1870 until its demise in 1929. It had a weekly circulation throughout the nation. He also authored several books.

Stephens was interested in science. His laboratory, known as "the Old Shack by the Lake" (Pennesseewassee), had fifty rooms where Stephens hoped to gather scientists from the world to search for a way to halt the aging process. He predicted the splitting of the atom and the construction of television sets long before any progress had been made on either.

He envisioned a "steamboat" college in which learning would be acquired by constant travel, around the world. And he endured being the husband of LaScala, whose dictatorial manner he accepted with grace. His laboratory home has been razed, but his name lives in the Stephens Memorial Hospital, in Norway, Maine.

In 1961, Edward Cony, of Maine, won a Pulitzer Prize for reporting while employed on the *Wall Street Journal.*

Nathaniel Parker Willis, of Portland, born on January 20, 1806, was called, at age thirty-four, the "most popular and in every way the most successful magazinist that America had yet seen." His articles were widely read and admired on both continents. Willis was a social lion with the women, a fact that showed as background for some of the most successful writings which were gossipy reports of high society. His biggest contribution lay in his founding one of the most popular magazines in the country, *Youths' Companion.* He was also a foreign news correspondent for a New York paper and the Civil War correspondent for *Home Journal.* He became a national figure and died on his birthday in 1867.

Willis had a famous sister who wrote under the pen-name of Fannie Fern.

James Phinney Baxter III won the Pulitzer Prize for his "Scientist against Time," in 1947. It is an account of allied crash programs used to develop the atomic bomb, radar, sonar, and other technological advances in combat use during World War II.

Baxter was a Portland native, valedictorian at Williams College in 1914, professor at Harvard for 12 years, first master of Harvard's Adams House, and at age forty-four became the youngest president Williams College had ever had. He was historian of the Federal Office of Scientific Research and Development. After his death at age eighty-two, he was buried in the Williams College Cemetery, June, 1975.

Women writers for magazines were rare in the 1800s, but Harriet Elizabeth Spofford, of Calais, 1835–1921, wrote romantic tales of minor literary value, but of major importance to nearly every American household. Perhaps her best works were "New England Legends" and "The Elder's People." She made a substantial contribution to literary and household journals, some in serial form, others in poetry.

In an entirely different angle of journalism was Julius A. Dresser, 1838–1893. This Maine man was founder and originator of the "New Thought" which contained new theories of disease and philosophy, based on metaphysics. He founded *Mental Healing.*

Loring Williams, a well-known figure at Ocean Park, where he and Adelbert Jackman founded the Maine Writers' Conference, put out an international magazine of merit, *American Weave.*

Publishing houses have benefited from Maine people. Thomas Bird Mosher, 1852–1923, was one of America's foremost publishers and literary scholars. He was a native of Biddeford who insisted on high quality and reasonable prices in his publications. One scholar of publishing work has been said to have made the comment that Mosher was "responsible for fine printing in America." In publishing circles he was known as "The Pirate of Portland" as he took advantage of the unprotected European writers, publishing their works without consent and without paying royalties.

The Anthoensen Press, in Portland, is one of the most famous small printing presses in America, and has won various awards and honors for having produced fine books. The company was formed by a Dane, Fred Anthoensen, 1882–1930, in the early part of the twentieth century. As did Mosher, Anthoensen insisted that the company produce fine, outstanding workmanship.

C. M. Clark Publishing Company, of Boston, was founded by a woman from Unity, Maine. Carro Morrell Clark published books written by unknown authors, and her publications were widely and enthusiastically received.

The nation-wide publishing house of Ginn and Company was founded by Edward Ginn, of Orland.

The G. P. Putnam and Son Publishing Company was founded by George Palmer Putnam, of Brunswick.

The Munsey publications were started by Frank A. Munsey, of Mercer. He had several publications, including two of America's oldest periodicals, *Godey's Lady's Book* and *Peterson's Magazine*, in addition to many newspapers.

Martin Brewer Anderson, of Brunswick, 1815–1890, was an associate editor of *Johnson's Encyclopedia.*

Samuel Deans, 1733–1814, wrote *The New England Farmer or Geographical Dictionary.*

The first American to publish a magazine with a circulation of more than 1,000,000 paid subscriptions per issue was Maine's William H. Gannett, whose family still runs one of Maine's largest newspaper businesses, in Portland, Augusta, and Waterville.

A true "great" in publishing was Cyrus Hermann Kotzschmar Curtis, whose grandparents were from Greene, Maine. He was born in Portland on June 18, 1850, in a corner house of Brown and Cumberland Streets. He continued to live in Portland. His father was a temperamental musician. His mother, Salome Cummings, was also musically inclined. Consequently, his two middle names were taken from a Boston musician who came to Portland and became friendly with the Curtis family.

Cyrus began his career by selling newspapers that he bought for one cent and re-sold for three cents. He eventually acquired his own hand-cranked printing press and solicitations from businesses for advertising. He lost all of this in the horrendous Portland fire of 1866, which leveled 1,500 buildings.

An interesting anecdote is that his mother put her valuables into a sideboard during the big fire, looters took the sideboard, she and her teenage son and daughter followed the looters for two miles, reclaimed the furniture, scared off the looters, and saved both sideboard and valuables.

Cyrus then went to work as clerk and salesman in department stores; then into an advertising firm; then started his own paper again at five cents per copy or fifty cents per yearly subscription. Thus did he begin with one page and advance, with the help of his wife, Louisa, to total magazines: *The Saturday Evening Post, The Ladies' Home Journal,* and *The Country Gentleman*, three magazines spanning the continent and impressive in their circulation expansion for decades.

Later he turned his attention to newspapers and at age sixty-three bought *The Public Ledger* and *The Evening Ledger* in Philadelphia, and then the New York *Evening Post*. He donated much of his fortune to charity, from hospitals to the Kotzschmar Memorial Organ, 1912, an outstanding instrument even now, in Portland City Hall. The story of this great philanthropist is contained in a biography, *The Man from Maine*, written by his son-in-law, Edward W. Bok.

The literary world of Maine is without parallel. Within a radius of 100 miles from the state capitol in Augusta are more literary landmarks than in any other circle of similar size in America and quite likely in the world. Maine has often been referred to as "The Home of Writers," and in recent years has gone well ahead of its nearest rival, Indiana. It can count an even dozen Pulitzer Prize winners in writing alone, up to 1980: six for poetry, one each for fiction, music, lyrics, newspaper reporting, drama, biography, and non-fiction.

A complete list of prominent Maine prose writers would be almost endless, and surely far too long for the contents of one book. Many have already been published in biographical book form. Any list of Maine writers of prose, however, should certainly include the following:

ABBOTT, Jacob and John, Brunswick and Farmington; known mostly for Maine histories and the Rollo books for children. Abe Lincoln once said, of Jacob's *Histories*, "To them I am indebted for about all the historical knowledge I have." The more than 200 volumes were highly respected and the Rollo books were acknowledged as "undoubtedly the most popular series of juvenile books ever published in America," up to that time.

BACH, Richard, Kennebunkport. National recognition with his first published work, *Johnathan Livingston Seagull*. The movie version was disappointing

BAXTER, James Phinney; historian, Pulitzer Prize.

BURNHAM, Clara Louise, Bailey Island; *Jewel* was her best novel.

BUSHNELL, Adelyn, Thomaston; drama, fiction, TV series.

CALDWELL, Erskine, Mt. Vernon; *Tobacco Road* and *God's Little Acre*.

CARROLL, Gladys Hasty, North Berwick; novel *As the Earth Turns* inspired popular TV series "As the World Turns." Her works have a warm, nostalgic style.

CARSON, Rachel, West Southport; *The Edge of the Sea* and *The Sea Around Us* typical works. Most influential, *Silent Spring,* which alerted the country to destructive forces of pesticides.

CATHER, Willa, Northeast Harbor; only story with Maine background is "The Best Years."

CHASE, Mary Ellen, Blue Hill; best works are those of her own life and home town: *A Goodly Heritage, Silas Crockett, Mary Peters*, and many other novels with biographical foundation.

CLARK, Rebecca Sophia, pen-name "Sophie May," Norridgewock; forty-two books led the way for interesting children's reading, such as the "Prudy" series and the "Dotty Dimple" series. Known as the "Dickens of the Nursery." Many of her books translated into foreign languages.

COFFIN, Robert P. T., Brunswick; best known for poetry, but excellent prose in *Kennebec, Cradle of America; John Dawn;* and other prose works. His biography of his father, *Portrait of an American,* won him honorary life membership in the National Arts Group.

COLCORD, Lincoln, Lincolnville; known for sea stories and for helping Golvaag, the Norwegian, translate into English his *Giants of the Earth.*

DAVIS, Owen, Bangor; Pulitzer Prize for *Icebound,* 1923. Wrote several plays.

DEANE, Samuel, 1733–1814, *The New England Farmer,* 1790, was first encyclopedic work of its kind in the United States.

DIBNER, Martin, South Casco; most important work *The Deep Sea,* 1953. Several translations and a movie.

DRESSER, Julius, A., 1838–1893; metaphysical writer.

ELIOT, Alice C.; pseudonym used by Sarah Orne Jewett for her early stories.

FIELD, Rachel, Cranberry Islands; best known for *All This and Heaven Too,* 1938. Several fictional books for children.

GILMAN, Dorothy, Portland; Mrs. Pollifax books are famous internationally. At least one of the series has been made into a movie.

HATHAWAY, Katherine Butler, Bar Harbor; *The Little Locksmith,* based on her handicaps throughout her life as a humpback.

HAWTHORNE, Nathaniel, Casco; began his *Scarlet Letter* while drifting in a skiff in a grotto on Sebago Lake, in vicinity of the Image Rocks. Sold 2,000 copies within ten days.

HOWELLS, William Dean, Kittery; *The Rise of Silas Lapham* and *The Lady of Aroostook* among his works. Was once editor of the *Atlantic Monthly.*

JACOBS, Margaret Flint, West Baldwin; winner of the Dodd, Mead and Company and *Redbook* magazine Prize Novel Competition in 1940 with her *The Old Ashburn Place,* the best novel by an American with not more than two previously published novels. Jacobs won the $10,000 with her first one. Several other novels followed.

JEWETT, Sarah Orne, South Berwick, 1849–1909; once considered America's greatest prose writer. In 1901, was first woman to receive an L.L. D. from Bowdoin College. Has surpassed other writers in her genre in describing the old, the odd, and the eccentric in a mild and gentle manner. A favorite work is *The Country of the Pointed Firs*, 1896.

JONES, Rufus M., China; internationally known when serving on Friend's Service Committee and for helping young people all over the world. Over forty of his books related to the history of the Quaker religion.

JUDD, Sylvester; probably the only minister to have written a transcendental novel.

KELLOGG, Elijah, Harpswell; famed for his Elm Island books for boys. Taught religion to families on the spine of Harpswell Neck. Great orator, especially on "Spartacus to the Gladiators."

MITCHELL, Edward Page; first science fiction writer. 1897 story told of freezing and then thawing dead bodies, startling the world. In 1881, seven years before H. G. Wells wrote about it, Mitchell authored a time machine story; and his *The Crystal Man* preceded Wells's invisible man by about sixteen years. He could well have been Wells's basis of inspiration in the science fiction world.

MORISON, Rear Admiral Samuel Eliot, Northeast Harbor, 1887; two-time Pulitzer Prize winner. Primary works were about Maine adventurers.

MULFORD, Clarence, Fryeburg, 1883–1956; famous for "Hop-a-Long" Cassidy stories, which became popular movies, and for other western tales.

PARTON, Sara Payson, Portland, 1811–1872; author of juvenile literature and light essays. Pen-name was "Fannie Fern."

PATTEN, Gilbert Corinna, Camden; pseudonym Burt L. Standish. Boys' books, including the Frank Merriwell series.

PULSIFER, Susan Nichols; writer for and about children. Some poetry and some religious works.

RAY, Isaac, Portland; known for publishing the best books in the 1800s on all phases of insanity.

RICHARDS, Laura E., Gardiner; over seventy volumes of stories, biographies, and poetry. Most popular book was *Captain January* inspired by a lighthouse seen from Mt. Desert Island. Won a Pulitzer Prize in 1916 for the biography of her mother, Julia Ward Howe.

ROBERTS, Kenneth, Kennebunkport; his historical novels are rated as the only ones to successfully rival those of James Fenimore Cooper. Roberts's personal favorites include *Arundel, Northwest Passage,* and *The Lively Lady.*

SARTON, May, York; universally known for her fifteen novels, ten volumes of poetry, plus journals and children's books. Has received several outstanding awards: one for her novel *The Single Hound,* one for her poems in *Encounter in April,* and one for a non-fiction work, *I Knew a Phoenix.* She once said, "Old writers never fade away. They just ripen."

SAWYER, Gene; known for the Nick Carter stories.

SPOFFORD, Harriet Elizabeth, Calais, 1835–1921; romantic tales popular in every American household for a generation or more. Best works were *New England Legends* and *The Elder's People.* Wrote several magazine serial stories and some poetry.

STOWE, Harriet Beecher, Brunswick, 1811–1896. She has been credited with starting the Civil War by the response to her *Uncle Tom's Cabin,* 1852. She began the novel on a piece of brown paper, with a fish chowder simmering on the kitchen stove beside her and a baby in a basket at her feet. President Lincoln called her, "The little lady who made the great big war." She was somewhat impractical, a dreamer, but her books accurately represent her times. Even the famous Tolstoy conceded that she showed "an example of the highest type of literary art." From the sale of that first book, she received the largest sum of money ever previously acquired by any American or European writer: $10,000 within three months. In 1856, her *Dred* sold out 100,000 copies in less than one month; and her *The Pearl of Orr's Island* achieved recognition as a very successful Maine-oriented novel.

STRUNK, Justin, Eustis; *Bury Me on the Wind,* 1979.

SWEATT, Margaret Mussey, Portland; author of the first Sapphic novel in America. The first woman book reviewer in New England.

71

TARKINGTON, Booth, Kennebunkport; friend and helper of Kenneth Roberts. Author, among seventy-five other works, of the Penrod series, *Seventeen* (1916), and *The Magnificent Ambersons* (1918).

WHITE, E. B., North Brooklin; ecologist, nature and animal lover. Has what is termed the cleanest, loveliest prose in the American language, by the consensus of several critics. His farm is a sort of domestic animal complex, down to Charlotte, a spider, who lived in a "two-holer outhouse." Known for contributions to the *New Yorker* and *Harper's* magazines. Among his best known works are "Every Day Is Saturday," "Quo Vadimus," and "One Man's Meat."

WIGGIN, Kate Douglas, Hollis Center, 1856–1923. Three best known works are *The Old Peabody Pew, The Birds' Christmas Carol*, and *Rebecca of Sunnybrook Farm*.

WILLIAMS, Ben Ames, Union and North Searsport. One of the best short story writers and novelists of the nation. One outstanding historical novel, about Union, Maine, is *Come Spring*.

WOOD, Madame Sarah Sayward Keating, York, 1759–1854; first woman fiction writer in Maine and the first Gothic novelist in America. In 1827 she wrote the popular *Tales of the Night* and called herself "The Lady of Maine." Was the first writer to use American locales for plots. *Julia and the Illuminated Baron* is often named as her best book, but it lacks reality and is too ornate for current taste. She was commonly referred to as "Madame Wood." Up to her death, she considered herself to be a failure to the extent that she located every possible copy of her works and burned them. To her, Sir Walter Scott was so far superior that she had no claim to even being accepted as a writer.

YOURCENAR, Marguerite, the first woman to be admitted to the prestigious forty member *Academie Francaise*, organized in 1635, and in which only death can create a vacancy. She came to Maine in 1950 to live on Mt. Desert Island. She was admitted to the *Academie* on March 6, 1980, at age seventy-six, and traveled to France to be inducted, thus breaking a 346-year-old men-only tradition. Her prize-winning work is *Memoirs of Hadrian*, now published in sixteen languages. She is a highly acclaimed classicist and novelist.

A special category of Maine prose writers is that of its humorists, who have influenced to a high degree the lighter side of American literature, especially in the nineteenth century.

Charles Farrar Browne, "Artemus Ward," of Waterford, lived from 1834 to 1867. He added the *e* to the family name. He was responsible for the nation's awareness and appreciation of humor and yarns. President Lincoln admired Artemus Ward to the extent that he would read one of Ward's stories now and then at his Cabinet meetings.

Ward began as a printer's apprentice at the Norway *Advertiser* and the Skowhegan *Clarion*, then moved to Boston and later to Ohio. He wrote for several magazines, favoring exaggerations, debunking, regional dialect, self-depreciation, and preposterous ridicule. He started Mark Twain on his road to fame by sending Twain's "The Celebrated Jumping Frog of Calaveras County" to a magazine. Queen Victoria was a devotee of Artemus Ward.

His real source of recognition came from his lectures, which were in demand all over the country. At the age of thirty-three, he died of consumption in England; but by his previous request, he was buried in South Waterford, Maine.

Second only to Ward was Bill Nye, 1850–1896. Born in the Moosehead region, at Shirley Mills, he was the most natural of all his contemporary humorists; never posed as outlandish; used no gimmicks, no misspelled words, no slang. He simply exposed the pretense and superstitions, customs and characteristics of his day. He has been compared to Will Rogers, and termed the "Laureate of American Humorists." His Western humor was judged to be the best.

He tried being a newspaper man, a lawyer, and a justice of the peace, but he was not content with any of those professions. Once he started writing about the town of Shirley Mills, "where I first met my parents," he began giving lectures which took up too much time for continuing his career as a writer. He earned the highest income of any American humorist up to his time; and once he had earned $30,000 within a year, his fame was secure.

Nye founded the Laramie *Boomerang* and was its editor in 1885.

Seba Smith, 1792–1868, a third American humorist, was born in a log cabin in Buckfield, Maine, and rose to fame by his letters, presumably written by "Major Jack Downing of Downingsville." These consisted of political "squabbles and chicanery," especially aimed at the Maine Legislature. On October 13, 1829, he started the Portland *Daily Courier*, the first daily newspaper north of Boston; and he made it prosper by Major Downing's letters, written in Yankee dialect, the first use of a dialect in humorous writings by American authors.

He has had many imitators of his homespun political philosophy, notably James Russell Lowell, David Ross Locke, Charles Farrar Brown, Artemus Ward, Peter Finley, Will Rogers, Hosea Bigelow, Mr. Dooley, and Petroleum Nasby.

Smith received national recognition because he was the first political satirist in America, the first to portray the Yankee-type individual (the Major), to be proficient in numerous poems and stories, and to employ research. He closely paralleled Will Roger's style of later years. He spent most of his life in either Bridgton or Turner with his wife, the former Elizabeth Oakes Prince, of North Yarmouth. Mrs. Smith was the first American woman to go on a lecture platform in public and the first to speak out on women's rights.

Stephen Evans Merrill, of Skowhegan and Brunswick, was a well-known humorist, photographer, and public speaker. He also appeared on radio and TV. He died in 1980, thus terminating his newspaper column "Sand 'n Salt." He is remembered, too, for his recording of "Father Fell Down the Well and Other Maine Stories."

The prolific Sylvanus Cobb, Jr., was the first American humorist to apply mass production. He was born in Waterville in 1823 and died in 1887. He seemed to manufacture rather than to write. His output, of no great literary value, was amazing: one biography, one hundred sixty-six novelettes, one thousand thirty-four short stories, and two thousand, three hundred five sketches. In 1846, with his brother, he founded a magazine, the *Rechabite*, with overtones of temperance. It soon expired, as it freely libeled several notables of the day.

Justin Strunk, of Eustis, was a nationally-known comedian, author, singer of Maine folklore, and a member of the "Laugh In" series on TV. He, too, had a Will Rogers type of humor. His death came in an air crash of his own plane on October 5, 1981.

In direct contrast to the humorists is Stephen King, born on September 21, 1947, in Portland, now living in Center Lovell and Bangor with his wife, Tabitha. *Down East* magazine characterized him in one issue as "King of the Occult," and "Maine's Horror Prince" has also been used in reference to him. His early horror novels placed him on the Best Seller list for an extended time and made him a millionaire at age thirty.

When he was a child, his living conditions were those of near poverty. As young as age eleven, he started keeping clippings of murders. His introspective mind, cataloguing the everyday events and frustrations of the small town of Durham, led to his enhancing or enlarging his data, fed by a vivid imagination and a wide scope of reading. By age sixteen, he was writing; writing stories of horror, of evil, of terror, of fear. His first prize money came from a writing contest held by the University of Maine English Department, from which he won $69.81.

Although his best sellers have all been bought by television stations, some refuse to show the "too gruesome and too intense" tales. His *Carrie*, 1973, deals with an adolescent with telekinetic powers living a nightmare. *Salem's Lot* leaves the reader trying to separate the vampires from those who have not been tainted. And *Shining*, filled with supernatural evil, and judged by many as his best book to date, has horror, the occult, the alcoholic, and child abuse, all wound around the plot. The jackets of his books are equally morbid, one being a single drop of blood on an all black cover. His 1981 novel, *Cujo*, was predicted to outsell any other book ever published by the Viking Press. Of himself he once said, "All I am is the phosphorescent ghost at the funhouse. I'm the guy who jumps out and yells 'Boo!' "

With all the famous past and present writers in Maine, it seems only natural that the Maine Writers' Research Club was for many years the oldest writing organization in the United States and the only historical research group in the country which published its own books.

This prestigious club grew out of a prize contest offered by the Lewiston *Journal*, in 1915, for stories of historical value relating to Maine. The club was organized in October of that year, in Biddeford, and pledged itself to perpetuate Maine history. Cora Belle Bickford was its first president.

Its first published book sold all 1,500 copies in only three weeks. Several contributors had been contest winners in various categories of literature, and its subsequent membership continued to be versatile. On April 10, 1965, in the month of its ninth publication, the fiftieth anniversary was observed and the club was dissolved. Its purpose had been fulfilled. Stories and data about Maine were pouring off the presses in quantities. There was no longer a need for cooperative work. Younger writers wanted personal recognition. Maine was finally being given due recognition.

Maine has rightfully been called "The Poets' Corner of America." Maine natives have won more Pulitzer Prizes for poetry than have the residents of any other one state. These prize winners have been Edwin Arlington Robinson, of Head Tide, three prizes; Edna St. Vincent Millay, of Rockland; Robert Peter Tristram Coffin, of Pennellville (Brunswick); Ann Sexton, who lived in Boothbay Harbor; and, stretching a point, Richard Eberhart, summer resident at Cape Rosier since 1940.

Maine has also produced America's three leading sonneteers: Millay, Robinson, and Henry Wadsworth Longfellow. Longfellow has the added distinction of having written the first and greatest American epic, *Hiawatha*; of being the only American poet permitted to have a bust of himself in the Poet's Corner of Westminster Abbey, England; and of having been the most widely-read poet in the world. Robinson is acknowledged as having written the most famous American contribution to the Arthurian Cycle, *Tristram*.

A few time-established "greats" in poetry will be mentioned in conclusion.

First, the well-known "Maine Trio," with Longfellow heading the list. He was a poet of the children, a poet of the common man, a poet of the world. Born in Portland on February 27, 1807, he died there on March 20, 1882. Of his tremendous output of verses, he chose as his most personal one "The Psalm of Life."

His first printed poem, at age thirteen, was "Lovewell's Fight," reflecting the defeat of Chief Paugus at Fryeburg, Maine. He knew his topic well because he often visited his grandparents in nearby Hiram. His first book of poems was *Voices of the Night*, in 1839. Many of his poems are about the dark and the night, as evidenced in his titles.

He is attributed as being the first to recognize beauty in the soul of an American Indian, shown in *Hiawatha*, which broke a long-time barrier. His patriotism found release in *Paul Revere's Ride*. His *Evangeline* has been printed in twenty different languages. He was a poet of the heart and even today is thought of as the most widely-loved American poet throughout the world.

While teaching at Bowdoin College, in Brunswick, he introduced the first study of foreign languages, preparing his own textbook as there were none available.

Second of the famous poets of Maine was Edwin Arlington Robinson, who won three Pulitzer Prizes for poetry yet was fifty-three when he won the first one. He was an author of remarkable characterizations, such as those found in his "Tillbury" poems, depicting local townspeople in Gardiner.

He was born on December 2, 1869, and died on April 6, 1935. His output of poetry was remarkable, totaling twenty-seven volumes. He was a compulsive worrier and fearful of ridicule, two factors which are sensed within his characterizations. He showed himself in self-justification, in winning approval, and in admitting to his feelings of inadequacy and humility. The self-effacing may have been responsible for his remaining a bachelor.

Narrative poetry was most easy for him, and among the best-remembered characters are Richard Cory and Miniver Cheevy. Although morose, he had a touch of wit which occasionally shows through; and it does seem that his success came not because of him but in spite of him. The last line in his *John Brown* seems to justify and identify this poet: "I shall have more to say when I am dead."

The third of the famous poets was Edna St. Vincent Millay, of Rockland, the first woman to receive a Pulitzer Prize in poetry. She died in 1950 at Steepletop, her lovely Berkshire home during the latter part of her life. Her other home was on Ragged Island, off the coast of Maine, where she could fill her soul with her love for the sea.

The "Queen of Poetry" came from a talented family, her mother and two sisters being artistic in writing and/or acting. Her first published poem appeared in the *St. Nicholas* magazine when Vincent (as she liked to be called) was but eleven years old. Three years later, she was presented with a gold medal from the same publication as its most worthy contributor.

Recognition and reputation came easily at age nineteen with her "Renascence," which won a nation-wide contest of over 10,000 submitted poems. Later, her Pulitzer Prize was for "The Harpweaver," which has run well over fifty editions to date. She was named State Poet Laureate in 1933, and elected to the American Academy of Arts and Letters in 1940.

In her young adulthood, she was a non-conformist, dealing with the problems of her day, such as the Loeb-Leopold case. So filled with patriotism was she that, during World War II, her poems were banned in Germany, particularly her "Murder at Lidice." During that time, she gave up her automobile and bought a horse and buggy to save gasoline, as requested of all true Americans. She probed, she exposed, but she never sought to answer the prevailing questions of the day. She merely wanted to bring them to the attention of all whom she could reach.

The extent and variety of her writing is broad, ranging from personal emotions to nature to crime to war. So far, no other woman poet has reached the pinnacle of this tiny, soul-searching writer. She was honored in 1981 by having her picture on the eighteen cent U. S. Postal Service stamp.

The third Pulitzer Prize winner, Robert P. T. Coffin, won his award in 1936. He was born in the Brunswick area on March 18, 1897, and died in January, 1955, during the delivery of a lecture that he was giving at Westbrook Junior College. His work is world famous for portraying the Maine rural scene. In his poetry he describes life on his "Salt-Water Farm." Both the farm and his productions were simple, soothing, and satisfying. Nature and nature's creatures were a source of delight to him, and he glowed when hearing of any favorable contribution mankind made in their favor.

His "Strange Holiness" won him the Pulitzer. It contains lyrics of sunlight, of hope, of humor, of tears, all closely combined in beautiful appreciation of Maine background, from "The Marsh Spider" to "The College of Captains." One critic commented that "Coffin has made an original contribution to American poetry varied in beauty, musically rhythmic, stalwart of spirit."

Further space on Maine's poets will be limited to a brief mention of five who have proved beyond doubt that they shall remain a great part of Maine's heritage.

Holman Day, 1865–1934, born in Vassalboro, but later a resident of Auburn, called "Poet of the Maine Woods," won his reputation as a delineator of the state and its characteristic people. Novels, plays, and short stories also dripped from his pen; but the homespun "Pine Tree Ballads" and similar poems with Maine woodsmen dialect have been his foremost accomplishment.

Day also turned out films at Augusta during the 1920s. In 1921, the Day's Production Company released a "two-reeler" twenty-minute, black and white movie every two weeks from spring to winter, with a "seven-reeler" made during the summer. "On location" meant the Maine woods. One of his two-reel silent films received a big response in 1977 when shown at a Rotary Club meeting, a film indicative of Day's dry, Maine-woods humor. That same year, Everett Foster, of Rumford, produced a documentary called "All But Forgotten—Holman Day, Filmmaker," which won a Silver Medal at the twentieth International Film and TV Festival in New York.

Another whose verses will never be forgotten is Julia Ward Howe, the first woman elected to the National Institute of Arts and Letters, in January, 1907; and to the American Academy of Arts and Letters in 1908. She was the originator of the stirring Civil War song "The Battle Hymn of the Republic," written while she sat in a tent on the battle grounds, and sold to the *Atlantic Monthly* for a mere four dollars.

Another writer of hymn verses who left two books of them at his death, is Samuel Longfellow, brother to Henry W. Longfellow. A third book of his verses was published posthumously.

Samuel Francis Smith, 1808–1895, was the Maine man who wrote the words to "America," sometimes called "My Country 'Tis of Thee." Within one half hour he had completed the verses almost as they read today. He held a pastorate in Waterville from 1834 to 1842 and was a professor of modern languages at Colby College. He authored over 600 poems. One popular one, both in America and abroad, is "The Morning Light Is Breaking."

Finally, the "Poet of the Maine Coast" is Wilbert Snow, of Spruce Head. Snow had the theory that there is a subtle relationship between a man's spirit and the soil on which he was born. He was at one time poet laureate of Connecticut, and he served as lieutenant governor of that state in 1946. He was also an Alaskan reindeer agent. If these professions and locations seem far apart, one should remember his versatility in living. He was a professor in Connecticut, a teacher in Alaska, an artillery man during World War I, and a professor at Wesleyan University for thirty-five years. In addition, he was, at times, a lobsterman off the coast of Maine, the state he loved most.

This quiet, gentle, man died at the age of ninty-three at his Spruce Head home while watching a Red Sox baseball game on television, with his wife, the former Jeannette Simmons, a Rockland educator, beside him.

A verse writer of a different style is Reginald Holmes, of Jay, who writes for *Ideals* and Hallmark's *Treasures*. Over 355 of his some 6,000 verses have been sold to Hallmark, Rustcraft, Gibson, Paramount, and other popular card companies. Born in 1896, he did not start his greeting verse hobby until 1958, and it soon became a part-time vocation.

There are by actual census more than 100 living, published poets and verse writers in Maine. Although their names do not appear in this book, the value of their work is in no way demeaned. Undoubtedly national recognition will, in time, reach many of them.

3

Shipyards, Sea Craft, and Seamen

Explorer MacMillan's "Bowdoin" at anchor in home port Provincetown, Mass.

The *Bowdoin,* used by MacMillan on his Arctic exploration

Launching of a schooner, Rockland

"The Crane," at Bath Iron Works Corporation, is the largest of its type in the Western Hemisphere. When fully boomed up, it stands 400 feet.

The schooner *Constellation,* built by Frye Flynn & Co., Harrington, 1918, is one of the last big four-masters.

Wreck of the *Maine,* Havana, Cuba

The *Dirigo,* first steel sailing vessel in the world

Maine has always led other states in sea-oriented ventures, especially shipbuilding. In 1607, the first American trans-Atlantic trader was built in Phippsburg and launched in 1608. Johnathan Philbrook and his two sons launched Bath's first schooner in 1743. In the early 1840s, Maine led the United States in wooden shipbuilding and put out the first clipper in 1850. Only three clippers were built out of the 326 vessels constructed during the 1850s, when Maine continued to rank as the nation's leading producer of wooden ships. In June, 1851, the first four-masted schooner was built in Bath. In 1853, more vessels were constructed in the Kennebec Yards, Augusta to Bowdoinham, than in Portland and Bath Yards together.

In 1860, a new type of transport was built, "coasters," in Calais. These were chiefly for carrying lumber to coastal markets, and over 80,000,000 feet of lumber was shipped that year by this new style boat.

Between 1862 and 1893, Maine ranked as the center of wooden shipbuilding in the nation with eighty percent of all full-rigged ships being made in Maine, forty-four percent of which were built in Bath.

In 1885, more than one third of all ships launched in the country were Maine built; and soon, over one half of all seagoing vessels under the American flag had been launched from Maine shipyards.

In no other region of the country has there been such fluctuation from affluence to poverty, from hopes to failures, than there was in Maine's sailing ships. Today's maxim is that As Steel Goes, So Goes The Nation. In Maine, it was As Ships Were Or

Were Not Built, So Went The State.

Each town built its own type of vessels, and seamen could tell at a glance where and by whom each ship had been constructed. Launchings were filled with superstitions. For instance, a ship was never launched on a Friday: girls with empty buckets should not be anywhere around; there must be seagulls present. This was taken care of by throwing garbage overboard just before the launching; and someone then had to knock three times on the hull to drive out witches.

The first types of vessels or seacraft built in Maine were shallops, ships, pinnaces, galleys, ketches, pinks, snows, yawls, sloops, joggers, schooners, brigs, barques, clippers, and a riverboat called a gundalow which resembled a Dutch canal boat.

These were followed in time by the multi-masted schooner, and eventually by the steamer. The only windjammers remaining in the world today are in the mid-coastal waters of Maine, and comprise a fleet based in Camden. They are either remnants of the famous old sailing vessels, or are reproductions. Unique to Maine, they offer summer cruises along the Atlantic seaboard.

The most recent popular Maine-made boat, 1981, is the Saroca. It derives its name from the fact that it can be sailed, rowed, canoed, or motor-driven. The Lincoln Canoe Company makes them in Waldoboro.

The oldest naval shipyard in the country is in Kittery, Maine. The U. S. Navy purchased the land on Seavey's Island, about two miles from the coast, from a William and Sarah Dennett, in 1800, for $5,500. In 1870, Admiral D. G. Farragut died in what is probably the oldest house on the island, a seventeen-room dwelling atop a hill. The house has been headquarters for the commanding officer in charge since 1812. It contains seven working fireplaces, a hidden passageway, and a sort of lounge between the front entrance and the stairway. There are indications that the main part of the quarters, before the addition of carriage houses, porches, and wings, dates back as early as 1724.

Within the security complex is the site of the signing of the Russo-Japanese Pact in 1905, and an old prison graveyard.

Since its inception, the yard has become known throughout the world as a leader in design and building of submarines; and it claims the distinction of having the only totally enclosed ship-building ways in the United States.

The Kittery Yard currently employs around 7,000 civilians with a monthly payroll of $7,000,000. In 1974, it had additional naval personnel with a monthly payroll of $831,000. It specializes in overhaul and modernization of nuclear submarines.

The first Navy submarine, L-8, launched in 1917, came from the Kittery Yard; the first atomic submarine, the USS *Swordfish*, was launched there in 1956: the radar picket subs USS *Sailfish* and USS *Salmon* were designed and built at the yard; and the USS *Dragon*, 1959, the first submarine to traverse the Northwest Passage under ice, a feat attempted, but not fulfilled, came from the Kittery Yard.

The worst disaster ever involving the yard was when the *Thresher* went down off Cape Cod in 1963, with 129 aboard, and no survivors.

Allied in spirit, at least, with the Kittery Yard is the Naval Air Station in Brunswick, with personnel of around 3,000. The station is headquarters for the entire anti-submarine warfare surveillance for the nation. Farther north, in Winter Harbor, is a naval security installation with personnel of around 400 navy and civilian employees combined. And at Cutler Communications Center, at Mt. Desert, is the prime link to nuclear submarines of the U. S. Navy which are submerged in distant seas. Maine has had and still does have an all-important role in the naval defense of our country.

Another world-famous shipbuilding site is the Bath Shipyard which, by 1850, was fully equipped to build and outfit ships and therefore became a busy international port for the nation, with wooden schooners its specialty. Up to 1920 it had built the largest ones ever constructed in the world. After the era of sailing vessels, the yard became known as the Bath Iron Works with a work force of 3,700 in 1976.

The first Bath contract for a wooden steamer came in May of 1889 or 1890. It was called *Cottage City*. At the same time, the BIW received the first of all its subsequent Navy projects. From being a small iron foundry in 1826, it became the builder of the largest yacht in the world up to that time, the *Corsair*, a turbo-electric, for J. P. Morgan, the millionaire. Here, too, was built the *Ranger*, defender of the American Cup contest, authorized by Harold Vanderbilt, a contest that has yet to be won by any country other than America, which won for its twenty-fourth time in 1980.

BIW now turns out tankers, containerships, and the new class of merchant vessels called "Ro-Ro's" (Roll-on—Roll-off).

A new class of Navy destroyer was started in the 1970s, the patrol frigate. A name worthy of mention here is William Stark Newell, 1878–1954, a BIW worker who was influential in the basic success of this type of destroyer. He served under President Truman on the Atom Bomb Committee and observed the nuclear tests at Bikini. He oversaw the building of seventy-four high-speed destroyers during World War II, more ships than were built for the entire Japanese Navy during a comparable period, and one quarter of all destroyers built for the United States' government.

In addition to destroyers, there were mine sweepers, tugs, Liberty Ships, and the customary submarines.

The Bath Yard has a huge, white crane, soaring 400 feet when fully boomed up. It is the largest of its type in the entire Western Hemisphere, and uses enough electrical power to supply 1,000 residential homes for a year. Its main hoisting machinery has 500 horse power; it can withstand a 112-mile-per-hour gale; and it can operate under a full load in winds up to thirty-six mph. This $4,000,000 crane has for its primary purpose the lifting of sections of ships up to 220 tons. Its official name is simply "ship-building crane." The operator's cab is air-conditioned and juts out midway up the structure. Its only competition is two similarly designed and strengthened cranes in Japan.

In 1975, the BIW Yard sent down its ways the largest ship ever launched in Maine up to then, the S. S. *Maine*, captained by William L. Rich.

In 1982, it launched the HSTC-1-(Hawaiian Sugar Transport Co.), the largest ocean-going barge ever built in the United States.

In 1976, the BIW launched a new Navy guided missile frigate, the *Oliver Hazard Perry*. Prominent actor John Wayne gave an address following the ceremony.

In 1979, on December 17, a "production" model, the first of fourteen of a new type of U. S. Navy guided missile frigates was launched eleven weeks ahead of schedule and below the projected cost, a familiar accomplishment of the BIW, no longer even challenged. The *Flatley*, commissioned in June, 1981, was completed sixteen weeks ahead of schedule. Flatley was the first World War II American flier to shoot down the first enemy aircraft in the first American sea victory during the battle of the Coral Sea.

In 1981, the BIW was resting easy with a backlog of orders very near the billion-dollar mark: guided missile frigates, commercial tankers, a dredge ship, a seagoing barge, plus overhaul work on Navy ships. These contracts should ensure a prosperous future into at least 1986, and the request to work on the most efficient means of producing a new generation of destroyers could mean an even more satisfying future. This apparently spawned the yard's 1981 decision to establish a $46.7 million expansion in Portland. The Bath Iron Works is one of Maine's greatest assets; and the confidence shown in it is a clear indication of the high quality of workmanship at the yard, a tribute to its management, a respect for its integrity, and a belief in all three.

From a three-year trade apprenticeship program offered at BIW since 1941, Elizabeth Beck, of North Yarmouth, became the first woman graduate, in 1980.

The Percy-Small Yard in Bath has built seven of the twelve six-masted schooners in the world. This yard specialized in very large four-, five-, and six-masted schooners for bulk cargo trade, and adapted power machinery to its hand-crafted industry. It is the nation's only surviving shipyard where large wooden sailing vessels are still constructed, and is listed on the National Register of Historic Sites. Established in 1909, it was renovated in 1971 as a public museum. In it are exhibits of small craft, ship gear, machinery, tools, and related marine-oriented objects.

The oldest steam vessel under the U. S. Registry is the *Seguin*, a gallant old tug which is being restored by the Percy-Small Yard to preserve Maine's seagoing heritage.

Samuel Rogers Percy, Jr., after his sailing days, became mayor of Bath, 1901–1902, and then went to the State Legislature for 1904–1905. Frank Small, after his sailing days, became, in turn, mayor of Bath, 1911–1912; and his son was mayor in 1939.

The Percy-Small Yard is famed world-wide for its reputation of building a boat which has proved to be both stable and beautiful. Its special contribution has been the internationally praised and nationally commended "Downeaster."

Another Bath yard of high reputation is the Sewall Yard, prominent in supplying the world's need for sailing craft. In 1894, it produced the first steel sailing ship in the United States, and it built the last square-rigger in the world.

Arthur Sewall, 1835–1900, was one of the country's foremost merchant shipping agents. Joseph Ellis Sewall, 1854–1925, also of Bath, was called a "brilliant mariner and a brutal captain." He was in charge of his *William P. Frye* in 1900, the first American merchantman sunk by a German U-boat attack, on January 28, 1915, during World War I.

The Bath Museum of Ship Artifacts is, understandably, about the finest in the world for marine memorabilia.

Several other shipbuilding yards have existed and produced quality seacraft.

At one time, Searsport had over 1,500 men at sea, most of them captains. In 1889, more than ten percent of the Merchant Marine shipmasters were from Searsport, and twenty-seven of their collective sons commanded the tall-mast ships in their own days. Captain Jeremiah Sweetzer headed the list of these able seamen when Searsport was known as Prospect.

At Rockland, wooden vessels were built from native oak. The most famous of the Rockland ships was the *Red Jacket,* the story of which comes later in this chapter. Snow's Shipyard was the leading "wooden vessel" construction site in Rockland for many years. Lee's Boat Shop is currently active.

In Damariscotta, in 1878, A. A. Curtiss Company launched a Downeast square-rigger. In 1884, Henry B. Hyde produced the finest Downeaster ever built. And the only large square-rigger ever to go through Great Barrier Reef, a steamer's lane from Sydney, Australia, to Calcutta, was piloted by Maine's Captain Herbert Humphrey, who did not even take in any canvas. At Thomaston, the Dunn and Elliot Yards built the last five-masted schooner in the world. At Southwest Harbor, Maine's only ten-master slid down the ways. At East Boothbay, in 1968, was built the world's largest molded fiberglass sailing yacht. Sailing craft have come also from Blue Hill, Camden, Mt. Desert, South Bristol, Vassalboro, Waldoboro, and other small towns.

A dominant factor during World War II was the South Portland shipyard which gave the country some of its best seagoing defenses. At the Bliss-Portland Yard, the first all-aluminum submarine was constructed, for example. And when World War II was in progress, the South Portland Yard was claimed to be the best liberty port in the entire country.

The fact is that Maine ships are acknowledged to be first in size and speed over practically all ships in the world. They are the best constructed and cheapest in cost, possibly because Maine workers have both ingenuity and pride in product.

Maine also has the availability of several streams and rivers within the state, abundant water power, a multitude of harbors, and near-ideal sites for both building and launching.

Currently, the Bath and Kittery Yards are foremost, but at least seventy-five smaller ones are in operation.

A less grand water craft is an added Maine product: the canoe. The oldest was the White Canoe Company, which started in 1889. Their canoes were patterned from an Indian birch bark design.

90

The Old Town Canoe Company, formed around 1890, has built some of the best great lake and river craft in the world for nearly a century, and currently manufactures about 7,000 crafts a year. This company was the first to convert the famous Indian birch bark canoes into a design of canvas on wood. As of today, the company is producing crafts of vinyl and fiberglass, and even sporty white-water plastic kayaks in breakout design. In the 1970s, the company led all other canoe works.

The labor for the Old Town Canoe Company is done on Indian Island where the best canoe factory is always branching out. The newest type of racer is slim, low profile, minimal drag, and just a bit of sheer and hard chine (back bone) for easy entrance. The rugged racer is an excellent craft for tough whitewater courses. It is a competition canoe built to win, and does!

There are other canoe firms, perhaps the Hampden and Waldoboro ones being best known, in the state.

Two historical facts are allied to Maine canoes and bateaux. A canoe identified as a Maine product appears in a picture taken during the first Alaska Gold Rush; and the bateaux used by Arnold's men on his famous expedition to Quebec were built by Reuben Colburn and Thomas Agry, shipbuilders in Pittston from 1763 to 1775.

At the present time, the only cruise ship operating intracoastal waterways between Maine and Florida is the *American Eagle*, launched in June, 1975, from the Harvey Gamage Shipyard in South Bristol. The waterway is a system of bays, inlets, canals, sounds, and rivers that run the entire length of the East Coast. The *Eagle* is a 151-foot steel ship begun in October, 1974, and costing $1.4 million. It was built for the American Cruise Lines, Haddam, Connecticut, and was operating between Haddam and New England islands and coastal ports. Its owner was Charles Robertson.

The last three-masted schooner in the nation to carry passengers is the *Victory Chimes*, built in 1900 in Virginia, but now sailing out of Rockland for summer cruises.

The *Luther Little* and the *Hesper* are the two schooner hulks that have been grounded on Wiscasset's shore for nearly forty years and provide an excellent subject for tourist photographers.

Thoughts of ships and sea voyages lead to thoughts of pirates. Maine had only one—Dixie Bull, the first pirate on the Atlantic seaboard. Dixie was an over-sensitive person; and whenever slighted in any way, he became exceedingly annoyed. Abraham

Shurt, of Pennsylvania, once built a strong stockade around his new village. Dixie felt slighted! The stockade was soon demolished.

In June, 1632, a French pinnace had seized Dixie's shallop in Penobscot Bay and took away several "coats, ruges, blanketts." Angered by his loss, as well as by losses suffered by other colonists through French intervention, Dixie got two ships and crews and, turning pirate, he engaged with the pinnace. In the course of this battle, he was taken prisoner; but after six month's imprisonment, he escaped, organized a crew, and became a pirate of English vessels and settlements, being successful at the fort at Pemaquid.

He is supposed to have buried his loot in a cove on Cushing's Island when driven there on one occasion by wind and storm. Although sought by many, the wealth has never been found.

Finally, a small fleet of five ships set out to capture Dixie Bull, and this was the first time in the New World that boats had been assembled for the purpose of protecting the seas. It was likewise the first naval demonstration of the colonies. The weather favored the pirate, and it is believed that he escaped to England.

The first U. S. Coast Guard's sea-going officer was Captain Hopley Yeaton, of Lubec, commissioned by George Washington in 1791 to serve as captain of the *Scammel*, in what was then known as the U. S. Revenue Marine Service. Later this became the Revenue Cutter Service, and Yeaton soon held seniority among the ten merchant marine captains.

Yeaton was a civic-minded individual, and he was instrumental in forming the Eastport Masonic Lodge as well as promoting the incorporation of the town of Lubec. His efforts to have West Quoddy Light established were fruitful, too. He served in command in the Continental Army and as third lieutenant in the U.S. Continental Navy.

However, the major outcome of his civic service was the influence that he projected in establishing the Coast Guard Academy, 1790. He immediately became known as "Father of the Coast Guard." He commanded one of the ten cutters which comprised the nation's only navy at the time and which patrolled the coast against smugglers.

He died in 1810 and was buried in North Lubec. In 1975, his remains were removed from the Lubec gravesite and taken to a crypt near the chapel on the grounds of a three-acre memorial park, known as Chapel Walk, in the Coast Guard Academy compound. He had spent seventy years at sea; therefore, it was appropriate that the *Eagle*, which carried his body to the Connecticut resting place, was one of the world's largest and most magnificent sailing vessels of the day.

Another Maine naval commander of renown was Commodore Edward Preble, 1761–1807, of Portland. He was the first great commander of the American Navy. It has been said that he sank every ship with which he engaged. Enlisting at sixteen as a cabin boy on a year-cruise European-bound privateer, at eighteen he was a midshipmen in the Massachusetts State Marines. That same year he boarded and captured a British brig in Penobscot Bay. Later, aboard the *Protector*, he was captured and put into the *Jersey*, a perfectly horrible prison ship.

After parole and release, he became a peaceful merchantman until 1798 when he was commissioned as a lieutenant in the U.S. Navy, and was given command of a new frigate, the *Essex*, shortly thereafter. His objective was to escort some mercantile ships to the East Indies, and it was on this voyage that he became the first naval officer to carry the American flag around the Cape of Good Hope.

His outstanding accomplishment was his victorious campaign against Barbary pirates. After this success, he was given command of the *Constitution*, known also as "Old Ironsides." However, he turned down the commission and instead began designing gunboats and a bomb ketch for the Navy. Only two days after these ships sailed out of Portland Harbor, Preble died of consumption.

He was often referred to as the "Father of the U. S. Navy," as Yeaton had been, because of his outstanding contribution to assure its future and its prestige.

Continuing the tradition of "firsts" in naval history of the United States, in 1974 the *State of Maine*, from the Maine Maritime Academy, was the first U. S. Merchant Marine training vessel to visit the Soviet Union. There were 350 midshipmen, officers, and crewmen who began the cruise on April 30 and returned in June. They were met in Leningrad by several thousand people, bands, and Soviet dignitaries. Twenty-five of the Maine crew were feted in Moscow as guests of the Soviet Union: the trustees, the officers, and Deborah Deane, a young girl in her twenties, the first female midshipman in the Maine Maritime Academy.

Maine created one unique situation when the nine sons of Joseph and Jennie Drinkwater, all nine being sea captains of full-rigged ships, by sheer coincidence sailed into New York Harbor and dropped anchor on the same day. The authorities thought that they were being hoaxed, but it was soon clear that yes! nine

Captain Drinkwaters really were applying to clear nine Maine vessels in New York Harbor on the same day.

It has been written that Captain D. D. Willard, of Palermo, spent twenty-one years at sea without losing a ship or a man. Certainly as incredible is the fact that between July 1881 and July 1884, 423 American "Downeasters" made the long trip to California's grain trade center with a loss of only two ships. Well-made Maine boats and efficient Maine captains should receive credit for this statistic.

A renaissance in boatbuilding came in 1979, when Bruce Doughty, of Harpswell, and two friends, Washburn and Planka, established a full-fledged commercial boatyard in Woolwich. Their first launch was an eighty-six foot, 120-ton steel fishing boat for lobstering and trawling. And in 1981, Bar Harbor suddenly found itself as a busy port of call for international cruise lines.

Alphabetical List of Some of Maine's Famous Ships

Albion Cooper: a brig besieged with mutineers who were brought to court and hanged in Auburn, Maine.

Alert: first clipper ship constructed in Damariscotta, 1850, met the demands for a fast ship to get to the Alaska Gold Rush.

America: first three-decker battleship built in America, at Kittery Yard, 1782. Showed the world the ability and ingenuity of Yankee naval construction. Given to France as a gift.

Ames, Governor: first five-masted schooner built on the Atlantic coast, in Waldoboro, 1888.

Anna F. Schmidt: Kennebunk-built merchant ship. Left Boston on January 11, 1863, bound for San Francisco, with all kinds of cargo, from iron furniture to the latest invention for killing bedbugs. Deceived by the display of an American flag flying from a hostile ship on July 1, off the coast of Rio de Janerio, the crew became hostages. All goods were transferred to the pirate ship *Alabama*; the *Schmidt* was burned; and the Captain Henry B. Twambly was later put on board the *Star of Erin*, reaching London on September 22, with total loss of ship and cargo.

Annie H. Smith: last large vessel built at Calais, 1876. Was 1,452 tons, 222 feet long, forty-foot beam, twenty-four-foot hold. Seemed blessed with good fortune. No trouble although it went around the world for seven years on seven trips. Even rode out the great blizzard of 1888 which swept the seaboard and wrecked many vessels on the high seas. Was eventually reduced to coal barge status. While being towed in third place behind a tug, the tow line was rammed by a steamship and the *Annie H. Smith* sank in deep water.

Aras: became the most famous of all yachts built at Bath Iron Works up to her time. Even her launching proved to be spectacular as, when the craft slid into the waters, she heeled over on the port side and a few of the passengers went overboard. She was soon balanced and all went well from then on. She was a private yacht until 1939, and in 1941 the government converted her into a gunboat named the *Williamsburg*.

She was stationed in Iceland until 1942, then to the high seas on patrol as a station ship for about six months. After that, back to the high seas on patrol and escort duty, during which time she saw action with German U-boats on one convoy.

For the next three years she engaged in trial runs, anti-aircraft and submarine training cruises, and troop transportation to Iceland.

On November 8, 1945, the *Williamsburg* became the presidential yacht of President Truman, and the deck felt the softer tread after years of hurrying, pounding steps of Navy personnel. She was the conference room for many important decisions made by world leaders during and after World War II, including Churchill, Atlee, Eisenhower, and the French Prime Minister, Rene Mayer.

Even that did not conclude the days of the old *Aras*. In April, 1953, President Eisenhower ordered the yacht taken out of commission and used for afternoon trips down the Potomac River for wounded Korean War veterans. That May, the President and Mrs. Eisenhower and guests took a four-day cruise on the *Aras*, the last glamor voyage for the now-called *Williamsburg* before she was put into mothballs.

However, the by-now ancient yacht returned to service in August, 1962, when the National Science Foundation took custody of her and converted her into a research vessel for an International Indian Ocean Expedition, involving twenty-five nations and forty-four vessels; and once again her name was changed, to honor a noted Danish marine biologist who was chairman of the first such commission, and the *Aras*, alias *Williamsburg*, became the *Anton Bruun*.

It seems unbelievable, but her saga was not yet finished. After the expedition, she was leased by a couple who operated her as a restaurant.

She certainly seemed destined to lead one of the most colorful, dynamic, and diversified lives one ship could ever expect, this *Aras* built at the BIW in Bath, Maine.

Aryan: the last wooden square-rigger ever built in the world. Constructed not far from the launch site at Phippsburg, considered to be the location of the first ship ever built in the New World, the *Virginia*, the *Aryan* was a product of the C. V. Minot Yard, in Bath. Launched on July 14, 1893, she has often been termed the best of her kind in North America.

The last of the famous "Downeasters" to slide down the ways were the square-riggers

Acme: 1901, captained by Stanley Amesbury, Rockport.

Astral: 1900, captain unknown.

Atlas: 1902, known as the "hell ship," captained by Reuben S. Lawrence, Dresden. This was a steel square-rigger from the Sewall Yard.

Bangor: an iron steamship built in 1844, the first sea-going propeller steamer built in the United States.

Bloomer: launched at Mt. Desert Island, known to have been carrying stone out of Penobscot Bay eighty-two years after its launching; an enviable record.

Bowdoin: carried Rear Admiral Donald MacMillan on his expeditions to the Arctic. An eighty-eight-foot sailing vessel constructed in East Boothbay, 1921.

Cary and Tammy: the "World's Fastest Lobster Boat" in 1972. A thirty-footer which won championships at Jonesport-Beals on July 4, the traditional date for the contest. Defeated a four-time winner, reaching a top speed of thirty-eight knots. Built in Jonesport and piloted by Guy and Duane Carver of Beals Island.

Chase: one of the last two four-masted schooners ever built in Maine. Constructed at Boothbay Harbor, a yard which never built five- or six-masted schooners.

Chester: U.S. Scout ship, built at Bath Iron Works in 1908, was fastest in the world at the time, at 26.52 knots.

Constitution, (or "Old Ironsides"): completed in 1797 with its masts and spars from Maine pine. In 1934, Mrs. Grace Whiting Gulliver, a Maine summer resident, was the first person to be married in the Captain's cabin of this old frigate. She married a naval officer—naturally.

Dash: a privateer clipper ship, a "thinned down" version of the early schooners used in privateering.

Defiance: an extreme clipper-type vessel of 1,690 tons, built in Rockland in 1852.

USS Dewey: a frigate which was the first guided missile destroyer leader ever built. Constructed in Bath.

Dirigo: first steel sailing ship in the United States. Designed by Arthur Sewall, president of a ship-building and shipping operation in Bath. He decided to experiment with a steel vessel and re-conditioned the British four-master *Kenilworth*, a bark of steel construction which had burned in San Francisco. He was determined to produce a fleet of five four-masted steel barks of his own with help from British shipyards and supervisors.

He brought trained riveters to the western bank of the Kennebec River. Their duties were varied. One boy heated the rivet, then tossed it to a man who caught it in a bucket and, with tongs, thrust it into a hole. The other men, one inside and one outside the hull, then hammered it into place.

On February 3, 1894, during a snow storm, America's first steel sailing vessel slid down the ways into the Kennebec River and was christened *Dirigo*. It was 321 feet long, 45.3 feet wide, had a draft of 22.5 inches (one source states 25.6), and registered 2,845 tons net, 3,005 tons gross.

The cost was $157,000. She had two full decks and carried 13,000 square yards of canvas. Black at the time of its launching, it was later repainted snow-white from trunk to waterline.

On her maiden voyage, she carried 130,000 cases of case oil from Philadelphia to Hiogo, Japan, a 159-day voyage, which included a cyclone. At Hiogo dock, the crew took advantage of Captain George W. Goodwin's being ashore and consumed too much liquor. In the ensuing turmoil, the boat-swain was stabbed.

After cementing a small leak around the bow plates, on March 5, 1895, she returned safely in only 140 days, which was excellent timing.

Steel houses on the main deck were connected by flying bridges, and the helmsmen were protected by a steel wheel-house at the forward end. She could stand up without balance. Jack London, famous writer, and his wife were passengers on one of the West Coast voyages of the *Dirigo*. London was work-ing on a manuscript in which he called the vessel a "hell ship." But it was one that Sewall and Company, the most influential of the Bath shipyards at that time, proudly proclaimed. It coursed the seven seas for twenty-three years on its steel plates and frame, acquired from Scotland. The Sewalls built nine more similar vessels before they closed the company in 1903.

Captains and owners of the *Dirigo* changed from time to time. On what turned out to be her last voyage, around the awesome Horn, she left Seattle in October, 1915 or 1916, for Kalamar, Sweden, with 5,000 tons of barley aboard. Off the Scottish coast, on March 2, she was spotted by searchlights, hailed by a British patrol boat, and boarded in spite of her bearing the American flag on her side. She was accused of carrying cargo shipped by a German agent, cargo intended for Ghana. This information proved to be correct, but was not known by the owners.

The *Dirigo* was condemned; but she was of such solid structure she was not scuttled but ordered back, and left for France on May 4, 1917. On May 31, a German U-boat challenged her before she had left British waters, off the coast of Cornwall, as she was leaving port. The men were saved by lifeboats; but the twenty-three year career of the *Dirigo* was terminated when German submarines sent bombs through her. She now lies silent, deep in the English Channel.

Edna Hoyt: the last five-masted schooner built in the world. In August, 1934, she was so popular that at Pier 11, New York, over 50,000 visitors broke down her gangplank in their en-thusiasm; sixteen artists set up easels to sketch her; and 500 people asked for a berth with her crew, of which ten was the limit.

In November, 1935, she took the last cargo of barrel

shooks from Portland to Barbados. Three motion picture news-reel companies were present to shoot her departure; but she found a good wind and set sail before daylight, so the only reel taken was one from off the Portland lightship, by one of the photographers who just happened to have commandeered that spot.

The *Edna Hoyt* was built in the Dunn and Elliot yard at Thomaston, in 1920, for coal trade; 284 feet long, 41 feet wide, 20.8 feet deep, weighing 1,384 tons, yet could carry 2,400 tons. She had fifteen sails. Although still in her prime, she encountered a battering gale in the Bay of Biscay in November, 1937, and was too badly damaged to be reconditioned. She was sold as salvage and became a floating barge. Her captain, Hopkins, turned down numerous offers to command steamers, but instead decided to, in his words, "go on the beach."

Elliott: the first ship to be named for a naval hero of the Vietnam War. It is an anti-submarine destroyer christened in 1971 for a Thomaston man who was killed in action, December, 1968, while commanding a river squadron in the Mekong Delta.

Enterprise: defeated the English *Boxer* in the first American naval success in the War of 1812. Both captains were killed off Pemaquid, and both were buried at the foot of Munjoy Hill, in Portland.

Flying Cloud: a well-known clipper of Maine construction.

Flying Scud: a clipper that voyaged from Damariscotta to Melbourne in seventy-six days. It was from the Metcalf and Norris Yard, pioneers in clipper ship building in Maine during the early 1800s.

George W. Wells: world's first six-masted schooner, built by Holly Marshal Bean of Camden; launched July 1, 1900. She cost $125,000; had a beam of 48.6 feet; depth of 23 feet; net tonnage of 2,745; overall footage of 40 feet. Her captain was John G. Crowley.

She could carry 5,000 tons of coal although only a 2,920-ton vessel. She had for sails a fore, main, mizzen, spanker, and jigger. A new sixth sail was added and named "driver" at the captain's suggestion. At the launching, white roses were scattered in place of champagne, and white doves were freed.

Crowley and Bean wanted it this way.

The yard kept 150 men busy year round and turned out fifty-four vessels in about thirty years, as well as becoming involved in other enterprises. The George W. Wells was hailed in the world as the start of a fleet to restore the American Merchant Marine to its former glory.

Great White Bird: a huge, 3,185-ton square rigger never previously matched in size nor appearance. Built in the Sewall Yard in Bath. Her main mast towered 200 feet above deck and all three masts swung seven yards. She was doomed to hard luck and accidents, and on July 28, 1891, bound from Liverpool to San Francisco with 5,000 tons of coal, a gale stripped most of the canvas, the coal began to smoulder and emit coal gas, and eventually broke into flames. The cargo caught fire; the gas overcame some of the seamen; help came from other boats; and the vessel became warped into shallow water and was grounded.

Guy C. Goss: probably the first ship in American history to be arrested. Weighing in at 1,572 tons, named for a well-respected Bath shipbuilder, it arrived in Aukland, New Zealand, under Captain William H. Besse on April 10, 1896, with 10,000 pounds of lumber.

She was immediately boarded. A rigid bailiff even nailed a writ to the main mast, stating that the vessel was in default of 1,500 pounds of back pay to the master and crew.

Hualco: undoubtedly made the shortest voyage on record. She was launched in Belfast in 1856, fully equipped and found; weighed anchor in the morning; headed into Penobscot Bay; and four hours later, scooting along at eight knots, struck a pinnacle rock on Saddleback Ledge, ripping open her bottom. She sank within twenty minutes. Her crew took to the ship's boats and returned home the night of the day they had sailed. This event claims to have caused "the shortest life span of any vessel ever built."

Jacona: the first cargo ship in the United States to attempt to furnish portable power, 1930. It began operation in Bucksport and later supplied power to Portsmouth, New Hampshire.

John A. Briggs: a three-masted built in 1878, the largest ship ever constructed in Freeport. Over 7,000 people crowded the river bank for the launching.

Kaiulani: the last surviving American three-masted square rigger merchant vessel and the largest of the 17,000 square riggers built in the United States. Constructed at the Sewall Yard in Bath and launched on December 2, 1899, on the Kennebec River. Built for an Hawaiian trading company she began her varied career as a sugar packet between San Francisco and Honolulu in the 1890s. Passengers were accommodated.

From 1909 to 1927, she went to Alaska with workers and supplies for salmon canneries there, bringing back the canned fish. She was idle during 1927–1936, and then was used in the movie *Souls at Sea*. Her next venture was in World War II when she was used to carry lumber from Washington State to Durban, South Africa, in 1941. In 1942, she barely escaped from an encounter with the Japanese enemy.

Her name signified "Child of Love." She will be permanently berthed along Maine Avenue in the Marine Museum, Washington, D.C., as a floating museum, by an act of Congress.

Lamson: fastest ship of its type in the U. S. Navy in 1936, was Maine made.

Lash: the first "Lighter Aboard Ship," a pioneer in 1972. She was tried out in Penobscot Bay, Maine, when a six-barge lighter with 1,200 tons of newsprint, destined for Greece, was hoisted aboard *Lash Espana*, off Searsport. She never goes dockside, but gets a fifty-hour job done in four and a half hours simply by taking the lighter and contents on board rather than transferring the cargo.

Lyman M. Law: a 1,300-ton four-master that sailed from Stockton Springs on January 6, 1917, with 2,000 tons of wooden staves, destined for Palermo, Italy, to construct lemon boxes. On February 12, suddenly a shell banged through the rigging and across the bow. Members of a German submarine came aboard and gave the crew twenty minutes to abandon ship.

Captain Stephen W. McConough, of Winterport, reached Sardinia safely and explained that the American flag was very prominently displayed. President Wilson said that the seizure was the last straw in a series of ruthless incidents and asked that from that time on all merchant ships be armed. This incident hastened the entry of America into World War I.

Magnolia: the first three-master built in the world, at Blue Hill, 1833. It weighed 109 tons. After forty years she was changed into a two-master.

Maine, S.S.: This 684-foot-long cargo ship was built for a San Francisco company and was the largest boat ever launched along the entire northeastern coast of the United States. It was not a warship, but a vessel to carry food products and other merchandise of peace. It was built by the BIW and the 33,000-ton vessel went down the ways on May 24, 1975, about ten miles from the mouth of the Kennebec River where the pinnace *Virginia* of Sagadahoc was launched in 1607.

It was called both "cargo carrier" and "cargo liner," and cost $37.8 million. This was the first of the Roll-on, Roll-off cargo ships of five such freighters to be built, four of them in Bath. Motorized cargo can be driven on and off on its own power; and on shipboard there is mobile equipment for the cargo and its containers.

The tremendous size figures are ninety-six feet high just to A deck, 102-foot beam, and a "sail area" of over 50,000 square feet. She is 685 feet long and has a cradle weighing more than many World War II destroyers. Over $10,000,000 of the cost went toward wages and salaries for Maine people.

Other ships built in Maine and bearing the state's name include:

Maine: 1844, a three-master, 150 feet long, built in Patton.

State of Maine: 1878, a "Downeast" square rigger, 216 feet long, built in Damariscotta by A. A. Curtis.

S.S. Maine: 1881, the first *Maine* sidewheeler, 224 feet long, built by Goss and Sawyer.

Maine: a schooner built by the New England Company and used to carry timber, oysters, and salt around Chesapeake Bay for over sixty years.

S.S. Maine: 1917, the largest of its type until 1919. It was 402 feet long and constructed in the Sewall Yard at Bath.

Was one of these six boats bearing the name of *Maine* the one which was blown up in Havana Harbor, instigating the Spanish-American War? If so, which one? If not, what is known about the historical one? The identity has purposely been omitted.

However, the shield from the bow of the "Remember the *Maine*" ship is now on a memorial granite monument in Davenport

Park, Bangor. In addition, a plaque designates that the monument was erected in memory of the Maine servicemen of the Spanish-American War.

The Maine warship which was sunk in Havana Harbor on February 15, 1898, touching off the war, lay there in the harbor until a Maine man, Alfred King, a Civil War veteran, started agitating the government to raise the wreck and find the true cause of the explosion. His refusal to quit finally had results; and on March 16, 1912, fourteen years after the event, the then poverty-stricken man had his dream come true. The ship was raised by pontoons, and the bones of sixty-eight crew members were removed for honored burial.

Later, the rusty hull was towed to open sea with impressive ceremonies, and was consigned to oblivion by most historians.

Malcom Baxter, Jr.: a four-masted schooner built in Camden and launched in 1900. It was the only schooner known to have demolished a lighthouse, which it did all by itself.

On December 28, at daybreak, with all sails set in a strong breeze, she rounded into the wind; and defying the efforts of the helmsman, crashed into the Thimble Shoal Light, which was set on pilings. The house toppled; the coal stove tipped over; the hot coals set fire to the house; the keeper and his assistant barely escaped; and the *Malcom Baxter* retreated with very little personal damage, but left behind her the first lighthouse ever demolished by a schooner.

Marguerite G.: a thirty-foot lobster boat which won its fifth victory in seven years in the 1974 Annual Fourth of July race at Jonesport-Beals. With this win, it regained its title of "World's Fastest Lobster Boat" with a speed of forty knots.

Mary and Helen: first steam whaler, built in Bath in 1879; 420.5 tons, 138.2 feet long, 30.25 wide, with a depth of 16.06 feet. Registered September 8.

After the Civil War, Bath made most of the Arctic steamer whaling barks. Whalebone was highly sought for women's corset stays, a fashion which greatly increased the need for whalebone. Goss, Sawyer, and Packard also put on three masts for emergency. The *Mary Helen* was destroyed by fire.

Maui: a 720-foot container ship, May, 1978, largest vessel ever built by BIW up to that time.

Neptune's Car: a clipper, one of the fastest on record, out of Rockland. Captain Patten took his wife, Mary Brown Patten, on one voyage and she took to the clipper with unusual dexterity. She could read charts, plot courses, and spot the sun, all on her first trip.

On the second trip, the first mate delayed the ship to keep it from winning a time race, and he was put in chains. Soon after that, the captain developed brain fever. Consequently, Mary, nineteen years old, took command of the tall-masted, long-sparred clipper in the furious Cape Horn seas. For fifty days and nights she did not once go to bed, fighting snow, sleet, and for a husband who did not seem to fully recover.

Meanwhile, the imprisoned mate was released; but he turned the ship around, then made advances to Mary; so she had him put back in chains.

One week from her goal, the wind died down, her baby was due at any moment, yet she persevered and took the ship into port after 136 days. She is quite likely the greatest heroine of the seas, this woman born in Rockland in 1837. She received $1,000 from the ship's underwriters, who said "We know of no instance on record where woman has assumed command of a large and valuable vessel and controlled the crew and ship to its destination."

She became an international heroine. As for the captain, he never fully recovered and died in 1857. Before her son reached his fourth birthday, Mary, too, died of typhoid fever and tuberculosis, in 1861. Young Patten was taken in with his grandparents in Rockland; and King's Point Academy, in New York, named a newly constructed hospital for his mother.

Navarch: the last of its type succumbed to ice floes with two determined men still on board as it was carried northward to its destruction.

Nightingale: of South Eliot, abandoned at sea in 1893, once sailed from New York to Shanghai in eighty-eight days.

Noa: the U. S. destroyer whose crew recovered astronaut John Glenn from the Atlantic, was a Bath-built ship. The name is that of a Navy midshipman, Loveman Noa, who lost his life in the Philippines in 1901 while on anti-smuggling duty.

A previous destroyer had borne his name, but was lost in the Pacific during World War II. This second *Noa* was intended for use in the same war, but was launched too late.

O'Bannon, U.S.S.: one of sixty-seven Bath-built destroyers of World War II and later wars. Had unique distinction of carrying a citation for waging war with potatoes. One of the few destroyers ever to take on an enemy battleship at close range and emerge almost unscathed.

In 1943, in the Pacific, she surprised a surfaced Japanese submarine; poured in five-inch shells at close range; lobbed depth charges onto its deck; and the cook, wanting a role in the drama, plugged spuds at the sinking sub. Two years later the Maine Potato Growers presented to the ship a plaque reading "Tribute to the officers and men of the *U.S.S. O'Bannon* for their ingenuity in using our now-proud potato to 'sink' a Japanese submarine in the spring of 1943."

The destroyer was named for Presley N. O'Bannon, 1784–1850, a Marine Corps lieutenant who led a detachment of marines 600 miles across the North African desert in 1805, in a war with the Barbary States, and planted the U. S. flag in the fortified town of Derne. From that action came the phrase " . . . to the shores of Tripoli," in the "Marine Hymn."

The *O'Bannon* also did escort duty in repeated invasions of the Philippines; and with two other destroyers triumphantly escorted the *U.S.S. Missouri* into Tokyo Bay for the Japanese surrender ceremonies.

Decommissioned in 1946, it was put back into service and earned three battle stars in the Korean War, making a total of twenty earned stars. It also saw action during the Vietnam conflict. The *O'Bannon* surely lead a life of noble achievements in addition to the potato episode.

There had been another *O'Bannon* destroyer during World War I which had been scrapped in the 1920s.

O'Brien: a Liberty ship, or small freighter, which carried supplies overseas during World War II. It slid down the ways in 1943 and was retired in 1946. Built in cooperation between the BIW and the South Portland Shipbuilding Corporation, it was named for Jeremiah O'Brien of Machias fame. Now resting in the Golden Gate National Recreation Area, California, it will eventually hold a museum. It bears the inscription "Jeremiah O'Brien, Portland, Maine" on its life rings, and has been designated as the National Liberty Ship Memorial, being the only one of over forty such ships which once existed that remains unaltered and unmodified. All others have been scrapped for their metal, or scuttled.

The *O'Brien* proudly rests its laurels along with Old Iron-sides (the *Constitution*) in Boston, the *Constellation* in Baltimore, and the U.S.S. *Olympia* in Philadelphia.

Ocean Bird: built and rigged in 1853 at Vassalboro. On her return from her maiden voyage to Africa, she brought to the United States its first peanuts.

Priscilla Alden: a schooner that still exists in miniature of the three-master as produced by Jay Hanna of Rockport, in 1964. The model is now the property of the Smithsonian Institution, being the fifth of Mr. Hanna's models constructed and on display there.

Ranger: first ship to fly the Stars and Stripes. It was on a voyage to France to apprise the American commissioner of Burgoyne's surrender. Built on Badger's Island, it was commanded by the famous John Paul Jones.

The *Ranger* was built and launched in 1777, at Kittery. When it entered the Harbor of Quiberon, France, Jones saluted the town and in return was given a nine-gun salute, the first such salute given by a foreign power to a man-of-war flying the Stars and Stripes. The event was on February 14, 1778. Jones was its first commander.

The ship was considered "fat" because of its tremendous canvas spread.

Ranger: of a different type than the one above, was built in Bath in 1937 and won the Class J1 yacht race for the American Cup.

Rappahannock: built in Bath at the Clark and Sewall Yard. For several years the 1,133-ton ship was the largest ship in the world. On November 11, 1891, she suffered an explosion around midnight, and by the end of that day was a charred and smouldering mass. Once back in Maine, her captain, Dickinson, took out a brand new vessel, the *Aryan*, another Bath product, and the last wooden square-rigger ever built in the United States.

Red Jacket: built in Rockland, 1853–54. A remarkable clipper, designed by Samuel A. Pook, of Boston, who was the first naval architect in the United States who was not connected with some shipyard. She carried forty men and a watch, needing a big crew to handle her speed.

Her launching was indeed spectacular. She scooted across the channel and struck the schooner *Warrior*, causing but little damage.

Her feats include the following:

1. On her maiden voyage from Sandy Hook to Rock Light, Liverpool, she broke the crossing speed by twenty-one hours and thirty-five minutes, having completed the trip in thirteen days and one hour. This trans-Atlantic east-bound voyage has never been excelled by any other sailing vessel.
2. She went from Liverpool to Melbourne in sixty-nine days and eleven hours. Upon her arrival, Captain Asa Eldridge disregarded the escort tugs and backed alongside the berth without aid. People on the dock cheered wildly.
3. She circumnavigated the globe in five months and four days (one source stated ten days). This included stops at ports. To be sure, it was not the popular theme song to come later, "Around the World in 80 Days," but it was superior speed for the times. Again, she was cheered at dockside and purchased by an Englishman, thus relinquishing the American flag.
4. Her 413-mile run of one day has been bettered by only three other sailing ships in history, and it was a whole generation later before a steamboat equalled it. Few, if any, ships can match the feats of the *Red Jacket*.

In 1878, she sank as a result of a collision, but was raised and continued as a coal hulk at the Cape Verde Islands until her end in the late 1800s.

Red Jacket: a second ship by that name was documented in Rockland customs house in 1939.

Roanoke: a vessel in which the 98,000 tree nails alone outweighed the entire tonnage of the early *Virginia*. It was the largest successful four-masted wooden bark ever built in the United States. Johnathan Philbrook is credited with its construction in 1743, at the Bath Yard.

St. Mary: last of the Downeast square-rigged sailing ships to be built; launched in Phippsburg, 1890. Wrecked off Cape Horn in 1890; reassembled in 1978 to be put on display at the Maine State Museum in Augusta. It is the largest surviving wooden ship in the world, and the reassembled wreckage weighed forty tons, recovered from the Falkland Islands off South America. It is an historic prize, featured on the last postage stamp issued by the Falklands before the 1982 Argentine invasion.

Saratoga: In 1844, its 1,200 tons surpassed the largest ship built up to then. She was a product of the Trufant and Drummond Yard at Bath.

Savannah: the first privateer to receive a commission from the Confederacy, in 1620. Built on Richmond Island by George Richard, her first capture was a brig, the *Joseph*, from Rockland, less than twenty-four hours after leaving from Charleston. Flushed by this success, she then chased and fired at a ship which turned out to be, to her mortification, the U. S. brig *Perry*, a renown privateer hunter.

Sciota: Captain James Maguire, of Camden, served on her and commanded the U. S. Fleet when Admiral David Farragut gave his memorable order, "Damn the torpedoes. Full speed ahead."

Solimar: the world's largest molded fiberglass sail yacht in its day. Built in East Boothbay by Hodgdon Brothers in 1968. The fifty-eight-foot boat cost $150,000, and its Texan owner planned to keep her in southern waters.

Swordfish: the first U. S. authorized atomic submarine, product of the Kittery Yard.

Tammy: Maine's only miniature ten-masted, thirteen and a half foot schooner, built to scale by Elmer Davis of Southwest Harbor, and "launched" in a pond behind the town's fire house.

Typhoon: built in Kittery, the first American clipper to sail to Liverpool, in 1851. It was the largest ship to have arrived there to date. Became affectionately known as the "Portsmouth Flyer" for her unequaled record time for the voyage.

Vast Explorer I: not beautiful. Resembles a tuna boat. In high waves and a strong wind, she can cause considerable misery to her crew, which is usually changed every two days in such weather. In calm seas, she is a smoothly riding craft. Only vessel of its kind in the world. Maiden voyage was from Portland to Bristol, August, 1973. Capable of testing sonabuoys, devices dropped into the water by the Navy to locate submerged submarines.

After Bristol, went to the Virgin Islands and then to the Antarctic waters which had a different salinity. It can go from Iceland Gap to the Gulf Stream and test waters where sonabuoys are used.

Virginia: built by the English and launched on the Sagadahoc (Kennebec) River by Popham colonists, 1607, on the site where England first attempted to settle the northeast part of the country. It was a pinnace, which first was captained by George Popham, who had established the first colony in Maine, and was used for his return to England.

The boat was sixty feet long and listed from twenty to thirty tons; well built, with moss being used for calking and shirts being used for sails. It served for twenty years and was then cast away on the coast of Ireland with a load of tobacco from the Virginia Colony, ironically on the very shores from which the future population of Maine was to be enlarged. A model of the *Virginia* is in the Bath Maine Museum.

Washington: first warship launched in North America; built for the Royal Navy in 1690, in Kittery.

Wild Rover: built in Damariscotta, by Austin and Hall. On one voyage out of Shanghai, with lumber, there was on board a young Japanese stowaway who became friends with the crew and found a friendly welcome in Boston. He was the first Japanese to seek an education in the United States. He returned to Japan in 1874, founded a college there, became its first president, and was the internationally-recognized educator Joseph Neesima.

William B. Frye: the first American ship lost in World War I. A steel sailing vessel built in 1901 and owned by Arthur Sewall and Company. She left Seattle on November 4, 1914, for Queenstown, Falmouth, or Plymouth, with a cargo of about 186,950 bushels of wheat. She was sunk on January 28, 1915, by a German cruiser, the *Prinz Eitel Friedrich.*

William J. White: a four-masted schooner constructed at Bath in June, 1880, a boat with an enviable reputation.

Wind's Will: the smallest sailboat that has made a west-to-east crossing of the Atlantic Ocean. The designer and pilot, William "Bill" Dunlop, age forty-one, of Mechanic Falls, left Portland in his nine foot one inch boat on June 13, 1982 and arrived in Falmouth, England, on August 29. This voyage set a world's trans-Atlantic solo crossing record for a small boat.

World Glory: the largest tanker afloat at the time, ran the Rockland trial course just before discontinuance of the course in favor of electronic devices.

Wyoming: largest and last of only ten six-masted schooners that ever went to the open sea. All but one were Maine built, the first one being in the H. M. Bean Company yard in Camden, 1900. The other eight were constructed in either Bath or Rockland.

Of these ten, four foundered or sank at sea because of weather; four were wrecked or sunk by enemy submarines in World War I; one burned at the dock; and one ended her days peacefully.

The *Wyoming* sank off Pollack Rip at Cape Cod, laden with coal from Virginia, destined for the International Paper Company in Portland. The disaster came during a violent snowstorm, March 11, 1924, when the bow was parted from the hull; and no piece of the craft nor any trace of its crew was ever found.

The master builder was Miles M. Merry, and its first sailing master was Angus McLeod.

Some of its outstanding statistics are five cargo hatches, three decks, a capacity for more than 6,000 tons of coal, a length of 329½ feet, beams of fifty feet, a depth of 30.4 feet, and a net tonnage of 113,730. Its massiveness is evident in stockless type: 7,000-pound anchors, six 127-foot-high masts, and a thirty-two-inch-diameter foremast. The frame was of Virginia oak, and the three decks were Georgia and South Carolina pine.

The *Wyoming* was the last six-masted schooner to carry the U. S. flag in commercial service. She was called a "3,730-ton monster," which had been built at the Percy and Small Yards in Bath and launched on December 15, 1909. It had elaborate luxuries such as the rarity of running water in the bathrooms and a telephone connection to all parts of the ship: a true luxury liner in her class.

4

Mills, Industries, Factories, and Inventions

Lombard Steam Log Hauler, first to use caterpillar treads *(Photo courtesy of Harry C. Crooker)*

Norway, "Snowshoe Town of America"

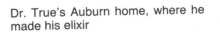

Dr. True's Auburn home, where he made his elixir

L.L. Bean (right) discussing his Maine hunting shoe with Don Williams

Home of Captain Gregory, instigator of the doughnut hole

Several types of mills in Maine were the earliest production plants in the New World. In 1620, Ferdinando Gorges chose a site in what is now South Berwick for a grist mill which was water-powered; but the first hand-powered grist mill was in Lisbon Falls. The first saw mill in the country, 1634, was at Gray; the first cotton mill, at York.

Maine had the first woodworking mills in the world. Spool mills were scattered throughout the state, the two earliest ones being at Locke Mills and Bethel. The Bethel mill, owned by Julius B. Skillings, once held the national title of the oldest one run by steam, having been in production prior to the Civil War. The area became known as the Steam Mill Community. In 1931, their spools were shipped over the entire country.

The last spool mill in the country was in Milo, which by 1976 was hard pressed by the invention of the cheaper, plastic models. Since 1902, the nationally popular spool mill in Milo had supplied the American Thread Company, one of the largest thread producers in the nation. The mill used about 2,000,000 board feet of white birch each year, and had about fifty employees.

Woolen mills, too, were abundant in Maine. The first powered woolen mill, 1791, in Gray, has an interesting story behind it. Sheep were continually sent to the colonists for food; but once satisfied with their meat, the colonists did not slaughter the creatures, but kept them for breeding. This fact displeased the English who no longer would send wool nor sheep, and laws were passed forbidding shipment of any equipment for carding.

However, young Samuel Mayall, an enterprising British subject of eighteen, tried to smuggle out parts of two carding machines. Discovered in the act, he was arrested and jailed. After his release, he plotted further by putting the parts of the machinery into bolts of cloth which went for trade with the Indians, and hid himself in the same hold of the vessel so as to keep track of the bolts and to arrive in Boston at the same time as the shipment. This scheme was successful.

The center for sheep growing was Gray; therefore, young Mayall leased an old grist mill and set up the first power-driven woolen mill in America. He had to send for parts, however, to England; and his reputation had been remembered. When one order reached him, the package of parts contained a bomb which was, fortunately for Mayall, a dud. Another delivery, which had not been ordered, came in a trunk. This he opened while standing in back of the lid, a wise decision, because when the lid was raised, a pistol fired.

Cloth from the Mayall Woolen Mill was used throughout the country, and Mayall expanded his business and set up mills in Lisbon and Phillips. Vice President Gerry, during the War of 1812, wore at his inauguration, a suit made of material from the Gray woolen mill. Newspapers alluded to the "American manufactured" material.

Mayall married Ann Hicks, of Danville, a wealthy spinster. As it was the custom for mill owners to house their employees, Samuel and Ann built a house for their twenty workmen. The authentic seal of the town of Gray pays Mayall tribute; and his tomb, in a pasture in Gray, has stood since his death in 1831.

In 1844, John Mayall, a relative of Samuel, set up a similar mill in Phillips. This mill was destroyed by fire in 1898, then was rebuilt by a "building bee." Once again, wool for this mill came from all over the world.

The Sabattus woolen mills once supplied a high grade of material that was world popular. The old brick building was razed in 1975.

During the 1850s, Maine led in nearly every enterprise connected with forest and sea. A partial list of the "firsts" in Maine production that have served the nation and the world would include the following:

First cotton mill, York
First carding mill, South Waterford
First paper mill, near Bangor
First pulp mill, Norway

First white flour mill, forerunner of the "Gold Medal" brand
   flour, Norway
First grist mill, Lisbon Falls
First water-powered mill, South Berwick
First power saw, Gray
First clothespin factory, Bryant Pond
First toy factory, Paris
First snowshoe factory, Norway
First spool mill, Locke Mills
First sardine factory, Eastport/Lubec
First blanket and carriage robe factory, the Thomas Good-
   all, Sanford, 1867
First oil cloth factory, Winthrop
First blanket factory, South Berwick, 1854, called the Bur-
   leigh Blanket Mills, on a site that Gorges had once chosen
   for a grist mill in 1620. Founded by John H. Burleigh
First threshing machine to use steam, Winthrop, 1793
First woolen mill, Gray, 1791. Parts of its stone foundations
   are still visible. Although some records attribute the mill
   to Brunswick, Gray is the rightful location
First woodworking mills in the world, throughout the state
First Pilgrim trading post, at Fort Western, in Cushnoc
   (Augusta)

By the last half of the nineteenth century, one small town,
Belfast, had what might be considered a typical list of available
goods, artisans, and producers in many other Maine towns:

sash and blind factory	watch and clock making
brick making	lumber and cord wood
carriage making	barbers
blacksmiths	hatters
barrel making	caulkers
tannery	painters
tailors	

Clothing

In Waterville, the name Charles F. Hathaway is a byword. He
closed his Massachusetts men's shirts factory around 1847, mi-
grated to Waterville, and became printer and publisher of the

Waterville *Union*, which consisted chiefly of sermons and moral stories from outside sources. The paper was filled with heavenly thought as he wanted to appeal to the crass world. But readers were few and the paper lasted only a short time.

Then he moved back to Watertown, Massachusetts, and returned to his shirt factory. However, restless between industry and religious convictions, he came back to Waterville with his younger brother, George; set up the C. P. Hathaway and Company shirt factory; and, while awaiting completion of construction, made shirts in his own home. This was in 1853; and the factory that he built then was where famous Hathaway shirts were made for over 100 years, and became a trademark for men's fine fashions throughout the nation. In 1959, this Waterville branch was known as the largest retail source of men's quality shirts all over the world. Later he established plants in Calais and Dover-Foxcroft.

In May, 1975, the company announced the closing of the Calais plant, which employed 150 workers, after improvements at the Waterville plant, which employed eighty-eight. There was no indication, up to 1977 at least, that the Dover-Foxcroft satellite would be discontinued. In 1981, plans were disclosed for a $3 million expansion for the Waterville factory.

Hathaway married Temperance Blackwell, of Waterville, in 1840. He was always torn between industry and worldly matters as opposed to his religious convictions. He would have abhorred the slick, smooth-haired, perfect profile of the gentlemen used in advertising Hathaway shirts. Such perfection would not have fitted in with his religious humility. So strong was his aversion to display that he would not let his wife have buttons on her dresses; only hooks and eyes which were not "showy."

Shoe factories have been plentiful throughout the state. Indeed, in the days of the buckle-type overshoe, the cloth for the tops was provided all over the country, almost exclusively, by Maine firms. Even in 1980, a report released by the American Footwear Industry Association showed Maine ranking number one in the nation in shoe manufacturing.

One special type of shoe was that invented by George Mitchell, of Turner. It was the copper-toed shoe, made when he was working in a North Auburn shoe factory, the H. M. Bearce and Company, between 1870 and 1883. His idea proved to be a big asset in the wearing longevity of footwear, and many shoes were exported to England and Scotland. Although Americans have discarded the copper toe, the same two European countries were still promoting it as late as the last half of the twentieth century.

Freeport, Maine, lays claim to at least two facts of fame: its being the alleged site of the signing of papers which gave Maine its statehood when it separated from Massachusetts, and its having Leon L. Bean, 1872–1967, and his store.

Bean, a native of Bethel, and descendent of the Scottish Highland clan of MacBean, was born on a farm; but during his lifetime he rose to own a $5,500,000 business in Freeport on the premise that every customer is a friend. The L. L. Bean Company, founded in 1876, is of world renown.

Bean is perhaps best known for his world-famous "Maine Hunting Shoe," made by stitching a leather top to a rubber bottom. These boots have been worn by General Ridgway in Korea, by Rear Admiral MacMillan in the Arctic, and by the U. S. Marines in Iceland. He has included among his "friends," such personalities as President Coolidge, "Babe" Ruth, Eleanor Roosevelt, Ted Williams, and countless other famous customers.

His Freeport store, which opened in 1912, specializes in camping clothing and equipment, and stays open twenty-four hours a day. It now handles over 600 items, having expanded since the death of L. L. Bean. In the first week of December, 1980, the store supplied over 16,000 separate transactions, with an expectation for 18,000 the following week, the most popular one for December sales. The statistics for 1981 were: 225,000 packages shipped in one week; 43,221 packages shipped in one day; 116,000 orders received; and phone calls on December 19 alone totalled 5,542. These figures broke all records.

During 1980, sales reached about $120,000,000; and the more than 600 employees produced an average of 540 pairs of Maine Hunting Shoes, 800 pairs of hand-sewn footwear, and 2,000 speciality items per day. The catalogue mailing reached 34,000,000 the following year.

An indisputable proof of the popularity of this man Bean and his store is evidenced in a piece of mail that reached him from Hong Kong, addressed:

Bean
Maine
U.S.A.

After his death, his grandson Leon Gorman carried on the

business in the cluttered, friendly establishment; and he also observed the same friendliness and honesty that has always characterized the L. L. Bean store.

Another shoe company, the Sebago Shoe, in Westbrook, is one of the nation's largest shoe exporters; Quoddy Moccasins made in Auburn has big foreign sales. Astronauts wear Acorn shoes made in Lewiston.

George Henry Bass, of Wilton, in 1876, offered his Bass Shoes, fashioned in a small, family-owned factory in his rural town. His shoes were light-weight and flexible, more so than were any other such shoes of that period. They are hand-sewn and styled from loafers to loggers' boots. The "Weejun" pattern has become especially popular, a name derived from the words *Norwegian* and *Injun*.

Famous wearers of the Bass shoe include Charles Lindbergh, on his 1927 "first solo flight across the Atlantic," and World War II troops on all fronts, who wore Bass combat boots. Since the death of Bass, in 1925, his sons have succeeded him, have expanded to Bangor and New Hampshire facilities, and have considered leasing a plant in Puerto Rico.

Sid Kahn, of Old Town, hand crafted, in 1965, a moccasin that became the rage in Paris, New York, Rome, and London. Some of the shoes were "prettied up" in pink kid and alligator and fashioned in "lady-like styles." They sold for thirty dollars a pair in 1965 and were bought by the world's best-dressed women of the year, both at home and abroad.

One should also note the long-popular Dexter Shoe Company owned by Harold A. Alfond, and the Penobscot Shoe Company, both long-time Maine producers. Alfond has been a philanthropist to the University of Maine and to Colby College, in the area of sports.

Earmuffs, known everywhere in the world, were designed by a fifteen-year-old Maine boy, Chester Greenwood, in 1873. He got his idea one day after skating. His mother made pads out of two old socks, for his ears; and he shaped a wire over his head to hold the pads in place. The idea worked, and soon earmuffs were manufactured commercially by Greenwood. Individuals made the muffs in their homes, and the steel bands were attached in a factory. Later, his mother used hunks of beaver fur, and his father made an attachment of spring steel.

At age nineteen, young Greenwood decided to make a million dollars, so he filed a patent for "Greenwood Champion Ear Protectors," and designed a machine for mass production. Thus, his town of Farmington, Maine, became the earmuff capital of the world, and made Greenwood rich. In the 1930s, over 400,000 were sold throughout the world. One order from Michigan asked for "an extra small pair" for her canary, so it could "not hear her husband's foul language." A wanted felon in Pennsylvania asked the wrong woman where she got hers. She was a police officer, recognized the inquirer, and immediately handcuffed him!

Greenwood also ran an excursion steamboat business; helped to establish the first telephone company in Franklin County; operated a bicycle factory and machine shop; and built a business block in the center of the town of Farmington. His steel spring garden rake is now used universally.

He had a large Victorian home with high ceilings, huge windows, a tower, fireplaces, mirrors, and other ornate furnishings. And it was he who had the first Stanley Steamer in his hometown.

In 1977, December 21 was legislated to be the annual Chester Greenwood Day, and Farmington schools close for a half a day of local festivities.

In Waldoboro is a 100-year-old factory originally built as a shoe factory, but now used for manufacturing buttons. It produces millions of plastic buttons, hundreds of thousands of poker chips, and rods to make scores of dominoes and dice. Since 1979, it has been operated by the Ball and Socket Manufacturing, Inc. In its early days, buttons were made from shells which were hand cut and drilled; and today, behind the factory, is a pile of many-colored shell scraps from which the buttons were cut.

Other nationally popular clothing from Maine includes Jack Nicklaus personal golf shirts made in Waterville; jogging suits, in Rockland; Maine Guide flannel shirts, in Bath; Van Baalen men's robes, in Rockland; Margaret Smith (not ex-Senator Smith) handbags, in Gardiner; and hand knits, from The Unique 1, in Camden. Bob and Sur Dunlap, of Mt. Desert Island, have hand-woven accessories, such as shawls, scarfs, and mufflers, sold in department stores from coast to coast.

Food and Drink

The first commercially produced crude chewing gum, "State of Maine Pure Spruce Gum," was manufactured by John Curtis, of Franklin Street, in Bangor, 1848. Two years later, he went to

Portland and had "Sugar Cream," "Four-in-Hand," "Biggest and Best," "White Mountain," and "Licorice Lulu" paraffin gums, plus "American Flag," "Trunk Spruce," and "Yankee Spruce" spruce gums.

In 1850, John Davis, of Portland, developed the formula further and had his first spruce gum factory in 1852, when he put in a more "chewy" substance. Then in 1871, he added chicle, and began selling all over the world.

Later Horatio Adams, of Belgrade Lakes, made America's first chewing gum with a real "chew" as we recognize it today. He sold his Adams Chewing Gum Company to Chiclets for several million dollars after having begun with a formula cooked originally on his kitchen stove.

The first canned food in the New World, lobster, was presumably done by Stowers Treat Upham, in 1839 or 1840. His factory was in Eastport. Later, the company enlarged and shipped to foreign ports.

In 1978, Bertha Nunan's Lobster Hut was listed as perhaps the best lobster restaurant in the world.

Dependence H. Furbish established an experimental plant in Portland to manufacture sugar from molasses, which at first was ridiculed; but ten years later was producing 300 barrels of excellent granulated sugar per day. The Portland Sugar House was one of three in the United States in 1845; and in 1860 was second only to New York's. The company also produced 30,000 hogsheads of molasses a year.

In 1885, Dr. Augustin Thompson, of Union, started the production of a soft drink more popular then than now—Moxie! He also built Fort Popham, at the mouth of the Kennebec River.

Maine is a "hen" state, too. Hillcrest Foods, Inc., at one time was shipping thousands of pounds of cooked frozen chicken over the entire country, coast to coast. It closed its doors in 1981, with hope for a successor.

The largest brown egg industry in the world is that of the DeCoster Egg Farm, in Turner. Their eggs go even to Baghdad, Iraq (via Turkey), which buys up to 3,000,000 at a time from Maine, New Hampshire, and Massachusetts.

The world's largest Egg Contest is held annually in Pittsfield, Maine.

Aroostook County supplies most of the state's fifteen to twenty percent share of the entire United States' potatoes. Its peak production year was in 1946 when it led the nation, and it was reported that one out of every seven potatoes grown in the United States was harvested in Aroostook County. The 4,000 potato farms of the 1940s have dwindled to only 1,000.

The potatoes are used not only for consumption, but for seed in several other potato-producing states and in various foreign countries, especially France, Germany, Greece, and Italy, which have been the biggest buyers. Maine ranks first in the production of certified seed potatoes.

Fort Fairfield claims to be the "World's Potato Producing Town," and its Potato Blossom Festival, first held in 1947, is unique in the United States. It includes all of Aroostook County, an area greater than that of the states of Connecticut and Rhode Island combined. The festival lasts for four days and nights. There is dancing in the streets, canoe racing, beauty contests, hang-gliding spectacles, and other events, including pie eating. It is estimated that one sixth of all the nation's potatoes are grown in Aroostook County alone; and the sight of the acres and acres of the plants in bloom is exquisite.

Much of the potato starch from Aroostook was used for sizing in the textile industry. In 1904, there were sixty-six starch factories in the county. The Industrial and Labor Statistics Report for the state of Maine that year gave a detailed description of the process followed at a factory in Monticello, the largest such factory in the world at that time.

Gardiner, Maine, is nationally famous for its Fairview Wine Company.

David Robinson is reputed to have made the first ice cream in America when he served a frozen custard to General Lafayette, in Wiscasset, in 1825. A type more like our present-day consistency is attributed to Wilbur Cross.

The A & P (Atlantic and Pacific) stores, popular for so many years, were founded by George Huntington Hartford, of Augusta. This was the pioneer of all chain stores in this country.

In 1978, David and Frank Frisbee celebrated the 150th year of service of the oldest continuously operating family-owned grocery store in the country. The first building was William Pepperell's marine store, in 1680. During the five-generation days of Frisbee ownership, such famous people as Mark Twain, Margaret Truman, Chief Justice Earl Warren, and decathlon champion Bruce Jenner have patronized the store.

The original Frisbee to run the business was Daniel and a partner, Mr. Williams, who together bought a building at Kittery

Point. Changing times have reduced patronage of the family store which has reciprocated by putting up an adjoining restaurant which is successful enough to counteract the store's losses, a store which still accepts telephone orders and makes Friday deliveries.

Everyone in the state associates canned baked beans with Burnham and Morrill, of Portland. They canned their first ones in 1875 for the fishermen to take when they sailed to Georges Bank, and missed their traditional Saturday night menu. B & M puts out the only true baked beans in the nation. When the slogan says "Oven Baked," that is what they are; baked in a brick oven, in iron pots, on slaughter-house tile floors. The beans are baked for seven hours at 700 degrees, after being put into a rich, brown sugar and mustard sauce.

They are then steeped for three hours. Pork has to be added manually as no machine to do this chore has yet been invented because the chunks are so irregular. Two women can plop a section of pork into the cans at the remarkable rate of 400 chunks a minute. Unless the label on the can says "oven baked," beans are stewed.

Each bean is checked individually from two sides, and rejected if not the right color. About 100,000 pounds of beans are baked in a single day, and it takes 3,000 to equal one pound. B & M produces an average of 200,000 cans per day; and the pots, when full of beans and their sauce, weigh about 700 pounds. The warehouse contains up to half a million cases at a time. In the course of one year, B & M cans about 70 million pounds of baked beans.

The beans come from Michigan, California, Minnesota, Iowa, and, of course, Maine, plus a few from foreign countries. Since the discontinuance of Friend Brothers of Boston, the Portland factory has become the baked bean center of the nation, and quite possibly of the world.

In 1888, B & M finally accepted sweet corn to can. Housewives were slow in accepting this new product, but stores such as the A & P and S. S. Pierce began buying wholesale. Later, frozen corn became a widespread Maine product.

In Sargentville, on the shore of the Punch Bowl, a local cove, there once stood the largest natural ice plant in the world. The firm was known as The Maine Lake Ice Company and had four giant storage houses. Four- and five-masted schooners carried 120,000 pounds of ice annually to cities all along the Eastern seaboard; to the Caribbean; to South America; and even to India. The years 1900–1916 were the best years of production. Artificial refrigeration brought the business to a standstill.

Maine ice was second only in volume to Hudson River ice, from the early 1800s to the 1920s. The peak year for Maine was in 1890 when it had a 3,000,000 ton harvest, which was called "Kennebec Crystal." In 1899, Charles Morse, of Bath, merged all Maine ice companies that supplied New York, Boston, Philadelphia, Washington, and other large cities in the States, into the mammoth American Ice Company.

Huge pieces were floated to the ice house at the Punch Bowl, where a dock for landing was built on the shore. This dock was connected with an 800-foot-long runway, to convey the ice up an eighty-three-foot vertical rise. Ice blocks had to be at least eighteen inches thick, yet not so thick that they could not go under the first blade of the planer. In the 1800s, any willful damage of ice within the state carried a fine of $500 or eleven months in jail.

During the busy season of blueberry picking, outside manpower took over for the local crew. Delivery was made by horse-drawn ice carts. The driver would chop off a piece of ice approximately the size required for that particular home or business ice box. Then he would sling the chunk over the thick, rubber pad that protected his shoulder, using big tongs. He would then enter the home or business and deposit the ice into the container. A card in the window of a residence indicated the need for ice that day. Prices per chunk ranged from ten cents to twenty-five cents. There is a splendid section on Maine ice in Robert Coffin's *Kennebec, Cradle of America.*

The story of the doughnut hole began in Maine. Captain Hanson Crockett Gregory, of Clam Cove (Glen Cove), at age fifteen, 1857, commented to his mother, who was cooking fried cakes, that the centers never seemed to cook through unless the edges were overcooked. Thereupon, he supposedly thrust a fork through the center of one of the cakes, with surprisingly good results in the finished product. His mother accepted the change and at his advice made a hole in the center of her fried cakes; and when he signed on as cook on a vessel, and later became captain, he found that the holes were "mighty handy" for hanging a couple of doughnuts on a spoke of the ship's wheel when he was at the helm, and was ready for his coffee break, known to seamen then as a "mug up."

On the corner of his homestead, on Old County Road, a plaque reads:

In Commemoration
This Is the Birthplace
of
Captain Hanson Gregory
Who first invented
The Hole in the Donut
In the year 1847
Erected by his friends
October 31, 1947

This bronze plaque commemorates his contribution to the culinary art conceived in Maine, now an accepted recipe. Captain Gregory died in 1921 at age eighty-nine, at Sailors' Snug Harbor, New York. His grandfather, William Gregory, was a soldier in the expedition against the British at Majabigwaduce, and Revolutionary War soldiers were once billeted at the Clam Cove home.

In the 1970s, it was reported that in 1872, John F. Blondel, of Thomaston, had patented a device to make a better hole in the doughnut by his "Improved Doughnut Cutter" which removed the dough automatically from the cutter tube by the use of a coil spring and a plunger.

Captain Gregory probably never imagined that even the "holes" would become a delicacy in the twentieth century.

It is generally conceded that the molasses doughnut originated in Maine. In a poll conducted throughout the nation, the only people who had ever had a molasses doughnut had originally come from Maine!

Mechanical Inventions

More inventions have come from Maine than from any other state in the United States. Cyrus McCormick and his friend Hussey, Maine men, invented the reaping and mowing machines. Johnathan Fisher, of Blue Hill, invented the wind-driven sowing machine, and other farm equipment. And in the 1800s, Hiram and John Pitts, of Winthrop, invented the first steam threshing machine.

It had three parts: First, the wheat, oats, rye, barley, or buckwheat were fed into the thresher. Second, the grain was sifted. Third, the chaff was blown away. Three mechanical parts did the entire job. Selling the machine for anywhere between sixty and seventy dollars, the men prospered after receiving their patent on December 29, 1837.

J. B. Mayo, of Kingfield, produced, in 1881, the first spinning roll bosses in the country. Chris Sholes invented and patented the first American typewriter, June, 1868. After 1873, it became known as the popular Remington. Moses Fellows, of Fayette, invented the first hand cultivator and other home and farm equipment, plus a cannon and ammunition known as the "ball and chain;" and a "Rail Car Protector," a device which used steam to quickly reverse any colliding locomotives on the railways, by pressing the brakes and retarding motion.

Alvin O. Lombard, of Waterville, invented the steam log hauler, the first successful caterpillar tread vehicle and the forerunner of the U. S. Army war tank, first used in World War I. His hauler could pull up to twenty sleds loaded with pulpwood across the 3,000-foot intervale between Eagle and Chamberlain Lakes, in the Allagash Region. Called the "Mary Ann," it was a series of two-wheeled dollies bolted every ten inches to the circulating 8,000-foot cable; and could move 500,000 feet of pulpwood in one day.

Lombard was born in Springfield, Maine, in February, 1856. At age seven, he had made miniature sawmills from wood, powered by water with a balanced paddle wheel. His saw blade was made from a steel stay taken from his mother's hoop skirt. He made many mechanical toys for himself and his brothers, and rigged a pulling system from a stream near the house to ease the task of churning butter.

In the 1880s, he built his own sawmill. He then made the first log-hauling working model after a lumber firm's owner told about the loss of horses pulling heavy loads of wood and asked him to invent a machine to haul the heavy logs. A few blocks of wood and his pack knife were all that he used in making a working model.

From there, he worked out the problem of traction on snow without using wheels which dig into the snow and ground. The result was the world-famous Lombard Log Hauler. It looks like a steam locomotive with bulldozer treads, the first "caterpillar treads," with bobsled runners for steering. His patent was approved on April 21, 1901. He continued to make improvements and eventually had a factory located between Waterville and Fairfield.

The hauler had a top speed of five mph going downhill. At

first, horses pulled it and a driver steered it. Then a steering wheel was added and the steersman sat in front, in a small cabin-like structure, with no brakes for reducing speed and no protection against the elements. The roads were tracks like a bobsled run, except that there were two tracks. In all, Lombard built eighty-three of these haulers. Three went to Russia. Of the rare ones left, one is in Ashland and another in Patten. In 1976, Harry C. Crooker assembled parts and restored one hauler at his Old Bath Road office site.

Lombard later invented the turbine water wheel control, a machine to remove bark from pulp, and a machine to separate the knots and sawdust from whipped wood. This he called a "knot separator."

The first steam-powered automobile was made by the Mc-Clench brothers, in Hallowell, in 1858, in their machine shop on Bombahook Stream. It was not too successful when compared to the model made by the Stanley twins.

F. O. and F. E. Stanley, born in Kingfield, became known as the Stanley brothers, inventors *par excellence*. Both taught school briefly and whittled incessantly. In fact, F. O. whittled his first violin at age eleven and his last one at age eighty-four, meanwhile supplying others for the Boston Symphony.

Together they invented and manufactured a home generator to make illuminating gas until the town gas works put a stop to it. They invented dry photograph plates and manufactured them until Kodak bought them out at an exorbitant price. They invented early models of X-ray equipment, diving helmets, farm tools, submarines, and wood-working tools. Had they lived longer, they might have beaten Einstein in his work on the atom.

Most of their inventions were later discarded in favor of scientifically improved ones, but in 1896 they saw a French automobile and decided that they could do better. Therefore, they made the first Stanley Steamer and by 1899 had produced 200 of them, the world's first mass manufacture of automobiles.

Freelon drove his wife over dirt trails to the summit of Mt. Washington, a feat that made headlines around the world. In 1952, a Springfield, Vermont, man drove his 1902 Stanley Steamer over the same route through a rain and wind storm. His kerosene lights blew out. His water feed-pipe broke. The trip had to be finished in total darkness. But he reached the summit!

Even in 1902, the Steamer clocked over 120 miles per hour, and for a short time the identical twins tried racing. They were pranksters. One would pass a policeman while driving over the speed limit. While the police was making out a ticket, an identical car and identical driver would speed by.

The emergence of Henry Ford's gasoline car mass production did not disturb them at all. They still enjoyed making one car at a time, the forerunner of all automobiles in this country.

Francis E., it is said, coming from Newton, Massachusetts, to Poland Spring, in 1912 and 1913, was often arrested for speeding. The brothers' cars were the first ones that could travel two miles in less than one minute. In 1918, he was on the Newburyport Turnpike, speeding as usual, returning to Boothbay Harbor, Maine. To avoid hitting two farm wagons ahead, he steered for a pile of cordwood, and was killed. Freelon O. then sold out the business and the Stanley Steamer industry closed for good in 1925.

The Poland Spring House consistently used a Stanley Steamer to transport guests from the Danville Junction railroad station, the nearest point of rail connections.

The entire Stanley family was inventive. The grandfather of the brothers had invented hogshead-shooks, a pre-cut do-it-yourself kit for making barrels, circa 1832. During the latter part of the nineteenth century, other family members made ingenious contributions to the bulging number of inventive geniuses in Maine at that time.

In 1981, support was strong for developing a Stanley Museum in Kingfield. A school building had already been donated for the project.

The first person in the United States to make and test "flying machines" was Charles Lamson, of Portland. His creation, shown in an 1897 magazine, was on Diamond Island, off Portland, where he had tested a machine designed by Otto Lilienthal, of Germany. Lamson later made his own design, and called it his "airship kite."

The Tibbetts firm in Camden is one of the largest, if not the largest, producers of microphones.

The Fairchild Camera and Instrument Corp., in South Portland, started its semiconductor plant with fewer than 100 people in 1962. In 1982, it had 1,160 employees, who turned out more than a quarter of a billion semiconductors, small instruments of which 100 would fit nicely in one hand.

These are but a spattering of the ingenious inventors and companies that Maine has spawned. Two others certainly deserve recognition among the remaining names. One is Philo Farnsworth who, in 1927, began working on the invention of the first electronic television system and perfected it at his home in Brownfield, Maine. It was the original model of the many TVs which were to follow. The other name is that of T. S. Hussey, of North Berwick, who fashioned the first steel fire escape at his Plow Works. The schools of nearby Sanford had the first completely steel fire escape system in the country. In time, the third generation of Hussey men designed portable bleachers and theirs became the pattern of all types of bleachers, especially the roll-out seats, or telescopic seating, of which the company is now the leading producer in the nation. In addition, they built ski jumps and possibly the biggest steel tower-type jump in America.

America's first breechload rifle was invented by a Portland gunsmith, John Hancock Hall. This was a major development in the history of military arms, and is an important part of the American heritage, as it excelled as a sharp-shooting implement.

Hall was born in 1781, son of a minister who later operated a tanyard on Fore Street, in Portland. He applied for his patent on March 16, 1811; kept on using all his funds; even went without the necessities of life.

Hall's gun was judged to be the best in cutting raiding parties in the War of 1812 and was later put to use in hunting down mysterious sea monsters in the Gulf of Mexico. Yet, his business lagged.

In July, 1817, President Monroe became impressed with the usefulness of the weapon; and in 1818 the rifles were tested in Missouri, and Hall was asked to leave Portland to work full time at Harper's Ferry armory at sixty dollars a month plus one dollar for each gun produced. By 1819, his rifle was the standard infantry weapon.

Hall lived until 1841, having spent twenty-three years working for the army, and most of his adult life trying to convince the military of the superiority of his breachloader.

A different type of weapon was the automatic machine gun, firing ten shots per second, invented by Hiram Stevens Maxim, of Sangerville. Born in 1840, eldest of eight children, he died on November 24, 1916. He was known as "Maxim the Magnificent," a title based on his vanity.

Maxim, sturdy in build, was from a poor family, and had but little rural education. He used to tinker in his father's workshop and eventually became a carriage builder and an ironworker. His invention was rejected by the United States Ordinance Department, but the British army adopted his rifle in 1889; and the Royal Navy, in 1892. An English poet once wrote:

Thank God that we have got
The Maxim gun and they have not.

Maxim became an English subject and was knighted in 1901 by Queen Victoria, one of her last official acts. His invention had helped win the Egyptian campaign for England. He was decorated as a Chevalier of the French Legion of Honor. Germany, too, saw the potential of the gun and gave the Maxim rifle a major role in their military planning.

Oddly, Hiram's first-of-its-kind machine gun, using the force of the recoil reloading and in great demand all over the world for past and present warfare, was intended, in Maxim's words, to "strike fear into the hearts of mankind" and prevent war. Unfortunately, it accomplished just the reverse.

Hiram Maxim's wife was attractive, six feet tall, and brilliant; but unwisely she developed Maxim's conceit. He, too, was six feet tall, rugged, and the holder of 122 American and 149 British patents. He may have been, as historians portray him, "vain as a peacock"; but among his and his brother Hudson's inventions were such worthwhile items as incandescent light, hair curlers, riveting machines, a new coffee extract, a steam-powered airplane, smokeless gunpowder, an aerial torpedo gun with delayed action fuse, automatic sprinklers for fire extinguishers, automatic gas-generating plants, steam and vacuum pumps, and even an improved mousetrap!

The two boys had vowed in childhood that they would become wealthy, and this they did; but later in life, jealousy separated their paths. Hudson was more skilled in explosives; and he produced one, called "Maximite," that was more powerful than dynamite.

A third gun inventor from Maine was George F. Evans, of Norway. The site of his factory was in Mechanic Falls. Adner Denison, also of Norway, was his original sponsor. His invention became so world-famous that the Russians sent a delegation to supervise its construction and to make suggestions; and the Russian Flying Squadron, organized in America, were all armed with the Evans Repeating Rifle. Two able assistants of Evans' were Charles F. Nason, of Lewiston, and Abel Spauling, of Buckfield.

For a long time a gun factory in Saco, Maine, was the only one in the United States making the M-60 machine gun. They were made to be mounted on American war tanks. From 1961 to 1975, about 200,000 were produced at the Maremont Corporation, which employed more than 1,200 workers. The U. S. Government, however, changed its patronage in 1976 in favor of a lower-bidding firm in Belgium.

Sanford is the amphibian-building capital of the nation. In 1969, it was the only community in the country turning out new amphibian planes from two local companies.

The electronic cranes used on the Balboa Dock of the Panama Railroad, Panama Canal, were made in Maine.

Valley Engineering, Inc., of Gray, manufactured the snow grooming equipment used at Innsbruck, Austria, at the 1976 Winter Olympics.

Gardiner is the only place in the world today where one-piece plastic toys are made.

The numbering system for patents was introduced on July 13, 1836; and patent number one under the new system was issued to John Ruggles of Thomaston, for "traction wheels for locomotive steam-engine for rails and other roads." Ruggles was chairman of the Committee on Patents of the United States Senate and introduced the new system after 9,957 unnumbered patents had already been granted.

Paper

In 1977, Maine moved into the lead as the major paper-making state, surpassing Wisconsin. A survey showed a capacity of 3.4 million tons per year. No country in the world now manufactures more paper than the United States, and only a few of these countries put out more than the state of Maine.

The International Paper Company's Androscoggin Mill at Jay has the world's largest paper machine dryer roll. Called a "Yankee Dryer Roll," it is sixteen feet in diameter, over twenty-one feet long, and weighs around 150 tons. Its surface is polished to a smooth, mirror finish, and must not be scratched. It is used in the process of manufacturing a type of carbonizing paper. The trailer bearing the roll was built in Spain and is unique in itself: sixty-five feet long, twelve feet wide, nine axles which turn hydraulically, seventy-two wheels, and other interesting features. It arrived in Jay in April, 1976.

Millinocket still has the largest newsprint mill in the world, thus promoting Maine's supremacy as the largest newsprint producer of the nation.

Orono, the hometown of the state university, is famous for

the fact that the university was the first college in the United States to introduce a special course in the making of pulp and paper. Sarah Medina, of Kennebunkport, was one of the first two women ever employed in this industry.

The Keyes Fiber Company, in Waterville, is the home of the largest producer of molded pulp plates and containers in the United States.

The Boise-Cascade Paper Company, formerly the Oxford Paper Company, in Rumford, leads the world in the manufacture of standard book paper, and may boast of having been selected as the recipient of a government monopoly grant for manufacturing and printing United States Postal Service postcards.

In Westbrook, the S. D. Warren Company produces the largest amount of high grade magazine and book paper in the country, and possibly in the world. Its success in treating waste water provided pollution clean-up standards for the nation.

Closely behind the Warren plant in importance are the Penobscot Paper Company of Topsham and the St. Regis Paper Company of Bucksport.

A different kind of "paper" was manufactured in Hallowell in the 1800s when Ben Tenney established a sandpaper mill.

Health

One Maine lady stands forth in the field of health. She is Marion G. Parsons, R. N., of Fort Fairfield and later of Fryeburg, who headed the first American unit to go to the assistance of the Allies in World War I. Her career included being personally decorated by King George V of England, with the "Royal Red Cross" medal; receiving the honor of "Order of the White Lion" from the Czechoslovakian Government, a distinction rarely offered to a woman; and establishing a nurses' training school in Prague, in 1919.

Her nursing carried her across the width of the United States, often working under adverse conditions, but ever eager to go on with the job. She was truly dedicated to the nursing profession and devoted most of her life to it, even to giving classes in home nursing and first aid during World War II, after she had retired in Fryeburg.

Dr. John Fogg True devised a worm repellent medicine for children. This he experimented with and later bottled in the kitchen of his home in Exeter, Maine, 1851. Not feeling well, he prepared a medication for himself with good results, and a neighbor named his concoction "Dr. True's Elixir." After he moved to Auburn, he developed a multi-million dollar business, the peak year being 1923 when 155,000 bottles of "Dr. True's Pin Worm Elixir and Family Laxative" were sold throughout the world, with "Auburn, Maine" printed on each label, a profound advancement from the days when he peddled his product on foot.

He also made "True's Triumphant Tincture," a sort of vitamin dispenser, "True's Headache Tablets," and "True's Sore Throat Gargle." Varying his line, he also produced in his laboratory a hair shampoo, a worm powder, and a liniment for aches. Quite frequently he sold his products to South America, so dosage orders were printed in Spanish as well as in English.

His death came on May 3, 1900, in his eighty-third year. He had made not only himself nationally known, but also made the city of Auburn known. On May 30, 1975, arsonists were unsuccessful in destroying an empty True warehouse. On August of that same year, however, they did succeed in completely ruining the factory and laboratory used to manufacture the old-time "best in the market" remedy for children. His adjoining home, although damaged, was not a loss and still stands on Drummond Street.

Lydia Pinkham, of Maine, was the first woman to have her face in all the newspapers of the United States and even across the seas, where she distributed her famous compound, guaranteed to cure any and every ailment.

The Lydia E. Pinkham Medicine Company was incorporated in 1882, and Maine was chosen because its tax laws for enterprise were more favorable; and, also, the state had some available cash. That meant that Maine courts were responsible for the several bitter legal suits for over thirty years when the two brothers and the sister in the corporation quarrelled unceasingly.

At least the two boys agreed upon one issue. They concurred that they should "Advertise widely in Maine. Those Maine folks will buy if you spread the advertising on them thick."

One of the popular songs of Lydia's day included these lines:

> Oh, we'll sing of Lydia Pinkham
> And her love for the human race;
> How she sells her "vegetable compound"
> And papers publish her face.

A prestigious recognition came to George D. Snell, of Bar Harbor, in 1980 at age seventy-six. He won the Nobel Prize in medicine in October of that year. His work was in accepting organ transplants and combating cancer and other diseases. He shared his prize with one other American and one Frenchman.

Snell, retired from the Jackson Laboratory in Bar Harbor, is a senior staff scientist emeritus. He did pioneer cell research between 1940 and 1970 that made organ transplant operations almost universally acceptable. In 1978, he received the Wolf Prize for medicine, after being awarded honors from the National Cancer Institute in the 1960s and being elected to the National Academy of Sciences in 1970.

Dr. Charles Herbert Best, of West Pembroke, was the one who discovered insulin. Born in 1899, he was killed in a plane crash in 1941. Through an error of good judgment, his colleague, Frederick Banting, received the 1923 Nobel Prize. Angry at the omission of Best, Banting divided the prize money with him.

A medical first unique to Maine is a system of emergency services for rural, central Maine, with its base in Waterville, The key word is *rural*, where medical services are not readily available.

Fabrics

The original, highly popular Palm Beach cloth, so cool and easy to care for long before drip-dry material was known, was made in a Sanford mill; and from that same town came practically all of the plush used for railroad car seats and automobile seats over the entire United States. These are in addition to the products of the Thomas Goodall factories previously mentioned.

Charles William Moss, of Camden, is a tentmaker, especially for Arab sheiks. He was a former designer for Ford Motor Company, from 1948 to 1958, then started his own business for revolutionizing tenting and camping textiles. Ford was his first client. He also built a paper house on North Haven which, at last reports, had stood for nearly ten years. His design for this house is currently used throughout the nation, but the dwellings are now built of fiberglass.

He also made a paper field hospital for the army, and a disposable command post. But his special interest lies in tent material and designing. His products are red, round, come in a five-pound bag, and use nylon in place of canvas. He calls them "Pop

Tents," and makes them in various shapes and colors. These are a popular item with thousands of campers. They are not fancy, but are useful primarily for hiking, bicycling trips, and camping. The Trilliam design has three sleeping compartments for six people, weighs under thirteen pounds, and in 1976 cost $350. He calls his factory "The Tent Works." His home is a farm overlooking The Bog just outside Rockport.

European companies feature his products, and the Smithsonian Institution has one of his tents for museum service, complemented with electrical wiring within the fiberglass structure, an aluminum support, and air conditioning.

Transportation

In the area of transportation, Maine developed the smallest narrow gauge railroads in North America around the turn of the century, one, at least, with cross rails of only two feet. Among these small railroads, the only one to be consistently in the black was the Sandy River and Rangeley Lakes Line, with which the Franklin and Megantic Railroad and the Kingfield and Dead River Railroad consolidated. It had over 100 miles in Franklin County and boasted of having a Pullman parlor car.

Other lines included the Bridgton and Saco Valley, which later became the Bridgton-Harrison line and used a nine-car train for over sixty years, spanning the nineteenth and twentieth centuries; the Waterville, Wiscasset, and Farmington run; the Kennebec Central, Randolph, and Togus Railroad, which used to haul coal to Togus, and charged thirty cents for a passenger's round trip. This last one had fewer derailments and serious accidents than did any of the other narrow-gauge railroads. On the Togus run, the worst calamity was when one of the cars flipped onto its side, and even then the only damage was the breaking of a few windows and the ruffling of the feelings of a female who was soon pacified by the gift of a new dress.

Among the other narrow-gauge railroads was the one which was a cog railway. This took passengers up Green Mountain, (now known as Cadillac) on Mt. Desert.

John A. Poor, of West Andover, established the Montreal to Portland rail line, and became known as the "Father of the Maine Railroads." His was the first international link with Canada, a route that later became known as the Grand Trunk Railroad Line.

Roldin S. Whitney, of Auburn, is said to have invented the

first steel auto body, around the turn of the century, probably 1881.

The Mt. Abram Monorail was the first of its kind in the nation, 1978. Each car has a handbrake and a safety strap, and goes one mile down the slopes of 1,030-foot Mt. Abram at about one mph. The cars cannot jump the tracks as the wheels travel broges, winding their way through wooded paths that are not too steep. Each car takes only one rider, unless an adult with a small child wishes to ride. In 1978, the fare for a trip was three dollars.

William Howard Gannett, 1854–1948, has been called a pioneer in the development and promotion of aeronautics.

Wood

The forests of Maine have been one of its main sources of industry, aided by the many rivers, lakes, and streams. For several years, during the 1700s, all the navies in the world flew pennants at the peaks of tall sticks made from Maine trees. They were much in demand; and the King of England, as early as 1609, had scouts select those to be used for his royal fleets by putting a special mark on each tree.

The state holds an international reputation in production of wood turnings.

During the 1840s and 1850s, Bangor, the "Queen's City," held the honor of being the greatest lumber shipping port in the world.

The state legislature showed recognition of the value of Maine's lumber when it led the country in forest protection by instituting the first continuously-operated forest fire lookout, at Squaw Mt., on June 10, 1905. Watchmen were in constant service. The tower was 3,267 feet high. In 1921, the legislature appointed the first forest entomologist to lessen forest pest losses, the first such action in the country.

The Lumbermen's Museum at Patten houses the largest and most complete collection of old-time logging artifacts in the world. It was instigated by Dr. Lore A. Rogers, who became its curator. At ninety-six, he was the oldest living University of Maine alumnus in 1971, and was a world authority on Maine's old-time logging techniques and equipment.

Henry Franklin Morton, in 1860, began a wood trade by crafting a few oak sleds for local children, using his kitchen as a workshop. His art turned into the Paris Manufacturing Company, the world's major sled makers; and the nation's oldest and biggest ski, sled, and toboggan firm. Especially popular are his American sleds called Flyer, Flexible Flyer, Dirigo Clipper, Clipper, and Speedaway. His Champion Clipper, which sold for about six dollars, was two feet long, of the best oak, and adorned with a majestic eagle.

The earliest and largest sleds and toboggans made in the United States came from his South Paris factory. Explorer Donald MacMillan prized his Maine sled used in crossing Greenland. After thirty years of leading in its product, the company was purchased by the Gladding Corporation; but its former reputation was upheld. In 1980, the plant employed 230 regulars with extra help in summer and fall. Morton's grandson, Henry, is still active in the company.

The decorations on those early sleds were attractive enough to have been made for wall decorations: birds, flowers, and various scenes.

The C. P. Kimball Company, of Portland, made the best carriages and sleighs in their day, and held a nation-wide reputation for excellence for many years.

Golf tees were first produced in Norway, Maine. Today, they are being turned out by the millions in Guilford, where the Pride Manufacturing Company produced three out of every four golf tees used in the United States during the 1970s. Their production was begun in 1930 by Fletcher Pride, who had previously manufactured wooden tips for cigars in Tampa, Florida. His tees are trademarked "Pride of Maine." In 1970, the firm produced 250,000,000 tees.

Joseph Peavey, a blacksmith in Stillwater, got an idea in 1858 to make a cant dog, or "Peavey," to help rivermen break up log jams. He fashioned the tool which has since been used universally by lumbermen. The factory was moved to Oakland after a fire at the Brewer plant, but the Oakland plant also burned in May, 1965.

The racquet factory of C. A. Thompson, in New Sharon, is one of only five in the United States.

Perhaps the only lobster barrel manufacturers in the world are at the Warren Barrel Shop, where owner Josef Vinal and his four-man crew provide for the increasing demand for this type of container. Most of his are barrels within a barrel, a special kind used by lobster dealers. Others are constructed for furniture. Vinal and his family live in Rockland and never advertise. He has all the business that he and his crew can handle. His best customers are coffee houses and country stores.

Quite possibly the largest manufacturing company of wooden lobster traps in the country is that of Lewis Anderson of Yarmouth and Richard Anderson of Cumberland, who produce between 45,000 and 47,000 traps a year. This company is unique in that it started from their father's snowshoe factory, where the smaller pieces of wood were made use of, rather than letting them go to waste. To satisfy different customers, the traps may be round-topped, square, three headed, four headed, and even extra large and heavy for deep-water lobstering.

Another use of Maine wood is the production of toothpicks. Nearly 100 % of the nation's supply comes from Maine. After the Civil War, an exporter's agent, Charles Forster, went to South America and sent home some so-called "toothpicks," whittled by natives. When he returned, the first thing he did was to invent a machine to make and market such picks. To introduce them to the public, he staged publicity stunts in Boston restaurants.

In Maine, the large plants were in Strong and West Peru. These plants were held by three companies and produced more than 100 million picks a day, each 7,000,000 picks requiring one cord of good, white birch. White birch was used because it has no tang nor taste, and the fibers are so tough that there is little chance of their splitting. The process is to peel long, thin strips from the wood, and then feed them into a cutting machine which shapes 9,000 picks a minute, two at a time.

There were flat picks, round picks, flavored picks (only the Forster Company made these), and red-white-and-blue picks. These companies have dominated the manufacture of toothpicks in the nation. The largest, the Forster plant, has produced up to 60,000,000 a day with a work force of 800. The other two firms, Diamond Wood Products and Strong Wood Turning Company, have turned out 43,000,000 and 25,000,000 per day, respectively.

Since the 1960s, the highest competition has come from Japan and from plastic toothpicks which, some people claim, may damage the gums, but are cheaper. Since 1967, American toothpick production has remained reasonably stable.

There are two methods for making the round pick. One is to cut and shape the pick from a dowel. The other is to cut square picks and then round and shape them afterward. Both methods are used.

From this industry have come allied ones, including those of popsicle sticks, tongue depressers, wooden ice cream spoons, croquet sets, baseball bats, ice cream sticks, and clothespins.

Clothespins have been made in Maine since the middle of the 1800s, when the Shakers at Sabbathday Lake made the last radical improvements in the design. However, by 1978 a quiet war was being waged against several Communist giants as their prices were undercutting our American factory prices, because their wages were much lower. This was still a problem with our clothespin manufacturers in 1981, with Poland, China, and Taiwan being the three greatest threats. Nearly 500 million pins, $2.8 million dollar's worth, were imported in 1978, half of the total sale of wooden clothespins for the year.

Maine factories supplied most of the other half: in Peru, the Diamond International Corporation; in West Paris, the Penley Corporation; in Wilton, the Forster Manufacturing Company. Add to these a small company in Vermont, the National Clothespin Company, and they constitute the only four such factories today in the United States.

As to the output of one of these factories, consider the Penley Corporation. It can turn out 1,250 pins per minute; 75,000 per hour; 600,000 per day; 3,000,000 per week; and a typical year's output is 156 million. This, the largest mill in the nation exclusively devoted to clothespins, uses beech wood. It is a family-owned corporation that started in 1923. It designs and develops its own machinery. Asked how the firm could stay in business so long, as the ordinary clothespin lasts for years of use, Donald Penley grinned, then said, "The lawnmower has been a great factor in replacement. And, of course, children like to play with them and dogs like to chew them."

The advent of electric clothes driers has cut badly into the clothespin industry, as would be expected. But the primary threat still is foreign imports which, although they are financial bargains for the consumer, are not nearly as well made nor are they as durable.

In 1973, Robert T. Duarte, formerly of Lewiston, invented the "polyethelene disc" to replace the conventional style clothespin. It can be used on any line in any direction, and is called a "solar disc." It is particularly advantageous to the elderly, handicapped, or arthritic individual.

There is a firm in Bangor that turns out the most popular fly-fishing rods in the country. It was begun by Hiram Lewis Leonard, in the 1800s. He was a Sebec native whose rods took first place in Vienna and London competitions. His daughter Cora was the first woman fly-rod competitor to make the record books, with a seventy-three-foot cast in New York's Central Park, in 1898.

The Fred P. Sanders Company mill in Bridgton was established in 1812, made small dowels, and shipped them all over the world. Many small buildings comprised the plant.

A few scattered wood mills in Maine are still in operation, mostly by special request for small orders which do not justify the cost of having a plastic model prepared. One of these, the Dixfield plant for Coates and Clark thread, will produce wooden spools by request, although it primarily produces plastic. The American Thread Company was the last mill to phase out wood entirely.

Turning now to living wood, Fryeburg's Western Maine Forest Nursery is one of the very few in the nation that deals in evergreen seedlings and transplants. In mid-century, the total sales were over 5,000,000 seedlings a year, mailed to all parts of the world. During World War II, the owner of the nursery, Clifford Eastman, while on military duty in Germany, sent home several pounds of excellent European seed. Unfortunately, he was ambushed after the signing of the Armistice and never lived to see those seeds become trees.

Miscellaneous

Ezekiel J. Bailey started the first oilcloth factory in the nation in Winthrop, 1845. He had seen a sample among a peddler's wares and with his sons, some burlap, a filler, and an added ingredient for body, the material was scraped and then painted. Later, he made oilcloth rugs (linoleum's ancestor). He had a factory by 1845 with ten employees, became established financially during the Civil War by the demands for waterproof tents and clothing, and became a millionaire.

In 1882, his widow, Mrs. Hannah Johnston Bailey, took over the factory, was successful, and simultaneously continued her influence in obtaining a reformatory prison for women in Maine. Previous to her intervention, they had been jailed in the same prison as the men. She became president of the Maine Equal Suffrage Association and was on the National Board of Charities and Corrections.

In Dover-Foxcroft, 1964, a tiny company of four or five constituted one of the nation's largest dye companies. Their dye was widely used for Navajo rugs of the Venezuela Indians in the West. This one-story plant sent products as far as Equatorial Africa in 1968. Wainwright Cushing, its founder, in 1897, was a Civil War veteran, and the only color that he produced was "turkey red," a predominating color nation-wide at that time and even into the early 1900s.

Today, his shades and colors number over ninety. The leading clientele are character actors who want specially tinted colors for stage or TV adaptation. Cushing died in 1918, but the business continued under his son, then reverted to an employee, and in 1968 became the property of a couple from Kennebunkport, Maine.

Bates Fabrics, Inc., in Lewiston, is the only company in the country fully owned by its employees. It produces about 10,000 bedspreads a day with a force of 800 helpers.

The outstanding mill in the world for making excelsior for stuffing furniture was in Milo. Now the excelsior is used for packing glassware and other fragile merchandise.

A common belief is that a Bowdoin College man was the originator of compound interest.

The Prudential Insurance Company, one of the finest in the country, was founded by John Dryden, of Temple Mills, Maine.

Carrie Gertrude Stevens, of Rangeley, fashioned in 1924 the "Gray Ghost," a streamer fly trout lure that still holds the record of 103 strikes on a single lure. It was an imitation of a smelt with gray wings, and is used throughout this country as well as in Canada, South America, New Zealand, and several European countries. A native of Upper Dam, Maine, she is still the national champion among women for fly casting. When she died in 1972, she was approximately eighty-eight years old.

At first, she used chicken feathers and dye; later she imported exotic plumage from all over the world. She was a perfectionist who never had any instruction in her art. She said, "I just use common sense." Originally being a milliner might account for the finger dexterity which made her the foremost fly-tier in America.

Edward Page Mitchell is credited with having invented the concept of an electronic computer capable of thinking. He was also a writer.

The invention of the telegraph, the founding of Western Union, and the creation of one of America's largest and most renowned universities are all connected with Baxter's Woods, Woodfords, Maine. Samuel Morse and F. O. J. Smith were Portland publishers in the mid-to-late 1800s. Morse was locally called "crazy man" as he wandered through the woods stringing wire after wire to experiment and to improve his idea. Smith, his host at the "Castle," Smith's home, edited *The Maine Farmer.*

A third figure in the experiment was Ezra Cornell, a plow salesman, who invented a machine to put the wires underground. Smith demonstrated the equipment by hitching eight oxen to the machine. In 1843, Cornell laid the pipe between Baltimore and Washington along the route of the B & O railroad and on May 24, 1844, there came over the wire those famous words uttered by Professor Morse: "What hath God wrought!"

However, the underground pipe had faulty insulation, so poles were substituted. Cornell finally made a fortune from the telegraph business and founded Cornell University. It all began in Baxter's Woods, Maine.

John B. Stearns, of Weld, made it possible, through an invention, to send two messages over a wire at the same time, called the duplex system.

Another Maine invention was the snow roller. It was like a barrel with heavy staves, weighted by stones and drawn by six or more horses. It created a good, firm street pavement and was used in some sections of Maine as late as 1920.

A so-called "water dress," used for submarine diving, was patented by Leonard Norcross on June 14, 1834. The Dixfield native fashioned an airtight rubber garment to which was attached a brass cap, or helmet, which rested on the diver's shoulders. The cap was connected to an air pump on the boat by a rubber hose, and the diver's feet were weighted by heavy lead shot.

An "air brush," a sort of atomizer for coloring pictures, was patented on October 25, 1881, by Leslie L. Curtis, of Cape Elizabeth.

Bernard Record, of West Minot, was talented in making violins. He moved to the West Coast, where he received most of his acclaim.

Harold Casey, of Passadumkeag, was one of the world's greatest taxidermists when he retired in 1952. He moved to Bangor and later worked for the New York Zoological Society. He and two companions prepared 168 Arctic owls for individual mountings in a mere two weeks allotted time, and no two poses were identical. His most exacting work was that done on an eighty-foot, 700-pound, leather-back turtle, caught off Rockland. He also mounted the first tuna pulled in by author Zane Grey, a 758-

pound tuna, world-record at the time. His most enjoyable moments were spent at President Teddy Roosevelt's "Sagamore Hill," where he could work surrounded by all sorts of game, birds, fish, and mammals.

A Portland glass factory was established in 1864 and closed in 1873. Meanwhile, in 1867, it produced over 100,000 ale and whiskey glasses, and a set of Portland Glass dishes, valued then at $47,000, for Mrs. Abraham Lincoln, the President's wife.

In 1982, Eric Hopkins, of North Haven, was a national figure in the art of glass blowing and acid-etched shells.

In Sargentville, flag makers Joe and Glenith Grey made the three largest fiberglass flagpoles in the world in 1974 and 1975: 100 feet tall, five feet thick at the bottom, tapering to an inch at the top.

In addition, there is a water preheating system to save electricity, wheelbarrows, brass candlesticks, and pinwheels made from used X-ray film. The list and variety is endless, ranging from a new type of artificial tooth to a system of roof gutters electrically wired to melt snow and ice. Maine people never seem to resist just one more invention or vocation.

Mark Mowatt, of Holden, made fur trading an international business in 1981, selling more in Europe than in the United States as Europeans place a higher value on furs and have more appreciation of them.

Bea Bryant, of the Maine woods, has what is believed to be the largest antique wood stove restoration operation in the nation. Her "junkyard," which may be the largest in the world, has around 1,000 rusted stove carcasses. She calls her restored stoves "prettier than poetry."

Probably the smallest, permanent, private international organization in the world is the Diary Publishers, first known as the International Board of Advertising Gift Manufacturers. The first meeting was at Poland Spring, in 1964, with nine firms represented. In 1973, eleven people from nine countries attended. The only American firm in the group is Geiger Brothers, of Lewiston, Maine. Ray Geiger, associated with numerous organizations, was elected to the Industry Hall of Fame in 1978. He has continued the yearly publication of "Farmers' Almanac," which started in 1878. From about 800,000 copies in 1934 it ran to over 6 million in 1982.

There are dozens of other people in Maine who have taken out patents in recent years, or who are waiting for an opportunity to do so, or who are already selling on a small scale. Just a sample of these devices are an air foil deflector, an ingenious revolution in car wheels, bi-vision motorcycle helmet windshield wiper, a "water miser," a chimney scrubber, a lawn mower that doubles as a garden mulcher, a radio rig designed to measure distance, and a novel incinerator.

To conclude this chapter on personal achievements and ingenuity attributed to Maine folks, a few additional names and their accomplishments are given, alphabetically, in brief form:

ARDEN, Elizabeth, or Florence Nightingale Graham, the "Cosmetic Queen." She had a salon in the Belgrade Lakes Region. In an area of over 2,000 acres, she augmented her business in beauty aids with raising cows and pigs, breeding thoroughbred horses, and growing vegetables and gorgeous flowers. Her own horse, "Jet Pilot," won the 1966 Kentucky Derby. She was the first woman to be admitted to the Business Hall of Fame, in 1974.

BANKS, Frank, University of Maine graduate of 1906, who engineered the Grand Coulee Dam.

BROWN, Herbert A., of Fairfield. Made miniature Santa Clauses playing Christmas music on tiny organs. The entire work was hand made, even the leather boots. He was the first to produce, in 1934, a Shirley Temple doll.

CROWE, Frank, University of Maine graduate of 1905, was construction engineer for the Parker, the Shasta, and the Hoover (Boulder) Dams.

DOWNS, Arthur, of Dexter, was the instigator of the idea for a sanitorium for tubercular patients in 1910. He practiced in Fairfield, died in 1913 at the age of thirty-nine; and had a building erected in 1923 in his name, for children who had TB. The compound was later known as Hebron Sanitorium.

DUNHAM, Alanson Millen, Norway, first produced snowshoes commercially.

FREEMAN, George, class of 1903 at University of Maine, gave directions on constructing the foundation for the Golden Gate Bridge in San Francisco Bay.

GREENLEAF, Moses, 1777–1834, "put Maine on the map." Was a surveyor, railroad corporator, cartographer, author, proprietor, prospector, and promoter. Discovered an entire mountain of a unique type of iron ore and slate deposits, and drew the first dependable map of inland Maine. Found the Brownville valuable slate quarries in 1876. Friend of, and authority on, American Indians.

HILTON, Maurice, of Freeport, in 1975 received the fifteenth Annual Award of the American Shoe Designers, from the Leather Industries of America. His improvement was on the famous Bean's Hunting Shoe of L. L. Bean, where he is on the staff.

MAYO, H. B., of Kingfield, produced in 1881 the first spinning roll bosses in the country.

PERRY, Walter, Mechanic Falls, constructed an exact replica of a steam engine which would actually run on a dime!

PHIPPS, William, has remained the greatest and most successful treasure finder in all the history of treasure-trove. Among his finds are sixteen Spanish galleons from around 1606, driven by hurricanes onto reefs north of Santo Domingo. In 1681, in a small brig, he recovered treasures as proof of findings in an unknown wreck. In his last dive, he recovered 160 one-pound silver ingots, plus a cannon and other artifacts, including gems and doubloons, amounting to thirty-two tons of riches, in just a short time. He was arrogant, tenacious, honest, and brave; and for his successful ventures, was knighted in England.

SKILLIN, Franklin J., of Portland, devised a simple way to find the number wanted in "Information" by a device known as a "Skill-Tracer" (a combination of his name and the purpose of the instrument). In 1963, he began production in quantity in his home shop on West Alna Road. The invention is now used as far as the West Coast. It has a colored scanning edge to facilitate finding the desired name and number on the white directory pages.

SMITH, Captain Leonard Burlington, of Mill Creek, South Orrington, built a floating bridge in the Dutch Antilles off the north coast of Venezuela, in 1888. This bridge, on the island of Curaçao, was replaced by a second floating bridge on pontoons, in 1939. Captain Smith also built a public water supply container and an electrical generating system for the island.

STEVENS, John F., born in West Gardiner on April 25, 1853. Attended Farmington Normal School. Took up railroad engineering. Made a treaty with the Blackfeet to build a pass through the Montana Rockies. A bronze statue now stands at this, the Maria Pass, in his memory and in recognition of his unbelievable hardships in the endeavor. Freezing rain, stinging snow, and Indian guides who refused to go higher with him were endured until he found the pass at dusk. He tramped around flaying his arms all night to keep alive until he could descend in daylight.

He also formulated the plans for the Panama Canal, and became its "master builder," although he was more familiarly known as "Big Smoke," in reference to the long, black cigars that he continually smoked.

He died in 1943, age ninety; and in 1946 his picture was on the Canal Zone postage stamp. He received many medals and other awards; and even Goethals, who finished the canal work in 1915, gave Stevens full credit for the monumental task. Stephens once said, "There are three diseases here: malaria, yellow fever, and cold feet—and the worst is cold feet."

WEYMOUTH, Frank, 1896 class at the University of Maine, conceived and planned a scheme to bring water from the Colorado River to Southern California, known as the Colorado River aqueduct.

5

History, Government, and Politics

Home of ex-Senator Margaret Chase Smith, Skowhegan

Knox Memorial, Thomaston

Fort Popham, Popham Beach, was built in 1861 and used during the Civil War and World War I. The white stones are grave markers.

Fort William Henry, 1692,
Pemaquid Beach

Hannibal Hamlin Memorial Library, Paris Hill, formerly the Oxford County Jail

Gateway National Soldiers Home, Togus

House of Colonel John Black, a land agent, Ellsworth

The approximately 3,500 miles of the coastline of Maine contain some of the most historic footprints in the United States, resulting from European upheavals. Ever since the first white man, Lief Erickson, and the Vikings came to the shores of Maine, around A.D., 992, the state has been an historically proud one, and with justification.

St. Croix Island, near Calais, Maine, was the locality where, in 1604, the first French emigrants settled on American shores. With eighty colonists, Pierre du Guast, better known as the *Sieur de Monts*, spent a winter there before moving onward to Nova Scotia. Samuel de Champlain explored the islands and made some maps of the Maine coastline. One boarded-up house and an automatic lighthouse still stand on the island which was placed on the list of historical sites in 1949.

Samuel Argall came to the coast of Maine by accident, blown there by a storm. He was the first man to report the Gulf Stream. Later, he was commissioned to destroy the French at Mt. Desert, which he accomplished in 1612. The following year, he annihilated the French settlements on the Bay of Fundy, at Port Royal. This was the first colonial warfare between France and England for possession of North America.

Captain John Smith began his exploration of Maine shores in 1614, when he charted the coastline from Penobscot Bay to Cape Cod. He named the region "New England," a change from its previous name of Northern Virginia. He made the first, remarkably accurate, detailed map of this new region and spent considerable time in Casco Bay, which he called Harrington Bay, and on the Isles of Shoals, known as Smith Isles. A bronze tablet commemorates his visit to Monhegan Island in 1614.

The first attack of the French-Indian War was on September 21, 1689, and took place in Baxter's Woods, Portland.

On May 8, 1725, the most severe battle ever waged in Maine was the subduing of Indian Chief Paugus at Lovewell's Pond, in Fryeburg. The event was spearheaded by Captain Lovewell and his thirty-four "King's Men" who were victorious over eighty tribesmen, in retaliation for numerous attacks on Lovewell's home.

A bronze tablet on a monument by the shore of the pond has a long inscription including the names of Lovewell's men killed in the early-morning until after-sunset conflict. This fight was the basis of Longfellow's first published poem.

It was off the coast of Maine that the first naval battle of the Revolutionary War took place, when Machias farmers grouped to drive off the British Navy, retain their Liberty Pole, and cause the death of the enemy commander.

Machias, a small town, was settled in 1763. Its men met in Job Burnham's Tavern on July 12, 1775, at which time they decided to erect America's first Liberty Pole. Many more were to follow in other towns. A British schooner, the HMS *Margaretta*, fully armed, was following two sloops of Ichabod Jones, the *Polly* and the *Unity*, which came to anchor in the harbor. The *Margaretta*, under British Commander Captain James Moore, sent its men to demand the removal of the Liberty Pole, which the Machias men refused to do. They were given until noon the next day to comply with the British orders; and were warned that the pole would be cut down if not removed. Machias men replied, "You do that and we'll burn the town."

The group met again, led by Captain Jeremiah O'Brien, his brother John, and Benjamin Foster. The decision was made to arrest Moore at church, but Moore saw some men headed for his ship, as he looked out the window from his pew. He leaped through the open window and reached his vessel ahead of the Machias group. A few shots were fired, but no one was hurt.

The next morning, the O'Briens and forty volunteers, armed with axes and a few fowling guns, with a limited amount of ammunition, and several pitchforks, assembled on the shore, took to their boats, and boarded the unarmed *Unity*. Moore hesitated to engage in battle with these farmers as his fiancée and her uncle were still ashore in Machias, held as hostages.

These events led to the first battle of the war. Jeremiah commandeered the *Unity* and ran the bowsprit through the mainsail of the *Margaretta*. Then the Machias men boarded her, led by

John O'Brien, and commandeered the *Margaretta*, with its sixteen guns, by merely leaping onto the enemy vessel with their assorted crude arms and shovels. They drove the amazed and terrified crew into the hold and took over the vessel. All of this happened before the Battle of Bunker Hill and was the first naval engagement in American history. The sole shot fired was from an old moose hunter's gun, from which one ball was directed at, but never hit, the *Margaretta*.

In the brief and somewhat bloody hand-to-hand skirmish, which was all over within an hour, Moore was mortally wounded as were three other Englishmen. The colonists lost two men before the British laid down their arms in surrender.

After the success of the "pitchfork brigade," the men of Machias solemnly went back to their sawing and fishing in the nonchalant New England manner. Moore's fiancée died within the year, many folks claiming that it was from a broken heart. The captured crew members were sent to Falmouth (Portland) as prisoners of war. James Fenimore Cooper called this battle "the Lexington of the Seas."

William Hutchins, of Bangor, 1764–1866, was the last man, at age 102, to have seen the British siege of 1779 and the occupation of Bagaduce (Castine). His pension was $21.66 a year until 1865. At that time, only four Revolutionary War veterans were still living, and their pensions were raised to $300 a year.

It is believed that there now exist only three Liberty Poles in the United States, one of them being in Bristol Mills, Maine.

Maine has several forts of historical distinction, one which predated any warfare. This was Fort Western, built in 1754, on the site of a 1628 trading post on the Kennebec River. It had been constructed to serve as a stonghold by the "Plymouth Proprietorys." Later, it was used to store supplies awaiting transportation by ox cart to Fort Halifax at Taconic Falls (Winslow). The Fort is unique inasmuch as it had been a trading post, a barracks for soldiers, and living quarters for Captain James Howard, its first and only commander. After the war, he purchased it, and it remained in his family for many years. Under new ownership, it was converted into a tenement building.

In time it suffered neglect, became a fire hazard, and, in 1919, Guy P. Gannett and his father, William Howard Gannett, bought it, restored it, and presented it to Augusta in 1921 as a memorial to Sadie Hill Gannett. It has sixteen exhibit rooms in which everything is "touchable."

Many people agree that the best fortification of the Revolutionary War was Fort George, in Castine, built by the British in 1779. It still stands, with its thirty-foot high bastions and an expanse of nearly an acre.

Fort Halifax, in Winslow, is the oldest surviving original block house in America. This was built in 1754 by the British at the confluence of the Kennebec and Sebasticook Rivers during the French-Indian War. With its sister fort, Western, it has served against invasion from Canada.

It has never been renovated nor restored in any way. Even the outside roof has been repaired only three or four times in more than 200 years, and the walls still contain the original timbers.

Fort O'Brien, sometimes called Fort Machias, was built in 1775 on the site of the first naval engagement of the Revolutionary War.

One outstanding Revolutionary War figure was Henry Knox, the youngest Major General in the War, at age thirty-one, and later the first Secretary of War for the nation. He was a good friend to Washington and presumably contributed to the planning of all the battles won by the general, who later appointed him to the Secretary post from 1875 to 1885. His artillery military encampment in 1778 is supposed to have been the forerunner of the military academy at West Point, thus making Knox its founder. He commanded at West Point from 1782 to 1784.

Knox was born in extreme poverty in Boston, 1794; acquired a good education; and was finally financially able to build a magnificent home, Montpelier, on the eastern bank of George's River, in Thomaston, where he spent the last ten years of his life. It was the most expensive country house in Maine, but was destroyed by deterioration in 1871. A replica, on a high rise just a short distance away, is now an historical edifice, open to the public during the summer months.

One humorous story about General Knox is that on one occasion he invited an entire tribe of Tarratine Indians for dinner who, once fed, finally had to be told to go home as they began to settle down for an extended visit.

The section of his estate termed the "Farmhouse," built in 1796, was later converted into the Thomaston Maine Central Railroad Station and is now the only original Knox building standing. It was the oldest railroad station in the country, antedating the two B. & O. stations by thirty-four years. It has been restored by the Thomaston Historical Society.

Knox was blessed with a popular personality, a strong character, and social charm. He was respected and loved by nearly everyone. His marriage to Lucy Flicker, daughter of the last British colonial secretary in Boston, resulted in a life of affection and closeness. He died in 1806, at age fifty-six.

Fort Knox, built on the Penobscot River during the Aroostook War, is but one of the many Maine landmarks bearing his name. This fort is considered to be the finest example of fort structure. It was built of solid granite, hewn by hand from the Mt. Waldo quarries. Reuben Smart, of Swanville, was instrumental in its construction, as well as that of three other forts in Maine: Gorges, Williams, and McKinley. Fort William Henry, at Pemaquid, built in 1692, is a strong contender of the excellence of Fort Knox.

Among the Maine men lauded for their part in the Revolutionary War were Stephen Boothby, Henry Dearborn, William Heath, Rufus Ingalls, and Henry Knox.

In 1775, during the march of Benedict Arnold and his 1,100 men to invade Canada by entering from the Maine woods, Falmouth lost 136 buildings, its custom house, court house, town house, and an Episcopal church.

The last survivor of the Battle of Bunker Hill was General Ralph Farnum. He was with Washington at Valley Forge and held his general in reverence during his entire life. He died circa 1860, at age 104. Unfortunately, Bunker Hill monument lists his birthplace as Lebanon, New Hampshire; but actually it was Lebanon, Maine. This same error has occurred in some printed publications, probably relying on the information from the monument.

Farnum enlisted at age eighteen, leaving his father's farm after hearing about the "shot heard around the world." At age twenty-five, he became the first settler in Acton, with his wife, Mehitable Bean. This was also the town where the "Muster Gingerbread" house stood, a name derived from the fact that gingerbread was peddled at all militia musterings.

At age 104, Farnum was invited to Boston, and he went! There he met the Prince of Wales, a high point in Farnum's life. A 104-gun salute was fired in his honor. He was at that time receiving a yearly pension of $6,166. For years, his code of living was to go to bed at 7 P.M. and get up at 5 A.M. He died the day after Christmas in 1861 or he would probably have enlisted for the Civil War.

During the War of 1812, a cannon was dragged to the summit of Mt. Battie, in Camden, in 1814, to protect the harbor. The novelty drew tourists to the extent that the Summit House hotel was constructed at the top in 1897, overlooking Camden Harbor, the bay, and out to sea. It was later torn down and the debris burned. Then, a field stone memorial tower was erected. It offers one of the most scenic vistas on the East Coast. A plaque to Edna St. Vincent Millay is also a part of the present attraction, because it was from the top of Mt. Battie that she wrote her "Renascence."

Maine is the only state in the Union that ever made war against a foreign nation. This was the Aroostook War, in 1839, in which no one was killed in spite of a few sniper shots. Governor John Fairfield called out the militia and thus created the first draft for warfare in the country. His political opponents have always called the event the "Fairfield Farce," and it remains the only bloodless war in which the United States ever engaged.

A battalion of reluctant troops was raised in Portland and started for Aroostook, untrained and afraid. Luckily for them, the battalion was halted at Augusta and returned home where the men received a glorious welcome after the brief campaign.

The reason for the Aroostook War was a boundary dispute between New France (Canada) and the inhabitants of Eastern Maine. Britain claimed that an American flag had been raised on their land. A counter claim that timber had been plundered and citizens of Maine seized and unlawfully imprisoned, was made. The Madawaska raids had resulted in the loss of much valuable timber.

On February 12, 1838, New Brunswick men surrounded the defenders and took the land agent, their leader. British regulars from Quebec carried eight pieces of cannon into the Madawaska area. Then young American men went into the Canadian woods and sabotaged the great pines, rendering them useless as masts for the British naval and merchant ships.

The Maine Legislature immediately appropriated $800,000 for the protection of Maine public lands; and Daniel Webster, a distinguished Maine man, served as chief negotiator. A "peace-without-dishonor" demand was delivered and surprisingly agreed upon by the New Brunswick governor, and the Webster-Ashburton Treaty of 1842 became a vital part of the state's legislation. The historical records show that Maine, standing alone, began what could have developed into a destructive international war; but instead it negotiated peace.

Then came the Civil War. The first name drawn in the national draft was Edward Francis White, of Portland. During this war, Maine furnished more army and navy men proportionally than did any other state. Out of the Union Army of 600,000 there were 72,945 Maine men, the highest state percentage recorded.

The town of Gray led in percentage rate among the Maine towns.

The state had fifteen infantries with seven batteries of mounted artillery. The First Infantry was made up of men from Portland, Lewiston, Auburn, and Norway. The Second and Sixth were known as the "coolest" and most efficient field artilleries during the entire war. The Third was once credited with having saved the entire army. Maine men seemed more eager, ready, and willing to do beyond their share than were outfits from some other parts of the country. The presence of Maine men in battle was considered a good omen.

However, it was the sixteenth Regiment of Volunteers from Maine that distinguished itself by its pessimistic attitude. Every soldier in the sixteenth had made his will. Yet, this regiment was unusually successful in warfare. Nevertheless, in one instance, at Gettysburg, the men decided to throw caution to the wind, a brave gesture for that regiment. This time their gloomy, dour predictions came true. Few members survived, but the Union was more quickly saved by this attack of the "Gloomy Sixth" from Maine.

The Twentieth Maine Volunteers actually did save the Union at Little Round Top, Gettysburg. And when Lee surrendered to Grant, it was a Brewer man, Joshua Chamberlain of the Twentieth who, as Commander of the Union troops, was given a post of honor to receive Lee's papers; and it was the Twentieth which paraded at the surrender ceremony.

The boots, saddle, and saddle pad used by Chamberlain, a three-time governor of Maine and hero at Little Round Top, the crucial battle of the Civil War, are on display in the Pejepscot Historical Society museum, built in 1827 and previously used as a church and as a schoolhouse. Chamberlain was also president of Bowdoin College for twelve years, and his erstwhile home in Brunswick still stands on Maine Street.

One of the first five men to enlist in the Civil War, at Lincoln's call, was Charles W. Bary, of Alfred, and he was the only survivor of Alfred's 165 Union soldiers. He was a brave and honorable serviceman.

Maine's Women's State Relief Corps, founded in 1883 to aid families of Civil War veterans, was the first such relief group in the United States. A similar national organization was later founded, but the Maine corps never joined it. At one time, seventy-five town corps with over 3,000 members served Maine. A second purpose of the group was to promote love of country and a sense of patriotism in their children. A great many flags and grave markers were distributed before the Corps disbanded.

The first city in the United States to adopt military training in the public school system was Bangor, which introduced the first ROTC, in 1862, as stated in the "Boys and High School and Selected Schools" report of that year. Survival training was added in 1959.

The course consumed two hours a week, when drills were held on Wednesday and Saturday forenoons. From 1862 to 1898, the group was known as the "Volunteer Drill Company." They wore gray uniforms of military type, each boy furnishing his own uniform and equipment.

At the outbreak of the Spanish-American War, 1898, the uniforms were changed to Army blue; and a larger unit, still at each individual's expense, developed into the Bangor High School Cadet Corps.

Rear Admiral William Kimball, of Maine, was the torpedo officer on two different warships and commanded the first torpedo boat flotilla in the Spanish-American War. During World War I he was on the Board of Examining Officers. He died in 1930, after finishing his term of being in charge of the Nicaraguan Expeditionary Squadron.

From 1921 to date, the ROTC of Bangor has won several championships. In 1933, the unit received the highest possible rating, that of "Honor Roll;" and cadets were allowed to wear a small red star on their lower sleeve. This honor was retained until the middle of World War II when they were called for serious duty; but it was reinstated in 1957. In 1962, the Bangor ROTC rifle team won the first U. S. Army match and also the ERA Regional match. Membership at that time was approximately ninety.

In World War I, the first American regiment to march through the streets of London, in 1917, was mostly Maine men. They arrived on August 15, crossed the channel on the seventeenth, and billeted near Boulogne on the eighteenth. Many more such regiments were to follow.

In politics, the first formally organized local convention for the Republican Party met at Strong, Maine, on August 7, 1854.

Among the many politicians from Maine, Hannibal Hamlin,

of Paris Hill, served as vice-president under President Lincoln; Nelson Rockefeller, a part-time Maine resident, was appointed vice-president following the Watergate Affair, in the 1970s; and George Bush, of Kennebunkport, became vice-president under President Reagan in 1980.

As for Hamlin, he broke from the Democratic Party on June 12, 1856, thereby becoming a national sensation. That same year, he became the first Republican governor of Maine. While governor, he resigned the post to work on the national slavery question. After his term as vice-president, he became minister to Spain. When he died, on July 4, 1891, he had completed fifty years of public political service and held the record for being the youngest speaker of the house in any state, having served as such at age twenty-seven.

President Harrison's administration in the 1890s might well have been thought of as the Maine, rather than national, administration. For example, on Capitol Hill were the following Maine men:

ALGER—Secretary of War
BLAINE—Congressman
BOUTELLE—Chairman of Navy Affairs in the House
DINGLEY—Chairman of the Ways and Means Committee to
    deal with the tariff
DOLE—First President of the Republic of Hawaii
FRYE—Congressman and President pro-tem upon the death
    of Hobart, around 1897
HALE—Leader of the Senate
LONG—Secretary of the Navy under McKinley
MILLIKEN—Chairman regarding public buildings
REED—Speaker of the House
SEWALL—Ran with Bryan as vice-presidential candidate in
    1896
STEVENS—Minister to Hawaii

Among the many other outstanding Maine political or governmental figures who have contributed to the nation's political welfare, governmental progress, and public service, with national or international recognition, are the following, in alphabetical order:

BENN, Col. Hazel E., Smyrna Mills; became colonel in 1968 and
    was highest ranking woman in USMC in 1971.

BLAINE, James G; defeated in candidacy for president in 1884 by close ratio of 48.5 to 48.2 in favor of Grover Cleveland. Had previously been defeated by Hayes, 1876, and Garfield, 1880.

Blaine was once part-owner of the Kennebec *Journal*, in Augusta. He was also one of Maine's five chairmen of the U. S. Senate Appropriations Committee, Maine having the highest number of such chairmen from any one state down through the years. He was Speaker of the House from 1869–1875; a Presidential candidate in 1876 and 1880; Secretary of State, 1888–1892; a fine orator with unfailing memory for names and faces; and a person of considerable charm

BUBAR, Benjamin C.; Maine's leading prohibitionist who had drunk alcohol only once in his life. He was a presidential candidate for the National Statesmen Party in 1880. At twenty-two, he had left Mars Hill Mountain to go into politics, the youngest ever elected as a state representative up until then.

CILLEY, Jonathan; speaker of the House, 1835. Last man in the United States to be killed in a duel, instigated by a heated debate when he was senator. Neither of the duelists was injured on the first three volleys, but Cilley was killed on the fourth one, at eighty feet.

CLIFFORD, Nathan, was U. S. Attorney General under President Polk. He had a special commission to Mexico where he negotiated the treaty securing California as a part of the United States. He once sat on the U. S. Supreme Court, under President Buchanan.

COHEN, William "Bill"; in 1975, became the first member of Congress to be awarded the honor of being one of the Ten Outstanding Young Men in the opinion of an United States Jaycee poll. His performance during the Watergate proceedings as a member of the investigating committee was highly commendable.

COUTURIER, Robert L.; in 1965, was the youngest mayor of any U. S. city, Lewiston. He won without a run-off, at age twenty-four. His opponents ranged from thirty to sixty-two years of age.

CURTIS, Kenneth; in 1966, at age thirty-five, was the youngest governor in the nation. Later became United States Ambassador to Canada under President Carter.

DIX, Dorothea; first woman lobbyist of more than local intent; often called the greatest American woman of the nineteenth century. She was born in Hampden, 1802; wrote children's books: devoted herself to prison reform and to bettering mental institutions for the indigent; and was given a special alcove in the Capitol's library for a conference room. Under President Lincoln she became Superintendent of Nurses for the Union Army. She died in 1887, and Congress voted a large sum of money for a memorial in her honor.

DOW, Neal, born in 1804, called "The Father of Prohibition." While mayor of Portland, he succeeded in getting the first State Temperance Act passed, on May 31, 1851. He eliminated the 11:00 A.M. and 4:00 P.M. bell ringing which signified "rum breaks." His law permitted no manufacturing, selling, nor storing of intoxicating liquors in the state. All in stock was confiscated and destroyed. It was nationally called "The Maine Law" or "Act for the Suppression of Drinking Houses and Tippling Shops." His home, named "Apostle of Temperance," was built in Portland in 1824. His tireless campaigning for prohibition resulted in the eighty-three year dry spell in Maine and became a model for several state statutes, leading eventually to the adoption of the prohibition amendment to the Constitution. He died in 1897.

EVANS, George, 1841–1847; first U. S. senator to receive mileage allowance for a trip that he never made. He did not have to go to Washington as he was serving as a congressman from Maine including the December 7, 1840 session, so he was already there; yet, by law, he had to be allotted his mileage expense.

FESSENDEN, William Pitt; Secretary of the Treasury in 1864, under President Lincoln. A Portland native, he was ready for college at age twelve; was accepted at Bowdoin College when he was thirteen; found the work entirely too easy; entered politics to avoid boredom. His closest friend was the Maine poet Longfellow. Politically, it is believed that he saved President Johnson from impeachment in 1868. He was another of the Maine politicians who were once chairmen of the U. S. Senate Appropriations Committee.

FRYE, William P., was President pro-tem of the Senate on February 7, 1876, when the office was rotated.

FULLER, Melville, associate Justice of the Supreme Court under President Buchanan, and chief justice of the Supreme Court under President Cleveland, in 1888.

JALBERT, Louis; a Lewiston native who, in 1974, had held the longest term of public service in both state and nation. In 1981, the National Conference of State Legislators ranked him as fifth in the nation in years of service in State Legislature.

JOSSELYN, Henry; the only royal chief justice any state ever had. He lived in Scarborough, 1636–1676. (Note: Maine also had the first and only Viceroy in the nation.)

KAVANAGH, Edward; the first Catholic governor in the United States. He assumed the position when Governor John Fairfield resigned to be a senator.

KIMBALL, Sumner I., of Lebanon; considered the "Father of the Coast Guard Life Saving Service" in America.

KING, Horatio, of Portland; Postmaster General under President Buchanan, and appointed by President Lincoln as a member of the commission to carry out the provisions of the Emancipation Proclamation, 1862, in the District of Columbia.

LADD, William; retired sea captain of Minot; first man to propose a united nations organization, after the War of 1812, to bring about world order through a congress of nations. Founded the American Peace Society in 1828 and was its first president. He advocated forming a Congress of Nations and a separate Court of Nations. He preached on lyceum circuits against war; published a book proposing practical approaches to acquiring world peace; opposed building the Bunker Hill monument on the grounds that it was vanity; and lived from 1778 to 1841, always dreaming of a warless world. The United Nations, 100 years later, fulfilled his dream.

LINCOLN, Enoch and Levi; first brothers to serve as state governors, Levi in Massachusetts and Enoch in Maine.

LITTLE, Mrs. Josiah Stover, 1859–1860; served as vice-regent for Mt. Vernon Ladies Association. Was one of the original fund raisers to acquire the building and donated a considerable amount of money to that purchase. (To date, Maine has had five vice-regents.)

LONG, John, a Buckfield native; Secretary of the Navy under President T. R. Roosevelt.

LONGLEY, James B., of Lewiston. Became the first, and so far only, Independent governor in the country. Elected in 1974, he won against candidates from both major parties. His untimely death in 1980 cut short a very productive life in business and government. The concept of a tax revolt which matured in California in 1978 was really begun in Maine four years earlier by Governor Longley. His campaign promise was "Less government and lower taxes," and he achieved exactly that during his term. This spark ignited twenty states which had or were considering some kind of constitutional limit on legislative power to tax at will. *Time* magazine, September 1, 1980, states that he halved unemployment, funneled a $10 million state surplus into tax rebates, and kept his promise of not seeking a second term. He also brought recognition to the state as a leader of action in the field of mental retardation concern throughout the nation.

MARTIN, John; in 1975 was a twenty-three-year old Maine legislator, representing Eagle Lake; and later was the youngest House speaker in the nation.

MORRILL, Lot M.; Secretary of the Treasury under President Grant, in 1876. Another of Maine's record-breaking five chairmen of the U. S. Senate Appropriations Committee. He was a Belgrade native.

MURPHY, Ward; first woman to become a chief executive officer of a United States correction system. Appointed in August, 1970, to the correctional institute in Gardiner.

MUSKIE, Edmund S.; governor of Maine, United States Senator, and appointed to finish out a short term as Secretary of State under President Carter. His home was in Rumford, Maine.

PINKHAM, Dora B., of Fort Kent; first woman to serve in the Maine Legislature and the first one in the United States to preside over a state House of Representatives, in 1923.

REED, John; ex-governor of Maine and twice appointed ambassador to Sri Lanka, under Presidents Ford and Reagan. He was born in Fort Fairfield, January 5, 1921.

REED, Thomas B.; weighed around 300 pounds and was the most powerful Republican in the nation during the last quarter of the nineteenth century. Witty as Mark Twain, oratorical as William Jennings Bryan, he is remembered for originating the sentence "A statesman is a successful politician who is dead." Clearly expecting to be elected Republican presidential candidate in 1896, he lost through manipulation of his own manager and the cleverness of McKinley. Teddy Roosevelt was a guest in Reed's Portland home many times. Reed was acknowledged to have the "greatest legislative mind in America"; was Speaker of the House from 1889 to 1891; and was internationally respected.

SANBORN, Guliema Penn, of Readfield; was a traveling seamstress and florist who pioneered the ten-hour work system for women.

SEWALL, Arthur, a Bath Democrat, the running mate for William Jennings Bryan.

SMITH, Frances Ormand Johnathan, called "Fog," 1806–1876; editor of the Portland *Eastern Argus* in 1827. Had a meteoric rise to riches; a decline equally precipitous; was a friend of the inventor of telegraph, Samuel F. B. Morse; and served as a secret agent for Daniel Webster when Webster was so deeply involved with the Webster-Ashburton Treaty.

SMITH, Margaret Chase; finished the House term of her husband, Clyde, at his death in 1942; became the first and, to date, only woman to serve in both Houses of Congress, serving four terms on her own election in the House and becoming the first and only woman senator in the United States. She once set a record of 2,941 consecutive Senate roll-call votes. In 1964, she was nominated for president on the Republican ticket. Her slogan was "Don't trade a record for a promise." Her trademark was a single, fresh, red rose which she wore every day.

Mrs. Smith was not only one of the prestigious five senators to serve as chairman of the Senate Appropriations Committee, but she went further by holding a record of thirteen years on this committee. No other state has had more than one Senator head the panel. At her retirement, she was the ranking Republican on the Armed Services Committee.

Senator Smith has more than eighty-five honorary degrees after her thirty-six years in Congress. In her retirement, she has not "retired." She is a visiting professor at the Woodrow Wilson Foundation, visiting twenty campuses during 1974–1975 and lecturing at six different colleges, at the age of seventy-eight. She is also a director of the Lilly Endowment Foundation.

At age eighty-three, in 1980, she was actively engaged in working on papers and records kept in her Skowhegan, Maine, home, now a national landmark. In 1981, plans were announced for a $1 million library center adjoining her home which, according to various reviews, "will rival presidental libraries," and will be called the Northwood Institute Margaret Chase Smith Library Center. She has permanent privileges for living in her Skowhegan home; maintains another home in Silver Springs, Maryland; and a summer home at Cundy's Harbor, Maine.

She will long be remembered for her "Declaration of Conscience" against Senator McCarthy, delivered in the Senate in June, 1950.

SMITH, Noah, Jr.; Secretary of State for Lincoln during the Civil War.

SOUTHARD, Gertrude, of Bangor, and

SKOLFIELD, Alice, of Lewiston. These two women vied for the position of being the first woman in the nation to cast a voting ballot, as the law permitting women's votes was passed about three weeks before Maine's state election and the state rushed into a legislative motion. State officials finally ruled informally that it was a tie. Actually, the first woman to register was a Portland lady who refused to give her age and was consequently turned down by a unanimous ruling of the Board of Registration.

SULLIVANS, four brothers from Berwick, Maine; distinguished themselves by becoming, among the four: an officer of the King's Navy, a prosperous ship builder, a brigadier general, a governor of Massachusetts, a governor of New Hampshire, a justice of the Supreme Court, and a successful lawyer.

Originally, they joined the Navy and were assigned to the same ship. The brother who became a Navy captain was lost overboard at sea during a severe storm. Another refused to take the Oath of Allegiance to the King and was confined to the dreaded Jersey prison where he died. A third, who became famous in law, was a New Hampshire governor and had many honors conferred upon him. He was a personal friend of General Washington. Not long before his death, at age fifty-four, he was appointed to be a justice of the Supreme Court. The fourth brother was judge of the Supreme Court at age thirty-two; was attorney general for the Commonwealth; and in 1804 was the presidential elector in the first electoral college, when Jefferson was elected.

THORNTON, Matthew; the last signer of the Declaration of Independence, because he arrived late and asked permission to add his name. He once lived in Brunswick and was a celebrated singer, physician, surgeon, soldier, theologian, lawyer, judge, councilor, and legislator. In 1745, he was the medical officer accompanying the expedition that separated Cape Breton from the British. He and his family successfully avoided an Indian raid on July 12, 1772. His grave marker reads:

MATTHEW
THORNTON
an
Honest
Man

WASHBURNS, seven notable brothers:

There is little doubt that any country can lay claim to a family of seven illustrious sons as were the Washburns, of Livermore. They lived during the mid-1800s and each son produced sufficient material for an interesting biography of achievement and philosophy. The following sketches of each are but a very brief introduction to the brothers. Together, they were incomparable in versatility and capability in many fields, although they grew up in the backwoods, in poverty and humble stature.

There were also three daughters, about whom little has been published. The sons were

Israel, Jr., 1813–1883; served five terms in Congress of Massachusetts; helped establish the Republican Party; elected Governor of Maine in 1860 for a two-year term; called the "War Governor"; authored the first history of Livermore; collector for Port of Portland, appointed by President Lincoln.

Algernon Sidney, 1814–1879; originated the first national bank in Hallowell; first to win financial success; helped each brother financially; bank president; alumnus of "the little red schoolhouse."

Elihu, 1816–1887; about eighteen consecutive years in Congress; helped elect President Lincoln; prevailed upon Lincoln to put Grant in command of Union Army; helped elect Grant to Presidency; Secretary of State under Grant; eight years as minister to France, under Grant; called "Watchdog of the Treasury" for his efforts to reduce expenditures; only foreign minister to remain at his post in Paris throughout Franco-Prussian War

Cadwallader Colden, 1818–1882; representative from Wisconsin for ten years. (At one time during those years, Elihu was representing Illinois and Israel was representing Maine in the same capacity); Governor of Wisconsin; helped fund Washburn Observatory at University of Wisconsin; had a flour mill in St. Paul that brought him the first gold medal ever awarded outside of Europe. From then on, he named his flour "Gold Medal," now a part of General Mills. Organized a cavalry regiment in Wisconsin; colonel of the Second Wisconsin Volunteer Cavalry; then brigadier general; then major general; influential in construction of Minneapolis-St. Paul railroad; actually achieved the most all-round success of the seven brothers, a fact concurred with by a collective vote of the other six.

Charles Ames, 1822–1889; came East carrying California's first electoral vote ever cast by the state, for Lincoln. This vote proved to be the decisive one; U. S. commissioner to Paraguay for four years under Lincoln administration; invented Washburn's Typegraph, patent for which was sold to Remington.

Samuel Benjamin, 1824–1890; only seafaring member of the brothers; master of own merchant ship before age twenty; captain in Union Navy during Civil War; commander under Admiral Farragut; war wound in hip brought naval career to an end, and from then on he served as caretaker for the estate, his father then being too old for the task; always added an *e* to his surname;

William Drew, 1831–1912; surveyor general of Minnesota; called "Young Rapid," because he made and lost fortunes so rapidly; leading promoter of Sault Ste. Marie Railroad Line; served three years in Congress following the year when his three brothers served simultaneously; U. S. senator from Minnesota; success was mostly in timber; had pink limestone, forty-room mansion; not included in most family business sales; his son, Dr. Cadwallader Lincoln Washburn, a deaf mute, was a renowned dry point etcher whose paintings hang in the Smithsonian Institution in America and in the Louvre in Paris, France.

The total contributions of these seven brothers lie in this compiled list:

> Four representatives to Congress
> Three lawyers
> Three historians
> Two governors of two different states
> Two U. S. senators
> Two bankers
> Two major industrialists
> One army general
> One navy captain
> One Secretary of State
> One editor and novelist
> One inventor

The family estate of these unusually accomplished individuals, is the "Norlands," in Livermore, and is a large nineteenth-century-type dwelling whose name was taken from Tennyson's "Ballad of Oriana" in which the poet wrote " . . . and loud the Norland whirlwinds blow." The estate consisted of a twenty-five-room mansion, a country church, a one-room school house, and a Gothic stone library in which each son had his own alcove. These buildings are open in July and August on a limited schedule, for public tours. The original birthplace was torn down in 1843; a more modern building replaced it; this burned in 1867; and the present house was then erected.

WHITE, Wallace; fifth and final of the five Maine chairmen of the Senate Appropriations Committee. Native of Auburn. Senate majority leader in Congress, 1946.

From a viewpoint of politicians, the town of Paris is known as the "Olympus of Maine" by claiming the distinction of having the greatest number of distinguished persons than has any other town had in the United States. Among these are the following names:

Hannibal Hamlin, Maine's first elected Vice-President
Horatio King, Assistant Postmaster General and the Postmaster General
Rear Admiral William Kimball, commander of the first torpedo flotilla, in the Spanish-American War
Sidney Perham, three terms as governor, Speaker of the House, and Secretary of State

In total, the list of offices from a small town of only 3,600 in the 1970s, and surely fewer in earlier years, there were

Eight U. S. Representatives
Five Governors
Three Presidents of the Senate
Three Speakers of the House
Two Rear Admirals
Two Senators
Two Supreme Court Justices
Two U. S. Marshals
One executive councilor
One Major General of Maine State Militia
One Brigadier General during Civil War
One U. S. Pension Agent
One U. S. Surgeon

The only father and son combination to have served the Maine Legislature were Eugene and Frederick Hale, of Portland.

The Legislature has often been sufficiently foresighted to enact laws that eventually have become nationally legislated. Others clearly advance the prosperity of the state.

Before the twentieth century, there were several noteworthy decisions. A few have been selected from among them.

1620— the first water power development grant ever given in the New World was allotted to South Berwick.
1623— the first bill of exchange, or deed, drawn in America was that by Abraham Shurt, upon Robert Aldworth and Gyles Elbridge, of Bristol, England, in favor of Ambrose Jennens of London who sold Monhegan Island for fifty

171

pounds sterling. This purchase was also the first written conveyance of real estate in America.

1625— the first deed of real estate from Indian chiefs to an Englishman was that of Samoset and Unongoit, of the Sagamore Tribe, when they conveyed to John Brown, of New Harbor, lands on both sides of Muscongus River, for fifty skins. Unongoit made his X. Samoset proudly drew a facsimile of a bow and arrow.

1642— the chartering of the first town in the New World, Gorgeana, which had been called Agamenticus and was finally named York, in 1652. The town was settled in 1624, near Alfred, where the oldest continuous court records in the United States, dating back to 1635, are currently in the courthouse vault.

1786— a treaty was signed on October 11 with Massachusetts to give Penobscot Indians of Old Town the right to have a representative to the state legislature, the only American Indians to have been given this right up to then.

1786— flood control in the United States began in Fryeburg. After the loss of a grist mill, nine houses, nine barns, four oxen, twelve cows, three heifers, four calves, four sheep, four swine, 572 bushels of Indian corn, ten bushels of wheat, 1,750 bushels of potatoes, and 400 pounds of tobacco, the farmers decided to take measures against a flood recurrence of the Saco River. Federal relief came to about 200 pounds off the town taxes.

The landholders demanded stronger action. Therefore, in 1812, the villagers discussed a proposed canal. This was on June 6. A delay of two years for approval by the Massachusetts General Court went by, and the residents then decided to organize and dig at their own expense, for a distance of one half mile. By then it was 1816.

After a narrow gulley was dug, it was believed that the spring freshet would do most of the remaining work. It did; and two ponds were drained and a new course formed. Only occasional deadwater backup ever occurred in the area after that.

1794— July 3, at a town meeting in Camden, a law was enacted that "eight hours be a day's work." That was more than a century ahead of the national law and possibly a world law on this particular labor question. The town also led the nation in forbidding drinking of "spirits" in stores and public places, in 1817. This Temperance Act was adopted by the Legislature's Act of 1851.

1848— a law for no smoking was legislated in Maine on June 21, banning smoking in public places, and the law is still on the books. Illegal smoking carried a fine of five dollars if signs were posted nearby. In 1939, this law was amended to include cigarettes as well as pipe and cigar. In 1951, an amendment included buses under the Maine PUC control. Its early purpose was to prevent fires; today, its focus is on health. Whatever the reason, Maine led the way.

1848— Eva M. Brown, of Camden, appeared in courts to transcribe testimony for all cases concerning drinking problems, and then wrote the Law of Massachusetts relating to "Intoxicating Liquors." This was a "first" for a woman.

1866— the first National Soldiers' Home, a hospital for Maine war veterans, was built. Over 100 years later, in 1970, the first state Veterans' Memorial Cemetery in the nation was dedicated, on Patriot's Day. It is operated by the state and looks like a park. There are no headstones, just simple grave markers flush with the ground.

The uniqueness lies in the fact that the operation of the project is without any aid from the Veterans' Administration or any other veteran organization. It is authorized and funded by the state legislature.

The 160 acre site has trees and shrubs; 1,000 grave sites; a memorial chapel with a fifty-bell carillon; a memorial circle with three flagstaff poles on top of the highest ground; and a metal sculpture of the lady's slipper, a Maine wildflower.

Eventually there will be room for 25,000 graves, each burial area separated and screened by landscaping and trees. Those eligible for burial are honorable discharge veterans who were residents of Maine either when they entered the service or at the time of their death, or a qualified dependent.

The chapel, dedicated in 1973, has a Carillon Schulmerich of twenty-five English and twenty-five harp miniature bell tone generators.

Maine is proud of its unique Veterans' Home, cemetery, and chapel, a complex so simple, so well-kept, and so expansive.

1880s— Martha Dorman Hanson, of Maine, was the first woman

in the nation to receive a driver's license for an automobile. She was born in Auburn, later moved to Portland, and lived there until her death in 1965. Her husband owned the first Stanley Steamer in Maine.

1800s— a group of nineteenth century buildings, known as Row House, Hallowell, received the first federal grant in the nation for restoration as a National Historic Site. It once housed mill workers.

Spanning the centuries, several Maine men were knighted by English royalty. The first native-born American to receive this distinction was Sir William Phipps, of Phipps Point, on June 22, 1687, at the age of thirty-six. Called "the first great Yankee," this deep sea diver for salvage, from what is now Woolwich, had treasures worth over $1,350,000 in gold and silver. He came from a poor family which had around twenty-five children. He went to Boston as a shipbuilder, married a rich widow, became an adventurer, and was the first royal Governor of Massachusetts. He died in London at age forty-four.

A second American to be knighted was William Pepperell of Kittery, who was the hero of Louisburg. He used to attire himself in red broadcloth trimmed with gold lace, and he lived like a baronet in a beautiful gable-roofed house facing the sea. Son of a prosperous boat builder and fisherman, he became a commander and merchant par excellence. For his conquest of Louisburg, on Cape Breton Island, Nova Scotia, he received the royal favor of King George II and was knighted and made a peer of the realm on September 28, 1745. This honor included command of the regular regiments raised in America, an unusual honor, which angered English soldiers.

Louisburg was considered to be impregnable, and its conquest took forty or more days of terrific combat aided by 4,000 men, mostly Maine farmers and fishermen, plus a fleet of ships. Together they laid the fortress low on June 16, 1745. Pepperell served as commander-in-chief even though he was not primarily a military man. He sympathized with the crown during the Revolutionary War. After his death, his family fled to England and the titles were lost.

In 1901, Howard Maxim, of Sangerfield, was knighted.

Another Sangerfield man, Harry Oakes, received knighthood. A graduate of Bowdoin College in 1896, he prospected for gold in the Yukon, Alaska, Belgium, the Congo, and Australia,

174

circling the globe for thirteen years.

In 1911, he was penniless; but on a tip from a Chinaman in Swastika, Ontario, he became a millionaire several times over, about 250 times. For his donation to the St. George's Hospital in London, he received attention from King George VI, as well as his knighthood.

In 1943, he was murdered in his Nassau home. His bed was set on fire; his skull was pierced four times with a triangular instrument. This was on July 9, when he was about to leave for Maine, where his wife was already spending the summer at Bar Harbor. The investigation was long and intense; and although the burden of the crime seemed to fall upon Count Alfred de Marigny, Oakes's son-in-law, he was acquitted and the case remains one of the world's most famous unsolved murders.

In 1950, the affair was revived by the murder of a woman lawyer who started to review the case; then the murder of a secretary who was among the guests at Oakes's home the night of the murder; and later, a watchman, who claimed that he saw strangers land on shore the night of the murder, lost his life.

Oakes's widow, Lady Eunice, an Australian, died in the spring of 1981 at her home in Nassau. The death of her husband, Sir Harry Oakes, gold prospector and philanthropist, will probably never be solved.

One other national open case of unsolved murder involving a Maine man is that of Judge Joseph F. Crater. He left his home in Belgrade one summer morning; arrived by train in New York; dined that night with friends; and was never heard from again. The surmise is that some decision that the judge had made had sufficiently aroused the Mafia, or else they feared detection of some sort; but this is all pure conjecture. His disappearance occurred on August 6, 1930.

The twentieth century has found the Maine Legislature even more productive and foresighted. For instance, the 1907 Rangeley Water Bill is one that surely belongs in history. It was a conflict in the legislature that produced world publicity and still may never be surpassed in its length nor intensity. The discussion lasted from January 5 to March 7 and reverted to old Roman, and even Egyptian, laws, bringing about the biggest lobby known in the legislature. As a direct result, the Union Water Power did not get its desired dam and the Rangeley Lakes still remain unblemished.

In 1921, Maine had the first forest entomologist, to protect the woods from pest losses, ever appointed in the country.

In 1923, Maine had the first standing Legislative Committee on Publicity in the nation. It was promoted by Speaker of the Maine House, Frank H. Holley, of North Anson.

In 1943, women served as pages in the Maine House and Senate, a "first" in the country. Mrs. Ruth Foster, of Winthrop, served the Senate; and Elizabeth Silver, of Hartland, and Rachel Bubar, of Linneus, served the House.

During the 1960s, Ray Geiger, of Lewiston, promoted the return of postmarks identifying the name of the town in which mail is cancelled. This identifying mark had been discarded in the early part of the decade. Now, all except a very few small postal stations have their own personal postmark.

Also during the 1960s, Maine became and remains the only state which officially recognizes the anniversary of the assassination of President John F. Kennedy. This is not even observed in his home state. In 1965, two years after the killing, the Maine Legislature enacted a law requiring special programs in the schools to memorialize the life and works of the young President. The law does not indicate a day out of school, but is considered as a "Remembrance Day," as is that commemorating the assassination of Lincoln.

In 1966, when Job Corps were popular, under President Johnson, Maine had the largest one in the country, at Poland Spring, a summer resort of fame and elegance. One thousand and eighty predominantly black girls, ages sixteen to twenty-one, were housed there, with a waiting list of 2,500. Dorms were the rooms in the Poland Spring House and the Mansion, and all major buildings were made available by decree of Maine's Governor John Reed. Each girl received a thirty dollar monthly allowance plus medical and dental care, work clothes, room, and board. In addition, fifty dollars a month was set aside for each girl. Of this amount, one half was allocated to the girl's parents by permission of the girl and, if such permission were granted, the parents' share was increased by another twenty-five dollars.

Many so-called "incidents" of vandalism occurred, such as wrenching fixtures from walls, setting fire to drapes, totally mutilating furniture, and complete destruction of floor coverings. The beautiful Poland Spring House was completely ruined and the entire plant was defaced. The resort never returned to its former elegance. The restoration price would have been astronomical. Some time later, mercifully perhaps, it burned to the ground.

Maine led the way in legislation for pollution clean-up in waters by clearing the Penobscot River, one of the most polluted in the nation. Assistance from the federal government helped. Other states soon followed the lead.

The 1970s brought many legislative rulings to the attention of the nation. In 1970, Maine legislated the most comprehensive system of land protection laws in the country. Called the Site Location of Development Act, it concerns development of over twenty acres or 60,000 square feet of building area. The state also mandated shoreline zoning; regulating filling or altering tidal wetlands, salt marshes, beaches, rocky outcrops, and flats between extreme high and low tides, plus the shores of most lakes and ponds larger than ten acres. The Land Use Regulation Commission also protects the 10.5 million acres which have no organized government. This was all legislated in Maine before the idea became almost universally accepted.

In 1972, Congress, pressured by Maine's Senator Margaret Chase Smith, permanently established an annual date for Father's Day. Such a day had been suggested and recommended in 1916, but, never confirmed by the Congress, it was a year-by-year designation.

In 1973, Maine became the first state in the nation to adopt a plan for voluntary contributions to the state's two political parties, by marking an appropriate box on the state income tax form.

In 1974, four outstanding pieces of legislation of national interest were enacted:

#1. The enactment of the Catastrophic Plan: it is not a hand-out, but gives help to families whose finances have been wiped out or whose medical bills far exceed income. Smokers pay for this through cigarette taxes. The plan went into effect on July 1; and six years later, medical bill payments had amounted to thousands of dollars. On the lesser side, aid is given to so-called "border-line" families unable to pay medical and dental bills but not sufficiently poverty-line applicants to get state assistance. At the beginning, it was judged that about 45,000 Maine families were eligible for the program because under this plan " . . . you don't have to be a poor person. This will help people over the hump." Other states have since duplicated the program.

#2. Some states had, in general, one or two specific protectional environmental laws. Maine, however, enacted the most comprehensive environmental laws in the nation: a mass of laws protecting air, land, and water. The state has a site selection act that sets standards for the locating of industry and large residential and business developments. Its mandatory subdivision and shoreland zoning laws are not yet duplicated anywhere, and controls over the transport of oil are exceedingly strict. The intent of this law has been copied in various states. The oil conveyance law placed a tax of one half cent a barrel on all oil transported through Maine waters, providing a $4 million fund for cleaning up spills when vandal ships cannot be identified.

#3. After several citizen complaints about the substitution of an October date for the original November 11 Armistice Day, the Maine Legislature returned the state to the November date for Veteran's Day; and the following year, Congress restored the original date, to be effective in three years. Once again Maine led the way, and once again Ray Geiger, Lewiston, was a dynamic force.

#4. In Portland, at the headquarters of the state chamber of commerce, is a log sheet which records consumer complaints and comments on bad business practices. One item logged in December, 1974, showed six inquiries about the ethics of specific firms, five reports of questionable business activities, and a complaint about a TV repair service. These logs are a part of what is considered to be the nation's only state consumer council, and the U.S. Chamber of Commerce has shown wide interest in the idea. The council is more advantageous than the previous Maine Better Business Bureau because it is a cooperative venture, involving fifty municipal chambers of commerce in the state. Each local chamber is now an arm of the State Council, which opened November 1, 1974, and already has been highly recommended as a model for other states to adopt. It takes the system into local areas rather than having one sole chamber for complaints. After appropriate screening, firms considered unworthy are processed.

Two laws of interest in 1975 were the Vietnamese refugee resettlement program in the state and the regulation limit of allowable noise, the first such law in the country.

When the influx of Vietnamese came to this country in 1975, Maine accepted over 300 and had the first state-sponsored refugee resettlement program in the East. The only other such program at the time was in the state of Washington.

The other law, regulating allowable noise, was focused on snowmobiles in conjunction with the International Snowmobile Industry Association. Under Maine's regulation, "no snowmobile manufactured after February 1, 1975, may be sold or offered for sale by any manufacturer, distributor, or dealer in the State of Maine unless such snowmobile is constructed so as to limit total vehicle noise to not more than seventy-eight decibels of sound pressure at fifty feet on the A scale as measured by the SAE Standard J-192a." Proof of this compliance was required by either an official certificate in sight on the vehicle or else by a legal letter indicating results of testing inspection for the minimum allowable noise.

One law that got its beginning in Maine and has now spread to every state and to major nations, is one promoted by Albert Ware Paine, of Maine: that persons may be permitted to testify in their own defense in court.

In 1977, Maine lead the nation in signing an aerosol ban, now a nationwide rule.

In January, 1978, Maine was recognized as having the lowest interest rates in the country. A cluster of banks in the Augusta-Gardiner area, led by John Gwazdosky, a maverick banker in Augusta, promoted the idea at his 125-year-old First Consumers Savings Bank, which had at that time the lowest rates in the country. New car loans led the business, and nearly every other bank in the area followed his lead.

Also in 1978, the legislature passed a law prohibiting mandatory retirement for teachers and state, county, and municipal employees, the first state to initiate such a law.

A law regulating sewage disposal provisions for seasonal dwellings converted into year-round use was the first of its kind in the nation, and is a boon for saving lakes and rivers.

In 1981, the Office of Maine CETA received the top rating given by the U. S. Department of Labor.

The largest civil action enacted in the United States came on July 3, 1979. It was the Maine Indian land claims case, the first Indian case since 1892. Two Indians were held responsible for an April 16, 1977 infraction of law, and the question arose as to whether or not the Washington County Superior Court had the jurisdiction to imprison men from an Indian reservation. The County Superior Court pronounced them guilty; the Supreme Judicial Court appealed, saying that the trial judge erred; and there the case was left, without further action to date.

One of Maine's legislative "firsts" was to enact legislation to provide help with winter fuel bills for the needy and the elderly poor. Other states have since followed suit.

Along the same line, Maine was the first state to institute

"Project Independence," a movement to make it possible for older people to live in their own homes as long as they were able, by providing necessary services that the elderly householder could not manage. Transportation was number one; health care, number two; need for information, number three; and recreation, number four.

In 1978, it instigated a new national concept in the Juvenile Code, sending violent or hard-core young law offenders into the regular Superior Court system for trial as adults, and the possibility of a heavy sentence if convicted. Non-criminal cases were sent to either their own families or to social service agencies.

In Farmington, in 1979, the first attempt was made to deliver comprehensive health care to the rural population. It was named the Rural Health Associates. It provides for those who cannot afford physicians, and gives people in rural locations their first regular health care. No other state had such a project at the time.

In addition, Maine was the first state to issue I.D. cards to the blind, realizing the need for such a card to take the place of a driver's license used so frequently to cash checks or use charge accounts. The first person to receive one of the new cards was Natalie Matthews, a food and drink stand operator in the Maine State House. At that time, there were 2,300 legally blind people in the state.

Maine is referred to as the leader in divorce law reform, especially in respect to family law which is in keeping with the social climate.

The largest land acquisition ever involved in the United States was in 1980, when Congress approved an out-of-court settlement of $54.5 million for the two major Maine Indian tribes, Passamaquoddies and Penobscots. This money was used to buy 300,000 acres of land they claimed belonged to them. The Malcite tribe members in Houlton were allotted 5,000 acres and $9,000 out of this settlement. The New Brunswick Malcites are currently making further demands. In addition, a $27,000,000 trust fund was set up to be divided among the Maine tribes. The Penobscots immediately chose to divide their first few million dollars equally among the members of their tribe.

In 1981, the legislature enacted what was considered to be the "toughest, most comprehensive (drunk driving) law in the United States," one which requires mandatory jail terms. It is called OUI (operating under influence). There are present indications that it is influential in reducing accidents and in saving lives.

In March, 1982, Maine was perhaps the first state to establish that the clients of prostitutes would receive the same fine of $500 as levied against prostitutes themselves. This, in an effort to deter the rise of prostitution in the state.

Many other impressive politicians and additional important and/or progressive legislation could have been added; and many historical facts of worth have not been given because of space. However, since the purpose of this book is to show the national and international impact of Maine's "firsts," "lasts," and "onlys," a varied and ample sample has been selected.

6

Education

Longfellow Statue, Portland, stands seven feet high and was erected in 1888.

The *State Of Maine,* training ship of the Maine Maritime Academy, Castine

Frederick Robie Hall, State Normal School, Gorham, now part of the University of Maine complex

Old Rock School House, Bristol

Raymond H. Fogler Library, University of Maine, Orono

In the field of education, the University of Maine is currently the largest postsecondary educational system in the country. Within a five-year period, campuses at Orono, Portland, and Augusta, plus five state colleges, were massed into one big complex. The total number of buildings including all major campuses, in 1980, was 339. This may have excluded an occasional building used for the C. E. D. courses offered throughout the state. Curricula have been diverted to specific needs, and several outreach programs have been instituted.

Payson Hall, at the Portland campus, was named for Payson Smith, not only an educator of renown, but also an assistant in a study used by President Franklin D. Roosevelt to formulate several New Deal programs. Payson wrote humorous articles for educational publications, and once turned down the office of Commissioner of Education, offered by President Coolidge. He was born in Portland, 1873, and died in 1963. He advocated separation of politics and education; was one of Maine's five delegates to the White House Conference on Education in 1955; and taught and lectured at the University of Maine and at Harvard.

The three miles of shelves at the University of Maine at Orono (UMO) Fogler Library contain the nation's only multi-state regional depository for government documents. Every document must be filed permanently for posterity, no matter how insignificant it may seem to be. This depository was established in 1963, soon after Congress authorized the system. The one at Orono serves New Hampshire and Vermont as well as Maine. Selective Canadian material is accepted. There are inter-library loans every week.

The University of Maine, then confined only to Orono, instigated national ROTC near the opening of the fall term, on October 21, 1916.

The first French-Canadian program in the United States was created at the UMO. The William F. Donner Foundation has provided a considerable amount of financial aid since the facility opened in 1967. Among the projects are teacher training in Quebec, provision of material, assistance in public schools, and cultural programs.

In 1969, the university appointed an undergraduate, Stephen T. Hughes, who was then president of the Student Council, to the Board of Trustees, the first student in the country ever named to such a board. He resigned his position in December, 1974, on the grounds that he had been elected as state representative from Auburn, and that he considered holding two important ranks of public trust simultaneously would not enable him to do justice to both.

On January 29, 1975, the reigning trustees sent him a resolution commending him for his conscientious efforts and objective approach to the board's work and its decisions.

The Orono campus has long had the best forestry school in the nation. It is noted nationally for its anthropological museum and extensive folklore archives. In October, 1980, Dr. Harold E. Young, one of the world's leading authorities on forest biomass, was awarded Germany's Burckhardt Medal at the University of Gottingen, the first American to receive the award in its 100-year-old history. Dr. Young was a university graduate in 1937, and is a forest research scientist in the School of Forest Resources, having been on the faculty since 1948.

A History Media Festival, in March, 1975, showed the results of students making history. Two showings were exhibited by the seventeen student-created multi-media and video-taped productions with titles ranging from "The Knight and the Tournament" to "From Maine to California, 1862." The course is considered to be unique because only one student creates and produces each production, rather than employing the customary group participation for each show.

In July, 1976, a first-of-its-kind conference among American and Mideast businessmen was held on the Orono campus. About 200 top business and government officials from Iran and several Arab nations accepted the invitation to meet with approximately 300 American executives.

The university has hosted many other national and international groups. In 1975, for example, the Biennial World Vegetarian Congress, founded in 1908, met for twelve days on the Orono campus, the first time the Congress had ever convened in North America. Previous hosts had been England, India, Holland, and Sweden. Over 1,900 members were in attendance to "study, socialize, eat, and argue." The Maine campus was selected as being the most pollution-free part of the country and having quiet surroundings. More than forty countries were represented. Menus included varying choices in vegetables, nuts, and berries.

Another group, the Blue Knights, a national organization, met in Maine for the first time, at the Orono campus. They are a motorcycle club formed in Brewer, in 1974, with no intention of expanding their membership, which is restricted to law enforcement professionals.

The 1975 meeting, at Squaw Mountain, drew over 300 members from 24 states and Canadian provinces. Maryland had 100 percent attendance. The purpose of the group is to fortify the image of the police, to show that they are considerate, and to confirm the fact that motorcycles can be both pleasurable and safe. One West Coast editor of a tourism magazine drove his cycle 7,800 miles to attend the meeting in Maine.

Bowdoin College, in Brunswick, graduated the first Negro student in the country, in 1826. This graduate was John Brown Russwurm, who was also the first black person in the nation to belong to a literary group, a forerunner of fraternities. He later returned to Liberia and became the first black governor in Cape Palma, an African colony.

In Washington, D. C., Howard University was founded on November 20, 1866, primarily by General Oliver Otis Howard, of Leeds, Maine. It opened its doors to four students. Howard was born in 1830, graduated from Bowdoin at the head of his class in 1850, and died in 1909. Until May 1, 1867, his university was known as the Howard Theological Seminary, and was the first such institute to establish undergraduate, graduate, and professional schools.

The University was once just a two-story frame house on a riverbank; but it currently has the highest percentage of foreign students in any American university, predominantly Negro, as they were the young men for whom Howard intended the education. Oddly, the first four boys to receive diplomas in 1867 were white children of the trustees and faculty. In 1967, one hundred years later, the college had an enrollment of 11,000 and a physical plant valued at over $50,000,000.

Howard served as its third president, 1869–1873. After that, he was superintendent at West Point for a short time before President Grant sent him to negotiate with the Cochise Indians, with whom he became friendly. He was also successful in treaties with Chief Joseph of the Nez Perce. In addition, he once managed the Lincoln Memorial University, in Tennessee, for underprivileged white children.

Originally, Howard had intended to study theology, but the call for volunteers for the Civil War cast aside this intention. He resigned from the regular army to take command of the Third Regiment Infantry from Maine, with its barracks in Augusta. In an 1862 campaign, he was twice wounded in the left arm, which had to be amputated; but he continued to command with distinction. He was a soft-spoken, no-drinking, no-smoking, no-swearing man who organized prayer meetings. Although quite opposite from his counterpart General Sherman, he was highly respected by Sherman, and aided him during the famous march from "Atlanta to the sea."

Bates College, in Lewiston, was the first American college to have a woman valedictorian, a Miss North, in 1869. In 1977, Janna Lambine, an alumna of the class of 1973, became the first woman aviator in the Coast Guard. She was a helicopter pilot. In 1981, it had the top individual debater among college freshmen in the nation, Steven Dolley, of Herman.

Colby College, in Waterville, is the only undergraduate college in the United States to have the authority to grant continuing education credits under the American Medical Association, although it has no graduate school and no medical school.

Oahu College, in the Hawaiian Islands, had a Maine man as its first president.

The Reverend Cyrus Hamlin, of Waterford, a cousin to Hannibal Hamlin, studied for the ministry at Bangor Theological Seminary; continued his studies at Bridgton Academy and at Bowdoin College; became librarian for Professor Henry W. Longfellow; demonstrated the use of the new electrical telegraph to the Sultan of Turkey while on missionary work there; and established a seminary at Bekek, a missionary school, and Roberts College in Constantinople (now Istanbul) in 1863, a college which is still in existence and has several distinguished alumni. Hamlin was its first president.

In addition, he was aided by Admiral Farragut in by-passing red tape in Turkey; and was praised for his "beer bread" and his successful remedy for cholera, by Florence Nightingale, during the Crimean War. He returned to the United States to teach in Bangor Theological Seminary from 1877 to 1880, and later became president of Middlebury College in Vermont for a few years.

His inventions included several useful articles, among which were washing machines, a watch, a rat trap, stove pipes, and a steam engine car which Admiral Robert E. Peary once started inadvertently and which ran wild, wrecking a room.

Born on January 5, 1811, he died in Portland on August 8, 1900, the very night after he had addressed a reunion in the Portland Church where he was ordained sixty-three years before. Called by the Chicago *Tribune* a "typical Yankee," Hamlin revered and appreciated another Yankee, Henry Wadsworth Longfellow.

Westbrook College, in Westbrook, was named for Colonel Thomas Westbrook, a pioneer of importance. The school opened in the 1830s with twenty-seven students, and was the world's first co-educational college. It was originally called a seminary, established as a result of the 1830 convention of the Kennebec Association of Universalists, at Greene. Its charter was signed by the governor in 1831.

At first, it was a boarding school for both sexes, three miles from Portland's downtown section, on Steven's Plains. The one original building still standing is Alumni Hall; and the second to have been built on campus seventeen years later, Goddard Hall, was living quarters for both men and women. It had a solid brick wall from cellar to attic, dividing it in half. Today, Westbrook is a highly respected college.

Brief mention should be made of the tiny College of the Atlantic, which offers only one degree, a Bachelor of Arts in human ecology. Located on Mt. Desert Island, about one hundred eighty students study ecological data. One group even lives on Mt. Desert Rock to study whales in the Gulf of Maine.

Bangor Theological Seminary, one of the foremost such institutions in the nation, owes much to Enoch Pond, 1791–1882. The school opened in 1804 and was one of the earliest theological schools in the country.

The Maine Maritime Academy at Castine had the highest tuition of any maritime school in the country in the 1970s. It recently has admitted many students from oil-producing nations whose tuition, due to their out-of-state status, is $2,000 higher than the normal fee. Leading in enrollment of these countries is Kuwait, followed by Libya and Saudi Arabia. Iran, once prominent on the list, has reduced its number of entrants because of the higher tuition rates. They now attend other maritime academies which have limited enrollment for foreign students.

The first so-called technical institute in the nation was the Gardiner Lyceum, which was the forerunner of present-day agricultural colleges. Founded by Robert Gardiner, it was the first secondary school to employ teachers of agriculture. Moreover, it was the first secondary school to offer electives, to adopt a system of student government, to teach sciences rather than languages, to have an experimental farm, and to receive financial aid from the state.

Incorporated in 1824, it became one of the first schools not sponsored by a religious sect. It opened on January 1, 1823, for "... giving to farmers and mechanics" a scientific education for "... becoming skillful in their profession." Benjamin Hale was the first lecturer. The curriculum had thirteen special courses, plus "... advanced mathematics and natural history."

The Bancroft School in Owls Head was a pioneer in individual instruction for handicapped children who are either emotionally disturbed or retarded. Since January, 1975, the school, which had offered only summer sessions, opened on a year-round basis. Some of its "students" are now in their seventies, people who cannot yet find their place in society.

The Hyde School in Bath is an unique college preparatory school with an unusual educational theory. Its philosophy focuses on character building as being more important than scholastic achievement.

It was established in 1966 under Headmaster Joseph Gauld, and became co-educational in 1971. In 1975, it had thirty-five graduates. The school's theory is being studied by various other schools because of the growing realization that there is a definite need in this country for character building.

It is the only known school now accredited for character development. The belief is that academic excellence will follow. At Hyde School, a student may fail in all of his academic subjects yet be progressed to the next grade, or level, through attitude and acceptance of responsibility. Gauld would like to expand and establish model schools in Texas and other areas of the Midwest.

Another widely-known school in Maine is the Outward Bound School, in Penobscot Bay. It began in the summer of 1964 at a former granite quarry site off the southern tip of Vinalhaven, and was restricted to men until 1971, when the 630-member student body included forty women. Entrants must be at least sixteen and a half years old.

The school offers a series of survival courses with rugged discipline. Icy swims in early morning after a two and a half mile jog, rock climbing, rappelling (descending by rope), rowing, sailing, manning radio distress frequencies, fire fighting, rescue work, survival roping, thirteen-foot wall scaling, and a host of similar requirements make up its curriculum.

The most exciting activity is the "solo survival," which means four days and three nights on an uninhabited, separate island, armed with only a knife, a few matches, a large can for cooking, and minimal clothing. The student must provide his own shelter and food.

This is the only sea-oriented survival center in the United States. All other such schools are for mountains. Surveillance is provided for emergencies by flag displays. Its motto is "To serve; to strive; and not to yield."

In the northern Maine wilderness are 4,000,000 acres known as the Maine-Matagamon Wilderness Base, an area larger than Connecticut and Rhode Island combined. It is available to all Boy Scouts of America, regardless of their home states. Estimated attendance runs at 10,000 boys a year having recourse to the scenic wilderness. The base was established in 1971, and is the first such facility for the High Adventure program of the Boy Scouts of America. It is a nationally-backed Scout base and is part of a chain that will eventually lead from Maine to Alaska, to New Mexico and Colorado.

Facilities at the Wilderness Base include a lodge of ten bedrooms, a first aid station, mail service, storage bins, a map room, and a supply house. All garbage is reduced to basic elements. Fire rings protect the environment. Litter is strictly forbidden.

The base lodge is the former Club Foster Sporting Camp on the edge of the Allagash, on Baxter State Park Road. The philosophy is that each boy pays his own way, thus promoting responsibility and avoiding freeloading. Jake Day, Maine's most famous cartoonist, originated a picture depicting the atmosphere of the camp by the use of animals galore at work and at play, a real appeal to a real boy.

A granite-walled, one-room schoolhouse, called the "Old Rock Schoolhouse," built in 1840, in Georgetown, served until

1912, and is possibly the only "rock" schoolhouse in the nation.

Peleg Wadsworth, 1793–1875, was probably the youngest American history teacher ever known, as he became a public school teacher at age eleven and took great pride and delight in his history course.

During the nation's Bicentennial year, Maine had the only statewide student bicentennial program. It evolved from the efforts of the high school graduates of 1976. Grants as high as $3,000 were given from the $13,000 provided by the Maine American Revolutionary Bicentennial Commission, which initiated the program in 1974. A statewide student film festival was included in the program.

In 1963, a librarian of Rockland Public Library, Mrs. Doris Scarlott, was awarded the Dorothy Canfield Fisher Award because the Rockland library was considered to have done the most for a community of its size throughout the United States. The schools, in particular, benefitted.

The first four-day school week was established in 1971, in Waldo County, Maine. It was originally inaugurated as a move to cut the budget. Other schools later adopted the plan. In 1975, it was voted by School Administrative District #3 to alternate four- and five-day weeks.

Bath was the first municipality in the country to provide free textbooks in its public schools.

Portland may have been the first city to practice integration in the schools. Between 1829 and 1857, the "Colored School" of about eighty students was integrated into the regular school system. Later, however, the decision was that it seemed best to serve the interests of those particular pupils by returning them to their smaller school.

7

Religion

Log Cabin Church, Oquossoc, early 1900s

"Smallest Church in the World," Wiscasset, the Union Church of All Faiths, was built by its pastor, Reverend L.W. West. It is never locked.

Williston Church,
Birthplace of the
Christian Endeavor
Portland, Me.

Williston Church, Portland, birthplace of the Young People's Society of Christian Endeavor

Interior of an old German Church, Waldoboro, 1773

Eldress Prudence Stickney of the Sabbathday Lake Shakers

St. Patrick's Church, Newcastle, the oldest Catholic Church in New England

In the field of religion, one of Maine's favorite attractions is the little Union Church, for all faiths, in Wiscasset. Having only two seats, it is supposedly the smallest public church in the world. It is four and a half feet wide, seven feet long, and has a floor area of thirty-one and a half square feet. A Baptist preacher, the Reverend Louis W. West, once gave Easter Vespers there, asked for a token offering, and got two pennies. Then he began to notice money tucked between the prayers in the Bible, so he provided a letter box for anonymous offerings. West died in 1966, at age sixty-one.

The first religious services in the New World were on Mt. Desert Island, in 1604. The first church in America was at Popham, in 1607, which conducted Episcopal services. The first Jesuit Mission in the New World was established on Penobscot Bay, in 1609. The first Protestant religious society organized in the country was in York, 1631.

In June, 1864, William Screven and Humphrey Churchwood, with a handful of Kittery men, went to Charleston, South Carolina, and planted the seed for all Baptist churches in the South.

The first mission, or monastery, east of California, was in Madison.

The largest Shaker village in the world is at Sabbathday Lake, in New Gloucester. Their technical name is The United Society of Believers in Christ's Second Coming. They organized in Gloucester in 1794 and their ingenuity and inventions constitute a list far too long to enumerate in this chapter.

Among their accomplishments were the first packaging of herbs for sale (and they still have the finest herbs in the country, with a sizable market), invention of the one-horse wagon, horse-drawn mowing machine, flat, brown clothespins, bricks for all the buildings in their village, ladderback chairs, circular saws, rotary harrows, and the first waterproof cloth.

All of these inventions were gladly shared without a thought of patents or copyrights, resulting in ruthless cheating by some firms. However, they did concoct an everwearing paint mixture, for which no ingredients were ever divulged and which Du Pont could not fathom in spite of its intense interest.

It was the Shakers who were the original promoters of Poland Spring water, still sold all over the world. A much longer listing of their achievements and contributions is available in many books.

The Shakers are an off-shoot of the English Quakers, a religious group of the eighteenth century. Although qualifying for tax exemption, as is any religious group, they have never made use of this privilege, declaring that they would prefer to pay for the use of the land and the town's public agencies. In the 1970s, Sister Frances Carr, of the Sabbathday Lake congregation, was the youngest Shaker in the world.

In December, 1978, with only six members at Sabbathday Lake and three at Canterbury, New Hampshire, the only other colony, all agreed not to admit any new members. Nevertheless, in 1981, the Sabbathday Lake Colony had fourteen members.

There was one Protestant church in New Gloucester in the 1770s which had various holes in the floor. These, it was explained, were for ventilation and also to serve as spitoons.

In Waldoboro is an old German church and meeting house, built in 1772 on a hillside. Box pews, balconies running the full length of the sanctuary on both sides, and a raised pulpit surmounted by a canopy which reaches almost to the two-story high ceiling, all present a charming picture. In its burial grounds is the grave of Conrad Heyer, an early settler who helped establish the first place of worship at that location, a combined church and blockhouse, destroyed by Indians in 1734.

Shiloh Temple, placed on the National Register of Historic Places in 1977, was founded by Frank Weston Sanford, born in Bowdoinham, in 1862. He considered himself a styled Elijah, and in time had created a large complex of buildings, known as Shiloh, in Durham, Maine, in a rural setting of several acres. The complex could house 1,000 persons; and he reached that number of followers. In time, he and his converts left Shiloh to sail to many parts of the "heathen" world, spreading their faith. Only the temple still remains of the once-ornate Kingdom, so spectacular that it was mistaken for the state capitol by Charles Lindbergh as he flew over it on his way to Augusta.

The first of the many St. Patrick churches in the United States was at Damariscotta Mills, and it is the oldest Catholic Church between New York and Quebec. Dedicated in 1808, it has the only authentic 345-pound Paul Revere bell owned by a Catholic Church. There are twenty-one of these still existing in Maine, the Damariscotta one having been cast in 1818.

The church is of mellow brick-red, and originally cost $3,000. When it was known as St. Mary's of the Hills, it was a temporary wooden chapel, eighty-feet long and twenty-five feet wide. The dedication of the church was given by a French missionary priest who later became a bishop in Boston, then an archbishop, and finally a cardinal in France: Father Lefebre. It is said that the church contains a more than 200-year-old altar piece from France.

Ellen Gould Harmon White, 1827–1915, of Gorham, was instrumental in organizing the Seventh Day Advent Church. This religious sect eventually went to all corners of the globe. She wrote more than fifty books and 4,500 magazine articles spreading her gospel, aided by her husband, James.

The first radio church in the country was beamed from station WCSH, in Portland. It was established by the Reverend Howard Oliver Hough, who was inaugurated as pastor of the Radio Parish Church of America. Nine different denominations were represented in carrying out non-sectarian pastoral work just as they would have carried out their usual duties in any ordinary parish.

The first permanent Lithuanian Franciscan Monastery in North America is located in Greene. Established on July 22, 1944, the friars were refugees who had left Russia in 1940. A chain of these monasteries has developed from this modest one in Greene, and it stretches all over the United States and into Canada.

At one time, Elizabeth B. Aageson, of Portland, was the oldest Sunday School teacher in the nation. Always in good health until she was 104, she died in 1975, at age 105.

It was in Newfield that two white congregations became the first to be under the pastorate of a Methodist Negro, Joseph Reed Washington, in 1958.

The Young Peoples Society of Christian Endeavor was started on February 2, 1881, by the Reverend Dr. Francis E. Clark at the Williston Church, in Portland. His suggested idea took root and soon became a worldwide organization with nearly 100,000 Christian Endeavor Societies in nearly 100 denominations. It currently has millions of members, bound by the solemn pledge to fulfill their Christian duty, to " . . . endeavor to lead a Christian life." In 1895, the World's Christian Endeavor was formed.

There is little doubt that the controversy of where and when the first Thanksgiving services were held will never be resolved. Maine's claim is that they took place on August 19, 1607, at either Phippsburg or Allen's Island, with George Popham, Raleigh Gilbert, and the colonists participating. It is told that an Episcopal minister lead a group of 100 in prayer of gratitude for their safe arrival to these shores. It is also claimed by some that this observance was a "fast day" for twenty-four years thereafter.

There seems to be less of a contest over the first Christmas services, which are generally accepted as taking place on seven-acre Dochet Island, in 1604. The group consisted of eighty French colonists led by Samuel de Champlain and Sieur de Monts. A quiet religious service was observed, even though one of the gentlemen was a Protestant and all the others were Catholics. A chapel had been built, and the leaders of both denominations took turns inspiring clergymen and colonists alike. Food and water being in short supply, the few survivors of that winter moved to New Brunswick to settle anew. The island, however, ringed with evergreen, was authorized as a part of the National Park System in June, 1949. It is now known as St. Croix Island.

The first ecumenical endeavor in history to later become a unified concept, belongs perhaps to the Papist Father Gabriel Druilletes, of Canada, and Puritan John Winslow, of Cussins Point Trading Post. They worked hand in hand and dwelt in close friendship. Father Gabriel built a mission where the town of Madison now stands. Both men sought betterment for the Indians and eventually produced a "Society for the Propagation of the Gospel in New England."

Finally, a fact which well may be unique to Maine is that of a country church which is divided right down the middle aisle by town lines. The Foreside Community Church once had the Falmouth parishioners sitting on that side of the church, and the Cumberland parishioners sitting on the Cumberland side. Today, the sermon is still preached in Falmouth, the choir still sings in Cumberland, but no doubt the collection plate is passed to both sides.

8

Recreation

The shortest title fight in the country—Cassius Clay (Mohammed Ali) v. Sonny Liston, in Lewiston *(Photo Courtesy of* Lewiston Sun-Journal)

Montreal observation streetcar, now on display at the Seashore Trolley Museum, Kennebunkport

Racing at Old Orchard Beach, early 1900s

John Bower, only American to win the prestigious Holmenkollen World Championship, 1968

"Longest Sled in the World," Naples *(Photo by O.B. Denison, Jr.)*

In the field of recreation, Maine fairs have been a statewide attraction for well over 160 years. The oldest fair in the country was held at Skowhegan, and that fair remains one of the biggest in the state. It began in 1818 and has one of the largest horse shows on the East Coast. In the 1970s, more than $55,000 was given in premiums, and a personnel of over 300 was involved. The 4-H building, known as the "Five Flag Expo," flies flags from the U.S.A., Canada, Maine, Quebec, and New Brunswick; and there is a special observance day for each flag.

One unusual innovation took place about twenty-five years ago when Fryeburg Fair constructed the first covered pulling ring in the country. In 1978, it was extended to a sprawling 112 by 157 foot permanent covering. This makes it the first all-weather ring in the world. Phil Andrews, finance committee member at the time, stated, "We probably have more pulling here at the Fryeburg Fair than does any other place in the world." Eventually, the pulling area will seat more than 1,000 people with provisions to accommodate the handicapped.

The Fryeburg Fair is considered to be the longest continuously-running fair in the nation, and one of the best. In 1981, its 131st year, more than 2,000 animals were on the grounds, and attendance reached an all time high. Future prospects seem encouraging.

Old Orchard Beach provides fun and entertainment for all ages. The rolling surf, the pier, the midway, and the rides all contribute to happy days. The state parks offer the sand and surf, too, but on a much smaller scale.

Near Old Orchard is Kennebunkport, where the most varied

collection of trolley cars in the world sits in the Seashore Trolley Museum. One-mile trolley rides are available to the public. Founded in 1939, it contains the elegant Manchester, New Hampshire, car, which carried charter parties to Pine Island Amusement Park. This car has ornate wicker furniture and genuine mother of pearl push buttons to signal the motorman. Also included in the display is the world-famous Montreal Open-Observation Car #2, with benches arranged in tiers, the only one of its kind in the United States. The oldest car is #38, built at Laconia, New Hampshire, in 1906. It ran between Manchester and Nashua. About 200 volunteers work at the museum, some from as far away as California and even England.

Dover-Foxcraft has an unique museum housing original blacksmith equipment: anvil, bellows, horse-shoeing tools, and ox-lifter. It is located on the Sebec Lake Route.

Robert Shapleigh's Museum, also in Dover-Foxcroft, is believed to be the only steam museum in the world. It has a wide variety of restored steam engines, a rock crusher, a snow roller, a Hyde Windlass Company 1890 engine, an 1898 steam automobile, and the oldest steam engine. This last one is a horizontal engine which once ran an up-and-down sawmill, and is dated November 3, 1804. It was located in Thorndike.

The Matthew Museum, in Union, is possibly the best in the country to display early farming equipment and transportation facilities.

The Boothbay Museum is reported to have the largest collection of railroad cars in the country.

The largest bean pit in the world, which can assure food for at least 3,500 people, is located in South Paris, where the annual Baked Bean Festival is held. The very first attempt to have such an attraction was held in the firehouse. Many more folks came than were expected, and the supply of food was far from adequate. At this point, Mother Nature stepped in and a heavy thunder shower sent many away.

The second attempt, the following year, was a disaster, too. The committee did not parboil the beans and they were served practically raw. This time, 2,000 people left in a hurry.

The third year, John Cox, of North Vassalboro, came to the rescue. He made his living by cooking and canning beans, and pointed out the necessary steps. After that, the yearly attraction was 100% successful.

The entire preparation for the Baked Bean Festival takes

thirty hours. The beans are washed at least three times. The sixteen cast-iron kettles are steam-cleaned and oiled to keep the beans from burning. Then the beans are parboiled, about 1,000 pounds of them, half kidney and half pea, over hardwood fires. Salt pork, spices, and molasses are added, and the kettles are immersed into the brick-lined pit with aluminum foil lining the iron lids. They then are buried under two or three feet of clean sand. The fire in the bean hold is started twenty-four hours in advance, and the cooking takes about twenty-four hours. Only the former year's raw beans may be used, as older ones might be tough after cooking.

The event is now held at the former Oxford County Fairgrounds. The pit is 200 feet long, the longest in the world. Hardwood slabs are fed into the bean holes on the first day. The second day, the beans are lowered into the pit in the afternoon. The third day, the beans remain buried, to be ready to serve on the fourth day.

A crew of twelve is needed for the cooking procedure. Attendants must wear protective special glass visors while hoisting the kettles from and lowering them into the embers. To complete the day, an auction is held, and bands march, and a carnival adds to the festival-like event.

The world's largest chicken barbeque is held annually in Belfast, and is called the "Maine Broiler Festival." The idea started in 1947 and usually has a Navy Band concert, the crowning of the Broiler Queen, parades, contests, square dancing, and fireworks. Belfast is often referred to as the "Broiler Capital of the World."

In Norway, there is a club known to be the only one of its kind in the country. It is the Weary Club, begun in 1922 by Fred Sanborn, editor of the *Advertiser-Democrat*, a local weekly paper. A group of old-timers met in a room in the Noyes Block, and called themselves the Norway Club. It changed its name when Elgin Greenleaf, upon the start of a discussion of a new name, merely yawned. After that yawn, Sanborn said, "The only possible name is 'Weary Club.'"

The Weary Club has stockholders who vote, non-voting members, no secret rituals, no fund-raising, no formal function, no regular meeting dates. The members voted not to install a coffee maker. Too much bother. They just sit, rock, talk, whittle, read, play cribbage with matches, and watch TV.

Each Christmas the club provides a sack of candy for every

child in Norway. Eventually, the members had a small building of their own. The minimum age for membership is 21. They once sent an honorary share of stock to President Coolidge who returned it, saying he could not accept monetary gifts.

In the early days, the club door was never locked; but that is no longer feasible. Women are definitely not eligible for membership, but no one seems to object. It is not a service club, but does contribute to the local hospital and to scholarships. It is a perfect example of lingering in the "old days": a substitute for the old country store with its stove, checkerboard, and barrel seats. No telephone is permitted, and the solution to all world problems is gratis.

The first youth-run Metropolitan summer camp in the nation is said to have been one organized by white and black promoters in Naples, Maine, 1975. About 400 high-school-age poor youngsters of both colors attended three sessions of three weeks each. Everyone was responsible for maintenance and sharing duties. The idea was originated by John Ertha, who ran a similar type of camp for suburban youths. It was called the Metropolitan Leadership Development Camp, and Ertha received no salary for his supervision.

The Camp Fire Girls were founded on March 17, 1912, at the Lake Sebago camps of Mrs. Luther Halsey Gulick. They soon became a national organization. Their watchword was "Wohelo," a derivative from its motto: Work, Health, and Love. Luther Gulick was a pioneer of the youth camp movement in Maine and also co-inventor of basketball, with James Naismith.

Jedidiah Preble, a Brigadier and a businessman of Portland, is the first recorded person to have climbed Mt. Washington, the highest peak in the East.

Maine people have always had an urge to break a record, but possibly the most unique effort was when Portland made a community effort to break certain world marks, the first such community project. On June 28, 1975, attempts were made to break existing records of various nature, especially some included in the Guinness book. Proceeds were to assist the Susan Curtis Foundation and to celebrate the completion of a $9,000,000 renovation of Congress Street in downtown Portland. There were three days of contests, open to individuals ages eight to sixty-two. Some of the records which were broken were

Basketball dribbling, passed the fifty-one hour mark
Lennie Smith clapped his hands for thirty-two hours

Robert Neales yo-yoed for eighty-nine hours
Rocking chair contest passed eighty hours
Portland High School baton twirling for forty-four hours
Portland High School Band played for forty-four consecutive hours
Boy Scout Troop #6 shined 1,094 pairs of shoes in twelve hours.
Art Pinansky told alleged jokes for four and a half hours in Monument Square, without notes, bettering the previous record of three hours

On July 27, 1977, Stan Lemelin and Rick Foss, both twenty-seven, of Lewiston, broke the world's record for most miles on a motorcycle within twenty-four hours. Their 1,142-mile trip cost $13 in tolls and the receipts were used for confirmation. Also in 1977, Norman Albert, of Lewiston, beat the Guinness record for treading water.

Among other Maine record-breakers are: Doug Kienia, of Kittery, who, in 1974, became the World Junior Champion of Horseshoe Pitching; Dean Emeritus Earnest Marriner, of Waterville, former Dean at Colby College, gave his 1,000th broadcast, called "Little Talks on Common Things," in February, 1974. The show set the longest record of consecutive broadcasts and the longest running show under the same sponsor, in America. He had begun in 1948 under the sponsorship of the Keyes Fibre Company of Waterville and was still at the job at age eighty-three. Alan Edwards, a disc jockey in Auburn, set a new marathon broadcasting world's record of 111 hours and eighteen minutes, making him the world champion DJ; and, although challenged twice, in 1975 he still retained the title. Rosemarie Samson, of Auburn, had won 420 trophies by 1975, been acclaimed the ten-year-old world champion in two-baton twirling, had repeatedly held the championship of the Maine Junior Grand Champion Association, and excelled in solo baton twirling, fancy strutting, flag twirling, and hoop twirling.

In addition, there is Perry Kerry, of Portland, a former auto and motorcycle racer and former Air Force karate instructor, who was successful on February 11, 1977, at Scarborough Downs, in driving over the tops of nine cars in his snowmobile, landing with the machine's back down, coming out unscathed, and setting a new world record. Bates College students, in Lewiston, in January, 1980, entered the Guinness Book of World Records with seventy-one continuous hours of volleyball, winning the record by a half

211

hour's time. Reluctant to miss out on their goal of three full days (with just a five-minute break each hour), they yielded to painful legs and feet, and lack of sleep.

Maine has also been a sports-minded state. A few of its outstanding women athletes have won individual honors in their field.

Joan Benoit, in 1979, became the new premiere women's marathon runner of America. She attended Bowdoin College at the time and shattered a record in the twenty-six mile Patriot's Day Boston Marathon. She became world champion in 1983.

Kathy Calo, of York, in 1979, became national champion of women's javelin throwing at the Junior AAU Olympics in Nebraska.

Cornelia "Fly Rod" T. Crosby holds the unique reputation of having shot the last caribou in Maine, at Square Lake, December 10, 1898. She remarked that it was not for the sport of slaughter, but just that if she had not done it, someone else would have.

Cornelia, born in Phillips, in 1854, was Maine's first publicity writer with lavish praise of the state in all her articles, and in 1897 was licensed as Maine's guide #1. She died in 1946 and was buried in Strong. Presumably, in her writing she coined the slogan carried for the past several years on Maine auto license plates: Maine—Vacationland.

Michelle Hallett, of Mars Hill, was called one of America's best high school cross-country runners in 1981. The seventeen-year-old girl was named an All-American cross-country runner by the national runner's magazine *Harrier*. Her goal is the Olympics, having finished third in the national Junior Olympics in Wyoming.

On the lighter side of recreation, youngsters and staff at Camp Samoset, Casco, around 1978, made a 101-yard-long banana split. This delicious dish required 600 bananas and seventy-five gallons of ice cream. It was longer than a football field. One thousand small cardboard containers were stapled together and formed the base for the bananas, ice cream, fifty pounds of strawberries, twenty-five pounds of marshmallow topping, twenty-five pounds of chopped nuts, three gallons of chocolate syrup, and three gallons of cherries. It was a Fourth of July project and was displayed on thirty picnic tables for dessert for the 200 campers and ninety staff members. This creation made the *Guinness Book of World Records*.

In 1895, Hervey Pearl built the longest double-runner bobsled in the world, and named it "Uncle Sam."

This sled was seventy-six feet, ten inches long and could seat seventy-five people comfortably. There was an attachment for thirty-five additional riders if desired. It weighed 1,510 pounds and had a speed, at times, of eighty mph. Pearl would drive it on the main road, which was closed to traffic for such rides. He would lie prone with a man sitting on his legs. The downhill course was one mile, and the sled was towed back to the top of the hill by horses. The sled is believed to be somewhere in the state today, but where?

Chris Hodgkins, of Rockland, was the first girl named to represent the East in the junior national competition in track, for two years in a row, 1974 and 1975. Her speciality was hurdles, although she also excelled in skiing.

Cyndi Meserve, of Livermore Falls, at age eighteen, became the first woman to participate in a men's varsity basketball game. She played forward for Pratt Institute in 1975.

Possibly the first woman in the United States, certainly in New England, to compete in men's varsity intercollegiate athletics, was Ellen Shuman who, in 1972, was admitted to the until-then all-male swimming team at Bowdoin College. In 1976, she surpassed the Bowdoin record in optional diving in men's competition and later won the one-meter diving in the New England Women's Intercollegiate Swimming and Diving Association meet. That same year, she entered a contest with Williams College for the NCAA Championships, the first woman admitted to men's swimming competition.

Ann Turbyne, of Winslow, is generally accepted as the nation's champion woman shot-putter. She broke the national shot put toss at Mt. Ararat High School in June, 1975, and set a state and national record of 51' 101/2" with an eight pound ball on her last attempt. She also won the AAU Senior Title and was rewarded with a trip to Russia. She set a state discus record of 123' 2" in 1975 and in the same year surpassed the world weight-lifting record for women, 410 pounds, on a dead lift. A French contestant had held the previous record of 352 pounds.

Maine has many male athletes who have won individual distinction in their fields, or have contributed to American sports.

Sandy Koufax, a former southpaw from Ellsworth played for the Brooklyn Dodgers and retired from major league baseball at age thirty-six, becoming the youngest such retiree. He had 382 strike-outs in one season, thirty-one of them in only two consecutive games. He pitched a perfect game against Chicago in September, 1965, and pitched four no-hit games in his career, which no other pitcher had ever done. He was the second Maine resident to be enrolled in baseball's Hall of Fame at Cooperstown, New York, receiving 344 of the 396 votes cast. He moved permanently to Maine in 1972.

He was preceded in the Hall of Fame by another Brooklyn Dodger from Maine, John W. Coombs, of Freeport.

Maine seems to have been jinxed by unusual circumstances in two main boxing events for titles. The first one was Al Couture's first-round KO of Ralph Walton, in Lewiston, September 29, 1946. It happened only ten and a half seconds into the fight. It is clear that Al must have been more than half way across the ring when the bell rang, to have caught Walton in so short a time, probably as the latter was adjusting his gum guard. At that time, it was listed as the shortest fight in the world.

John B. Gagnon, of Augusta, was considered the strongest man in the world in the 1930s, and he held the world title for weightlifting. Standing five feet ten inches, weighing 230 pounds, he could lift a total of 16,650 pounds.

George F. "Piano Legs" Gore, 1852–1933, started the practice of holding out for higher salaries in major league baseball by his demands in 1878.

Steve Halasz, of Kennebunkport, was, in 1974, the first high school football player to have a hearing aid fashioned within his helmet. Born with a forty percent hearing loss, he had previously played by watching the coach's lips, but rarely heard the ref's whistle, which resulted in several penalties. Stanley W. Wilner, a Portland audiologist, fashioned the hearing device. Steve had read that Larry Brown of the Washington Redskins had been successfully fitted for playing football, the only such accommodation in the country at that time.

Jack McAuliffe, 1866–1937, a Bangor boxer, was the U. S. amateur featherweight title holder in 1885. At age twenty, he won the U. S. lightweight title over Bill Frazier, of Eastport, who was twenty-four; and he inherited the world lightweight crown when England's Arthur Chamber retired. McAuliffe retired in 1896, undefeated. A spectacular fight in 1887 with Jem Carney, of England, went seventy-four rounds before spectators stormed into the ring.

George Murray, of Millinocket, at age thirty-three, left Los Angeles in a wheelchair on April 10, 1981, to cross the country, in observance of the 1981 International Year of Disabled Persons.

214

He became the first person to complete such a trip when he reached New York in August. He and his travel companion were given a major reception at the United Nations before heading for Murray's home, which he reached on September 19. He commented that he had no plans for future long trips. His average mileage was forty miles a day.

Paralyzed from the waist down since age fourteen, he had trained intensively. His competition has been in national games for wheelchair victims: shot put, discus, archery, basketball, weight lifting, and speed racing. In 1978, he won the Boston Marathon, competing with the runners. He has also won the Schlitz Light Marathon, the Orange Bowl Marathon, and the Gasparilla. In addition, he has set new records in the mile, the 1,500 meters, and the 10,000 meters. In January, 1981, he was appointed national consumer representative of the Easter Seal Crusade and also won the World Wheelchair Marathon.

As a Boy Scout, he helped raise the sunrise flag at Mt. Katahdin following the admission to statehood of both Alaska and Hawaii.

Frederick Alfred Parent, 1876–1972, was influential in getting the Red Sox to sign on George "Babe" Ruth, one of baseball's "greatest,"—past, present, and perhaps future. Parent was a charter member of the Maine Baseball Hall of Fame, in 1969, because of his achievements in the major leagues.

Louis Francis Sockalexis, 1873–1913, of Old Town, was the first native American Indian to play major league baseball. He played outfield with the Cleveland Nationals.

"Del" Bissonette, 1899–1972, of Winthrop, was another major league baseball player with exceptionally high batting averages.

Another Lewiston-based boxing confrontation took place on May 25, 1965, between professionals Muhammad Ali (Cassius Clay) and Sonny Liston. The fight began with a "goof" on the part of actor-singer Robert Goulet, who has yet to live down the fact that midway in singing the national anthem to open the fight, he forgot some of the words. The fight terminated in a most bizarre first-round KO by Ali before all of the 2,434 fans had even taken their seats. This was the smallest recorded attendance at any world heavyweight fight, and assuredly the most frustrating one to many who paid admission. One word describes the contest: *confusion.*

One minute and twelve seconds after the starting bell sounded, Ali shot an overhand right over Liston's extended left, and floored and confused Liston for an instant. Ali did not go to a neutral corner before the count started, thinking that Liston would get up. The referee thought so too, and did not begin to count, but instead waved Ali to his corner, and then began counting. If one may believe the news reports, he counted "at least up to twelve," expecting Liston to arise at any moment.

The timekeeper, flustered by the unexpected commotion in the ring, was not sure of the count, did not sound the bell at the end of the count by the referee, and finally, in all the confusion, a press man, with no legal right, shouted "The fight is over. Liston is out. Ali wins." One could say that in this contest Ali retained the heavyweight crown by popular consent rather than by legal announcement. This is surely a "first" in the world. And it happened in Maine.

On June 26, 1982, sixteen-year-old Joseph "Joey" Gamache, Jr., of Lewiston, became the United States Junior Olympic light-weight boxing champion.

As for outstanding Maine teams in sports, an incredible victory in ice hockey came to the Maine Mariners Club, of Portland, in 1978. At the end of an eight-month season, this new team, with a new franchise, in a new arena in Portland where professional hockey had never before been played, won the coveted Calder Cup, the equivalent to the famed Stanley Cup. Among their victims were hockey teams from Russia, Nova Scotia, New Haven, Rochester, Philadelphia, and other cities.

The Mariners became the only team ever to win the Calder Cup in the first year of their existence, a win that they repeated later during their first four years.

In 1978, the University of Maine baseball team won the prestigious Riverside National Intercollegiate Baseball Tournament in California. They were the first team from the East to win in the history of the tournament; in fact, they were the first Eastern team even to make the finals.

In 1981, the Maine Junior Boys basketball team defeated the Michigan team 68–66 in the final game of the Taiwan Youth Invitational Basketball Tournament, involving nine different states. The Maine team was the only unbeaten one.

The Maine girls' team was the only one which defeated the winning Taiwan girls' squad. Women's basketball is not only more popular in Taiwan than men's, but even superior. Girls' teams often complete an undefeated season.

The state of Maine has offered training facilities for various activities. Two lakes in the Augusta area have been hosts to national events, too. Lake Maranacook became known as an ideal place for oarsmen from all over the nation to train for single sculling. Contests were often held on the lake, the best sculling waters in the country. Lake Cobbosseecontee has the oldest yacht club in the nation, and in 1967 hosted the United States Flying Tern fleet.

The old Rigby Track was once a national favorite for horsemen who shipped their harness racers there from all over the country. The track had a firm, springy consistency which was considered about the best in the United States at the turn of the century.

When pony harness racing started officially, around 1950, the United States Pony Trotting Association was initially incorporated in Maine. The ponies had to qualify for the USPTA, have a height of under forty-six inches, draw a two wheel sulky, and have the driver's age between thirteen and sixty-seven. It is a much more informal and family-like affair than regulation horse racing. Area judges have been known to permit twelve-year-olds to participate if they were considered qualified in all other respects.

The Oxford Plains 250-race, in Oxford, is the richest short-track stock car race in the United States. The 1981 winner took home $20,000.

The Maine International Bicycle Race, 105 miles long, from the Canadian border at Jackman into the heart of Waterville, equals the world's toughest course for bike riding. It is hilly and twisting, and is sanctioned by the Amateur Bicycle League of America.

Golf is very popular in Maine, and the first course in the country was a roughed-out four or five holes in Skowhegan, prepared by a group of Scottish weavers. The Poland Spring course was the first modern-day course in America. It was laid out by the resort owner, in 1894.

At no point in Maine is anyone farther than thirty miles from a golf course, there being nearly 100 courses within the state, all considered among the best in the nation. Maine also publishes a booklet called "Golf in Maine," an unique publication. It has been published consecutively since 1974, and lists locations, facilities, tournaments, and other relevant data. Sandra Palmer, once the leading money winner in women's golf, started her career by playing on Maine courses. President Taft used to play at the Kebo Golf Club, at Bar Harbor, where, on one occasion, he used twenty-six strokes on the seventeenth hole.

The Portland Country Club course, in Falmouth, is acknowledged to be one of the most sightly and well-kept courses in the nation, and was said to be worth a half a million dollars in the 1960s.

Adjacent to the Waterville Country Club course are fifty acres of pine trees. It became the first golf club in America to have membership in the paper industry Tree Farm Program.

Quite possibly the highest number of honors in one sport that have come to Maine people are those won in skiing. Leon Akers, of Andover, was the first dealer on the East Coast to import Nordic Ski equipment from Finland. Only the best in the world is now used by serious Maine ski competitors.

Maine's outstanding slope is the Sugarloaf Mountain Ski Slope, which, in 1971, hosted both the World Cup ski races and the Arlberg-Kandahar Race, which for its forty-four years had never before been held outside of Europe. The Narrow Gauge Trail was used, 11,100 feet long with a vertical drop of 2,600 feet. In 1975, the first French ski team tour of the United States included Sugarloaf as forty skiers came directly there for a six-day skiing vacation. Several members of the French press accompanied them. The tour was promoted by a Paris travel service and it was arranged that the group spend some time at Sugarloaf each week for the fourteen week ski season.

For years, American skiers had been taking winter vacations at Chamonix, France; but 1975 was the first year of the reverse order. The French chose Sugarloaf because it provides some of the best skiing conditions in the country. It has the only gondola in Maine, a 9,000-foot, four-passenger lift. And in March, 1981, the thirteenth Annual World Heavyweight Ski Championship was held at Sugarloaf, where many competitors weighed in at over 400 pounds. Minimum weight for entry is 250 pounds, and the entry fee of three cents per pound is donated to charity.

An honor was awarded the slope in 1981 when it was chosen to host the Peugeot Grand Prix races.

John Bower, of Auburn, is still the only American to win an International Nordic Combined World Championship. He surprised the world in 1968 when he won in a field of the best Nordic Combined skiers and took the coveted King's Cup at the Holmenkollen Festival in Oslo, then a seventy-year-old competition. In doing so, he defeated the newly crowned Olympic champion.

Bower was on the Olympic teams in 1964 and 1968, and on

the U. S. Nordic F. I. S. teams in 1962 and 1968. In 1968, the U.S. Ski Writers' Association voted him the racer who had made the greatest contribution to the sport of skiing. In 1969, a forty-year-old requirement for admission was waived to admit twenty-eight-year-old John to the National Ski Hall of Fame. He then turned to coaching; and Bill Koch, who won a medal at the Winter Olympics of 1975, was one of his pupils.

John Bower was born in Auburn, in 1941; was a guest of President Johnson at the White House when a state dinner was given for Norway King Olave; and was named "Coach of the Year" for his Middlebury College teams which twice won the Eastern titles and finished at the top in five NCAA meets in the Eastern Intercollegiate Ski Association in 1971. He later left his Middlebury coaching to become the Nordic Program Administrator of the U. S. National Team, in 1975. Along the way, he collected several medals and honors. His wife was a successful coach of women's ski teams.

Thomas Upham, of Auburn, deserves mention, as he and Bower have won about every Nordic Combined distinction available in U. S. competition.

Nel Jodrey, also of Auburn, was distinctive for turning out four-event wins; and for being among the three young Auburn men by whom the Junior National Nordic Combined Championship was won for three consecutive years.

A fourth Auburn resident, Thomas Kendall, was the only competitor from the East to classify for the Senior A in four events on the Nordic Team U. S. A. competition in February, 1968.

Karen Colburn, of Bangor, won the Girls' National Free-style Ski Championship at Killington, Vermont, in 1975, when she was only eighteeen. This event, begun in 1966, consisted of compulsory forms of basic turns, snowplows, stem christies, parallel christies, and short swings, for the first half; and free style, two runs, for the second half, to demonstrate speed and control. Later, complete free style took over: mogul run, aerials, and ballet.

Karen is the daughter of a Bangor man and an Eskimo mother. She had skied since she was four, and won the Maine State Championship five times. Once she had such strong competition that her win was by only three fourths of a point. She later joined Professional Freestyle Associates.

Another Maine skier, Wendall "Chummy" Broomhall, of Rumford, was inducted into the National Ski Hall of Fame in February, 1981. He was Maine's cross country champion before

World War II, having begun the sport in the 1930s. In 1948, he was on the U. S. Olympic Team at St. Moritz, Switzerland; and in 1950 was to compete in the World Ski Championship at Lake Placid. However, there was a lack of snow at the lake, so he arranged to have the event transferred to Rumford, an unexpected thrill for Maine enthusiasts. He won several citations and championships in skiing.

Among other outstanding winners in skiing have been Kris Hodgkins, winner in 1974–75 of the Northeast Alpine Racing Association, with Jill Marshall, of Maine, coming in second place; Gail Blackburn, a National Downhill Champion of the U. S. "B" team; Karl Anderson, of Greene, top American finisher in six World Cup downhills during 1974–75; Leslie Bancroft, of Oxford, who established excellent results in Europe in 1979, including fifteenth in the World Cup 5K at Newkirch, West Germany, and third place in the National Championships 10K; and Dan Simoneau, of Livermore Falls, who tied for first place in 1980 in the Over-all Dannon Race Series and placed ninth at the Gitchie Games in the 15K. Cindy Nelson, of the U. S. Ski Team, at twenty-six, has won a bronze medal from the 1976 Olympics, six national titles, five World Cup Races, and Three World Cup medals.

There will surely be more Olympic ski champions whom Maine will give to the world as the sport becomes more popular each year.

9

Potpourri

Cribstone Bridge, Bailey Island to Orr's Island, constructed of granite cribstones
through which the tides rush

Graves of the commanders of the English *Boxer* and
the American *Enterprise,* killed during the War of
1812, Eastern Cemetery, Portland

The first balloon to cross the Atlantic
Ocean took off from Presque Isle, 1978.

Old Jail, York, 1653

The only octagonal post office in the U.S., Liberty, 1867

The toll to cross the Tupenny Footbridge, connecting Waterville to Winslow, was, in 1901, two pennies.

This final chapter will present some of the remaining superlatives and unique data which are part of Maine's heritage. As in the case of the other chapters, more could be written. It has been difficult to be selective throughout the book. However, there should be sufficient variety in all chapters to indicate the width, breadth, and depth of Maine's contribution to the nation and to the world, omitting with very few exceptions Maine's leadership in regional attainment.

People

The largest Indian burial grounds in the United States are on Sebago Lake, North Windham.

The first Indians taken to England were kidnapped by Captain Weymouth at Allen's Island, 1605.

The first land bought from the American Indians was by the British at Pemaquid.

Maine is the only state where Indians have representatives in the state legislature.

The *Wabanaki Alliance*, the only regularly-published Indian affairs newspaper in the East, was recently given a grant by an England-based trust to insure continuance.

The Indian Metallak laid out the route for the Atlantic and St. Lawrence railroad, later known as the Grand Trunk Line.

Although in this century, almost all of the presidents have visited Maine, the first one was George Washington, who spent October 15 to November 13, 1787, in Kittery.

225

Josephine Peary, wife of Rear Admiral Peary, was the first woman to be on a polar expedition. The group of Peary, his wife, four Eskimos, and a Negro left on June 6, 1891; but did not reach their destination because of travel complications. However, this voyage did prove one misconception: that Greenland was a land mass reaching to the Pole.

Peary reached the North Pole in 1909, the first man to do so. He was then fifty-three, a man who had wearied of his civil engineer work in Central America and had decided to explore. On September 6, 1909, he presumably wrote a postcard to his wife saying "I have the Pole." Upon hearing this, President Taft is supposed to have said, "Now that you have it, what are you going to do with it?" Other sources say that the message was "I have won out at last."

His final voyage was on the *Roosevelt*, which he had had built in Bucksport, expressly for him, by Maine laborers. The launching of this ship was so easily done that she continued across the Penobscot River and ran astern right into the bank on the opposite side, a position from which a tug had to free her.

Eagle Island, Peary's home, is now a Maine historical site.

His daughter, Marie Peary Stafford, always disliked being called "the Snow Baby," yet that is exactly what she was, being the first white child born so far north. Marie became an authority on the Arctic, authored several books, lectured, and was awarded the Order of Liberation by King Christian of Denmark, besides receiving many honorary college degrees.

According to most authorities, no other human being has walked to and from the Pole from his ship, as did Peary. The U.S. atomic submarine *Nautilus* crossed under the Pole; the *Skate* surfaced forty miles from it around 1958; and airplanes have circled it. Yet, only Peary has actually occupied it.

Donald Baxter MacMillan was the "Dean of Explorers" to many authorities. The Freeport man was the first Arctic explorer to use radio and airplanes, and the first to advance the idea that the Arctic glacier fields are slowly moving southward. He was also the first to compile an Eskimo-English dictionary, done primarily through his affection for the race. He was the last American member of Peary's 1909 expedition to die.

Dr. Mary Floyd Cushman was appointed by Governor Brewster to the Board of Medical Examiners, the first woman to hold that distinction in the United States. She attended Castine Normal School and later studied medicine in Boston. After that, she practiced in Castine and Farmington. In 1922, she was appointed for foreign missions, went to Chilesso, Angola, Portugal, and West Africa; founded modern hospitals and clinics; and retired in 1941. After that, she wrote a book about her foreign service; toured the country telling of her work; and finally insisted on going back to Chilesso, where she remained until 1953.

The first woman in the United States to become president of a board of realtors was Mary L. Cavanagh, of Lewiston. In 1949, she was named realtor of the year by the Lewiston-Auburn board.

By Mattawamkeag Lake, a marker was placed in 1921 to indicate the spot where Teddy Roosevelt, as a youth, used to go to read his Bible.

In 1919, Gail Laughlin, of Portland, was the first national president of the National Federation of Business and Professional Womens's Clubs, Inc., a unique organization with state federations and local clubs all over the world. Miss Laughlin was at one time a Cumberland County trial judge.

On Treat's Island in Parmachenee Lake, a marker was placed in 1970 to indicate where President Dwight D. Eisenhower raised his first Maine brook trout and landlocked salmon, in June, 1955.

John Hay Whitney, of Ellsworth, used to hunt with Eisenhower. Whitney was a man of great versatility: a newspaper publisher, a movie producer, a financier of such great movies as *Gone with the Wind*, a diplomat, an international polo player, a United States Air Force captain, an outstanding player of golf and bridge, and was listed as one of the wealthiest men in the country.

In 1947, Grace E. Fitz, of Auburn, completed her eighth survey of Maine women in public office. This was a task that no other state in the Union had undertaken at that time. Her surveys, the first of the kind in the country, won national attention and were the basis of several prize-winning news stories.

Joy C. Coon, of Millinocket, was the first woman in the world to graduate in an apprenticeship training course in paper making. She received her training at the Great Northern Paper Company, in Millinocket, and graduated in 1981.

It is claimed that the first women firefighters were in Gorham. They submitted an application in 1973 and were voted on by the entire department. Their restrictions were that they might not climb ladders, enter burning houses, or drive the fire trucks. Accepting these restrictions, Paula Ward and Rowena Murray were accepted. By 1981, there were seven or eight other women on the force.

John Darling, a ne'er-do-well hermit of Harpswell, instead of being jailed, was marooned on Pond Island some years ago. It was rocky; had no trees; yet he lived there for twenty years and grew his food, finally succumbing to the cold and freezing one night. This must have been a unique case of court authority.

Navy Capt. Sherwin J. Sleeper, of Owls Head, is responsible for keeping the nation's official clocks accurate. He is in charge of the 200 civilian technicians who tend all the apparatus required for the precise date.

The first Irish Community in the United States was at Pemaquid when Col. David Dunbar, commissioned to build a fort there in 1770, induced several of his countrymen to join him.

Mrs. Carolyn Brooks, as commander of the Mundt-Allen post, and her daughter, Jerri Brooks, as president of the auxiliary, were the first mother-daughter combination in the nation to hold these offices simultaneously.

In 1971, Wesley W. Ridon, of Portland, was named the nation's number one policeman. He was a veteran of fourteen years on the force and was not at all the hero type. He was a man who had worked silently to help the image of the police officer and to bring about better understanding between police and community.

The first woman to be president of a national bank was Mrs. Frances Estelle Mason Moulton, who assumed the position vacated by the death of her father, president of the Limerick National Bank.

Major General J. Edward Marks, of Thomaston, was the country's longest term state police officer when he retired. He first patrolled on horseback and then on motorcycle in his early days on the force. He died in 1980.

Garrell S. Mullaney, age twenty-seven, is believed to have been the youngest state prison warden in the nation. He took over the Maine State Prison in Thomaston in 1972 with a force of 120 guards and 370 felons to be rehabilitated.

The 1976 Miss America, Tawny Elaine Godin, was a Portland-born girl and a Maine summer resident.

Buckminster Fuller, a part-time resident of Maine, once had the longest entry in *Who's Who in America*: 139 lines.

Mrs. Alto A. Mottram, of Auburn, was appointed as court reporter in 1917, at age eighteen, the youngest female stenographer in the United States to hold such an office. Her trademark was the pencils protruding from her pugged, black hair. Whenever a lead wore down, she would automatically reach up, pull out a pencil, and keep on working without the loss of a second.

James A. Healy, of Portland, who died in New York in 1975, was a stock exchange member who, in the 1920s, handled the largest recorded single volume of orders within one hour—160,000 shares of U. S. Common Steel.

In June, 1981, the Lewiston-Auburn Jaycees won "every major award given away on a state basis" by the United Jaycees at their Convention in San Antonio, Texas. It was proclaimed the number one state Jaycee organization in the nation.

Places

Auburn is the fourth largest city, area-wise, in the nation, although its population, around 24,000, is smaller than that of the other three.

Bangor was named accidentally in a most unusual manner. Known in 1783 as Sunnyside Village, it wanted to be incorporated. The Reverend Seth L. Noble, chaplain in Washington's Army, owned a large tract of land on the banks of the Penobscot River, and was appointed to secure an incorporation charter. Being of a restless nature, he began to whistle an old hymn tune while the clerk was filling out the form. The clerk, waiting to put down a name, inquired, "Please, sir, may I inquire the name?"

Noble impatiently snapped back, "Bangor!" thinking that the clerk meant the name of the tune.

And so it was that the town became officially chartered as Bangor, the title of the hymn, because a man was whistling.

Calais, Maine, and St. Stephen, New Brunswick, Canada, share a unique relationship. The phrase "Hands across the border" could never be more aptly demonstrated than the fact that the two towns have joint water, gas, and fire departments, joint hospitals and medical clinics, and celebrate each other's national holidays.

Pemaquid had the first stone pavement in the country, in 1625, consisting of stones, rocks, and cobblestones.

Portland, on July 4, 1866, had the most disastrous fire in the United States up to that time. The poet Longfellow commented, "Desolation! Desolation! It reminds me of Pompeii."

Block after block burned flat. The town was literally wiped out. The cause? A youngster, around 4:30 P.M., may have thrown a fire cracker among shavings at a boat builder's shop. Or, less generally accepted, it might have been caused by sparks from a railroad engine. Whichever, the fire was still burning violently at 8:00 P.M.—that night? No. Not that night. At 8:00 P.M. the *NEXT* night! Lost were nearly 2,000 buildings, among them eight churches, seven hotels (one being John M. Wood's unfinished marble one, which could not withstand the intense heat), the City Hall, all seven banks in the city, every law office, and seven newspaper offices.

The fire path was one third of a mile east to west, and over one mile north to south. Two hundred acres were charred. A visiting circus loaned its animals and wagons to move furniture. Ten thousand of Portland's 13,000 inhabitants were made homeless. Many buried their valuables in the ground, hoping to find them later. Kegs of nails fused into a solid mass. Iron melted like lead. Yet, oddly, only two lives were lost: a mother and son by the last name of Chickering. In the jail block at City Hall, a forgotten drunkard slept through it all, safe and sound.

South Paris opened the first federally-funded elderly housing complex in the country, early in 1977, and named it Elderberry Hill. It had a ten-unit development on High Street and was subsidized under the federal leased housing program. There were three separate buildings adjacent to shopping facilities. Over 100 people applied.

Warren had the oldest canal system in the nation, the George's River Canal, built in 1793 and 1794. It was taken over by General Knox to transport lumber from the ocean to Seven-Tree Pond, in Union. There were two canals around the dams. Rebuilt in 1846, river navigation extended to Quantabacook Pond, above Searsmont. Some remains of the Old Powder Mill Locks are still visible.

Wilton, with a population of only 4,200 by 1977, had the first alternate energy-powered waste water treatment plant in the world, using solar and methane.

York was not only the first chartered town in the country, but also the first summer resort, as the Indians used to come there for a sort of playground long before the locale became a royal colony in 1641.

The two towns of Camden and Union had the first novel ideas of street decorating. Camden erected double flower pots on each light post, planted geraniums and petunias, using real moss to retain the moisture, and watered them three times a week all summer. It became known as "The town with the lamp-post flower

230

pots." The idea came from Cary Bok, son of the distinguished author Edward Bok, a Camden resident; and the Camden Garden Club has continued the idea. Union went Camden one better by having bird houses on each pole during the summer; and in the winter, before the energy crisis, had lighted Christmas trees on each pole.

No other state has as many towns named for foreign countries and cities. As a partial list, Maine has: Athens, Belfast, Belgrade, China, Denmark, Lisbon, Lucerne, Madrid, Mexico, Moscow, Naples, Norway, Paris, Peru, Poland, Rome, Sweden, Vienna, and Wales. It also has names unique to Maine alone, three of which are: Kennebunk, Skowhegan, and Wytopitlock.

Buildings

The first fur-trading post in the country was at Augusta, 1628. Trade was carried on with Norridgewock Indians. Some of the furs were kept for wearing apparel. Most of the pelts were sent to England.

The first known tavern "on the principle of no liquors" was in Winthrop, 1838. Many taverns advertised the slogan, but no other one enforced it. This national "first" may stem from the fact that the owner of the Winthrop tavern was a devout churchman, Deacon Daniel Carr.

The oldest existing English public building in either North or South America is the old gaol at York. The building is now a museum. Built in 1653, it was known as "the King's Prison," and many early colonists who spoke out against the king were thrown into its dungeons.

The Portland Observatory is the only nineteenth century signal tower left on the East Coast. Rising on the highest point of land in the city, the eighty-two foot tower is a landmark. Built in 1807, it was a traditional place for wives and families to watch and pray for incoming vessels which might bring loved ones.

Captain Moody, who spearheaded the construction of the observatory, could identify a vessel twenty miles off shore by use of a powerful French telescope.

Portland Head Light was the first lighthouse to be commissioned by President Washington, and it is the only one to have been in continuous service in the nation since then. One of the most famous historic landmarks on the Atlantic Coast, it is said

231

to be the most photographed lighthouse in the nation. Its appearance on the 1981 eighteen cent U. S. postage stamp marked the fifth time Maine had been depicted on U. S. stamps.

History recounts that an Edgecomb farmer-sailor, Captain Clough, once of Boothbay, was the last man expected to respect and sympathize with the royal family of France. He was described as a "hard-shelled, hard-bitten, straight-laced Maine Yank." Nevertheless, while in France he learned of the danger to the life of Marie Antoinette, and decided to smuggle her aboard his ship and bring her to Wiscasset, with his wife's approval, of course.

Although under espionage, he did manage to get some of her elaborate and valuable furnishings aboard his ship before he heard of the murder of the Queen. He then left France in a hurry. Being sentimental, he never cashed in the objects that he had secured, but put them in what might have become the Maine home of Marie Antoinette of France. The house is now privately owned.

It was this same Captain Clough who presumably brought to Maine and to the nation the first "coon cat," from the Orient. The species is broad-chested, shaggy-coated, bushy-tailed, and heavy. It has large, round paws. No other state is known to have had a special and distinctive breed of cats. In 1981, one kitten sold for $150. Restrictions, required of every buyer, are exceedingly strict.

The Bangor House, last of the so-called "Palace Hotels" in the United States, was built in 1843, when Bangor was a lumbering town. It eventually hosted many distinguished guests, from Daniel Webster in 1835 to Walter R. Shaw, former Premier of Prince Edward Island, in recent years. A fifth story was added around the turn of the century. The hotel is now on the National Register of Historic Places.

In 1903, the Mt. Kineo Hotel, on Moosehead Lake, was proclaimed to be the largest inland water hotel in the United States. Its design was very elaborate. In 1930, additions and renovations brought it the compliment of "the most famous fresh-water resort on the continent," and it acquired the affectionate title of a "small kingdom of content." As auto travel increased, hotel registration decreased; and the main building was razed in 1938.

For some unknown reason, only in Maine did homes have hinged doorsteps.

The nation's last Grange Store, founded in 1874 at North Jay, closed its doors in 1976. Gone are the cracker and molasses barrels, the round "rat" cheese, and the rubber boots. There are no longer spools of string hanging from the ceiling for tying packages. Old time advertisements are missing from the walls. Reduced prices, brought in by supermarkets, claimed the demise of the century-plus old store, now officially registered in the National Registry of Historic Places. At first, sales were restricted to Grange members, but later its doors opened to the public. A few cooperative Grange stores still exist in the Midwest, but only the North Jay store was ever a public convenience. During its final years, the health department capped the pickle and cracker barrels, rudely eliminating those familiar "free samples."

In 1972, a branch bank was established at Maine's largest psychiatric hospital, in Augusta. This was the first U. S. branch bank located within a mental institution compound. The superintendent said that most of the 900 patients were capable of handling their financial affairs, and that a bank would help them return to their outside environment when they were discharged.

In 1874, Portland boasted of having the best public houses and hotels in America, and even in the world, especially as many of the buildings had an elevator and "a bathroom on every prinicipal floor."

Castine once had a unique facade on its post office. Patriotism was the theme, and four large panels depicted Franklin, Washington, Baron Castine, and General Grant. Flanking the main door were panels bearing the Federal eagle and coat of arms of Baron Castine. Other panels were in formal design of scrimshaw patterns brought to America on whales' teeth, some the work of Castine sailors. The original brick building was erected in 1814, with an outer coating of sanded cement. The cement chipped, and wood sheathing was put on. Then the panels were installed, made by Kimball Devereux, who had patented a process called "kpotography," an ornamental process of chiseling and gilding. Progress being what it was in the 1970s, the lovely structure was doomed to oblivion in favor of a more modern edifice and additional parking space.

Another noted Maine post office was at Liberty, the only octagonal post office in the country. Built originally for a harness shop, in 1867, it was discontinued in 1961 when a new post office was erected across the street. However, the old octagonal building was purchased by Dr. and Mrs. Alfred Hurwitz in 1972 and, with the help of townspeople, the exterior was renovated. On June 19, 1973, it was entered upon the National Register of Historic Places. On May 10, 1974, the Liberty Historical Society received an award from America the Beautiful for "helping to protect the beauty of our nation." The old building contains photographs of parades, people, picnics, and places of interest as they appeared in the early 1900s, plus a few relics and historical objects.

But its most significant recognition came in October, 1974, when a special committee of the U. S. Postal Service approved issuance of a special bicentennial stamp commemorating the octagonal post office, from a painting done by a summer resident, Dr. Dorothea Vann.

Transportation

The first balloon to make a successful flight across the Atlantic Ocean took off from Presque Isle in August, 1978, with three Albuquerque men aboard.

An airport on Seal Island, the Hancock County Airport, in Trenton, is just about the smallest of its kind in the nation. It was the country's first small-size airport to receive a sophisticated approach lighting system.

It was granted by the Federal Aviation Administration, and used by Vice-President Nelson Rockefeller to reach his summer home on the island.

Called "A String of Pearls" by a poet, and a "gangplank more than a highway" by a more prosaic writer, Maine has the only cribstone, or cob work, bridge in the world. It connects two islands, Orr's and Bailey. No mortar and no cement were used. It is constructed of huge twelve-foot granite blocks from the Pownal Quarry, laid in honeycomb arrangement and held in place by gravity alone. Through the openings, the tides are free to rise and ebb without damage to the structure.

The cob bridge, built in 1927, was opened to traffic on Labor Day, 1928, and was fashioned after one at the Firth of Forth, in Scotland, which the Luftwaffe destroyed with bombs during World War II. It has but two narrow lanes for one fifth of a mile, with a curve in the center. A fifty-two foot elevation, midway across, allows small craft to go underneath. Not far from the Bailey Island end is the last point of land on the entire Eastern shore until one reaches Spain. The point is appropriately called "Land's End."

A second bridge of distinction is the last wire footbridge in the nation. Begun around 1838, it was opened to the public on

June 20, 1842, and was still serviceable in the 1980s. It spans the Carrabasset River, in New Portland, and may be used if one does not object to a sensation of rolling. There is a house-like structure at each end to protect the cables, guy lines, and fastenings. The bridge floor is composed of 100 cedar cross-ties and 100 upright steel wire stays fastened to the ties. It has been called the "Fool Bridge" of retired army engineer Col. F. B. Morse. The suspension cable came from England, by schooner, to Bath; then to Hallowell, up the Kennebec River; then, to its destination by sixteen yoke of oxen with special rigs; and finally reached the building site on the seventh day of its trip across the state. There is no record of any serious accident connected with the bridge.

A third bridge of notable consideration in Maine is the only known toll footbridge in the nation. This bridge was built by the Ticonic Footbridge Company in 1903, in Waterville, and has a one-room house midway across, where the toll keeper lived and collected at first two cents toll each way, thus it was named the "Two Penny Bridge." It is a cable suspension bridge, spanning the Kennebec River, and is now an historical landmark. Hundreds of workers at the local mills once used it daily from Winslow to Waterville.

Since 1935, the bridge has been referred to solely as the Ticonic Bridge, and the price was raised to a five cent toll soon after. When toll keeper, Leon Crowell, died in the 1970s, after eleven years of service, he was receiving eighty dollars per month plus house costs. Advertisements for his replacement brought in an unbelievable number of applications, one letter coming by special delivery, and others from as far south as Maryland and Virginia.

A fourth noteworthy bridge, is the Waldo-Hancock Bridge across the Penobscot River. This bridge has long been considered one of the most beautiful ones in the country.

A famous sight on the island of Curaçao, in the Dutch Antilles, off the north coast of Venezuela, is a floating bridge built in 1888 by Captain Leonard Burlington Smith, of Mill Creek, South Orrington. The bridge was replaced by a second floating one in 1939. Captain Smith also built a public water supply container and an electrical generating system for the island.

Another type of bridge built by Maine hands was the first pile bridge constructed in America, at York, in 1761. Thirteen bands of piles hammered upright, ends above the water, supported a 270-foot wooden structure. Designed and constructed by Major Samuel Sewall, this multi-span roadway was a feat extraordinaire at the time.

Before leaving the topic of bridges, mention should be made of the international one which connects the United States with Canada, at Campobello. It was dedicated in 1967 and offers an easy access to the Franklin D. Roosevelt summer home and the wide area of picnic facilities. A trailer site operates about two miles away for tourist accommodations.

One unique method of travel between Maine and Canada was the first-in-the-country dogsled mail service, which left Lewiston on December 20, 1928, led by Alden William Pulsifer, a Minot postmaster. It arrived in Montreal on January 14, 1929, an eight-foot mushing sled with six black-headed Eskimo dogs pulling it. The team averaged nine miles per hour and covered forty to sixty miles a day unless it encountered bare ground, where it made only seven miles per hour. The mail pouch had 385 letters in government-stamped, cancelled envelopes even though it was not an official trip. The sled returned to Lewiston on February 2, passing through four states and provinces and 118 cities. Total mileage was 600 miles.

Cecil "Mush" Moore, of Danville, set a record dogsled journey from Fairbanks, Alaska, to Lewiston. He started in November, 1950, and arrived in April, 1951. His six months on the trail covered 2,300 miles. Actually, he never used the word *mush* to start his team. He would shout, "Hike!" He died in 1968, at age fifty-nine.

Sherwood and Merrill Megquier, of Glenburn, near Bangor, are two of the few sled-dog racers in the country. Sherwood has raced in Alaska, Canada, and the Midwest.

PAS, which stands for "Passing Air System," indicating unnecessary speed passing on hills and curves, was experimented on a fifteen-mile stretch of Route #2, between Newport and Palmyra. This was the first attempt in the nation to give a highway test for speeding over hills and around curves. The system produced different colored lights for safety prognosis. The colors green, yellow, and red indicated safe or unsafe passing ahead.

This arrangement developed into the "Maine Facility," a more complicated device and the only one of its kind in the country. Promoted by the Federal Highway Administration, it is the first micro-electronic system that may, one day, beam signals to drivers as to speed and passing awareness. The computerized mechanism was established on Route #2, west of Newport, for experimentation. The flashing lights, which warn the driver that he is above legal speed or about to encounter a school zone or pedestrian crossing, were not too well received by the hurrying drivers, who "just won't slow down." Its future remains uncertain.

From Limestone, Maine, Military Base, David Carl Schilling took off in the first jet trans-Atlantic non-stop flight East to West.

The Fryeburg Horse Railroad was the last of its kind in the United States. It began as a means of transportation from the railway station to the Chautauqua Grounds, about three miles away. It stopped at practically any point along the route, and the driver would even assist a passenger with baggage to the extent of taking the time to carry it into a house and thence into any room designated, even the attic, as is known to have happened on at least one occasion. In cold weather, the driver had a cab arranged so that he could drive the horses by reins protruding through slots. He used a peekhole for sighting the road. In summer, the conductor often dragged a brush behind the car to clear the tracks of debris, stones, or other impedimenta.

Bemis once had the only railway station built of logs. It served the Rangeley Region and was a popular gathering place for the Bemis population to watch incoming and outgoing trains, and possibly catch a shipment of liquor being unloaded.

In 1953, Mrs. Doris Rosen, of Bangor, was the first woman in the United States to be appointed as superintendent of dining cars on any railroad.

Finally, where but in Maine would a seven-year-old boy leave his home (at Nubble Light) by a breeches buoy which transported him to the mainland where he boarded a bus for school. This was true in 1967 of Rickie, son of Coast Guardsman David Winchester, the lighthouse keeper.

Miscellaneous

The first international telephone conversation may well have been one on July 1, 1887, when service was opened by the National Bell Telephone Company of the state of Maine, between Calais, Maine, and St. Stephen, New Brunswick, two towns separated by the St. Croix River, which constitutes the boundary line.

The first trans-oceanic television program was sent from Andover, on July 10, 1962, thus making the mechanism the oldest space station in the world. Known as COMSTAT (Communication

Satellite Corporation), the station was built by the American Telephone and Telegraph Company for experimental purposes; and it readily relayed that first full-time commercial communication via satellite between North America and Europe.

Much could be and has been written about this intriguing and powerful construction handling international communications. Briefly stated, the giant radome, the huge white "bubble" with the "big ear" within it, and its large horn antenna, are 177 feet long. The horn antenna is protected by a dacron polyester and synthetic rubber radome, which is transparent to radio energy. The immense ball is held up by air pressure. Perfect pictures were received from the Brittany peninsula of France and from Goonhilly Downs, England, on its first transmission.

Known as Telstar, the first picture beamed to Europe was, appropriately, that of Frederick Kappel, Chairman of the American Telephone and Telegraph Company, preceded by a picture of the American flag flying in front of the bubble. This station is of great importance to the nation and the world; and although it now is a part of a worldwide system of satellite communications, the Andover Telstar handles the only international ones.

The largest nuclear power plant in the nation is in Wiscasset, and it holds the world record of continuous use with only minor breakdowns.

Maine is the first state in the Union to have the Coast Guard be able to call three different hospitals and talk directly to the doctors in Portland for treatment needed in emergencies before the ship could reach shore.

The Auburn-Lewiston Municipal Airport lists two "firsts" in the nation: it was the first municipal airport to install a wood stove in the terminal building; and second, it employed Suzanne Lindahl as the first female station manager of a major United States airline. An interesting sideline is that the wood fuel is cut from the airport's own surrounding property.

A special Maine study in 1977 was the first such study and report ever undertaken in the United States. It was to pinpoint some seventy communities in the state which had a need for a local physician. As a result, the National Health Service promised financial aid through federally-paid doctors.

The Maine Army National Guard won first place in 1979 among the fifty-three states and territories that make up the total Guard, based on their composite performance profile for the first six months of that year.

Since "burning dumps" became prohibited in 1979, Rockland found a novel solution. The city perfumes the dump each Friday, the day when the crews push back the refuse. Gallons of a sweet-smelling chemical are used. Costly—but efficient.

In the Jackson Laboratory on Mt. Desert is the world's unique collection of scientific volumes. It was started with a collection provided by the research staff in 1929. Many journals and books came from the laboratory's founder, Dr. Clarence Cook Little. In the raging inferno that covered the state of Maine in the drought of 1947, the library was destroyed, along with much of the island and the genetics laboratory.

An appeal around the world brought more than 20,000 research-paper reprints and hundreds of donated books and journals; and a special room was allocated for the library in the renovated laboratory. In 1950, the institution made its first large purchase and added 3,000 volumes. In 1975, the library served the needs of the thirty-four scientists of the world's largest center of mammalian genetics research, plus the more than seventy visiting investigators and students who conduct research work there every year.

The collection now boasts of having over 16,000 volumes, worth more than $500,000, in addition to over 42,000 different research-paper reprints, a priceless rarity in modern libraries. There is little use of an inter-library loan system, so adequate is the Jackson Laboratory's own library—a rare situation.

The lab raises about seventy-five different inbred strains of mice, plus some hybrid strains. It also stocks about 200 mutant mice strains, most of which cannot be obtained anywhere else in the world.

In 1888, the first European postcards were delivered to and distributed from the Portland wharves, from the Grand Trunk Station, and other Maine outlets, such as the newsboys on the trains. Around the turn of the century, the Hugh C. Leighton Company and the George W. Morris Company produced the first American-manufactured colored postcards. The factories were located in what is now the "Old Port Exchange" section of Portland.

The Olde Grist Mill in Kennebunkport is believed to be the only tidewater gristmill in the country. It once served as a refuge from hostile Indians; and from 1749 to 1937, without interruption, it provided the area with ground corn. The mill was converted into a restaurant in 1940, retaining the original works in the lobby. In keeping with its primal use, the menu offers john-nycake and baked Indian pudding as specialties. The mill is advertised as "Maine's Most Unique Eating Place."

The first women's club in America was the Female Charitable Society of Wiscasset. It met on November 18, 1805, with thirty ladies present. Seventy-eight dollars was subscribed; and Madame Wood, the country's first woman novelist, was elected president.

The first Women's Literary Union in the world was organized in 1889, in Portland, by Eunice Nichols Frye, later known as the "Mother of the Maine Federation." She was born in Vassalboro on January 8, 1852, and died in 1923. During the Civil War, groups of women would get together to knit and sew. After the war, they met in smaller groups of social and cultural nature. Ten of these clubs formed the first WLU to stimulate intellectual and cultural life among its members and to promote the spirit of co-operation within the community.

Maine was the first state to fly the fifty-star flag after the admission of Alaska, on July 4, 1960. This was before flags might be flown overnight; and since daylight comes first to Maine, the flags are raised earliest in the day.

On May 22, 1816, the Portland *Eastern Argus* announced that one might see the "only elephant in America" at a tavern in Portland from May 29 to June 4. It is commonly asserted that this was the first step taken in the later popular traveling circuses throughout America.

The first cows to arrive in America landed in 1634 on the shores of Salmon Falls River, that section later referred to as "Cow Cove." They came on the *Pied Cow* which brought the first sawmill to this country.

A possible record is that established by a blue-tick hound dog of Wesley, Maine. It is credited with tracking down over 250 bobcats within a twelve year period. Its owner, Ash Peasley, believes that this record will endure as the number of cat hunters has so greatly increased that the catch per man will diminish.

In 1981, two gray horses, owned by Dick Wallingford, of West Forks, pulled 22,000 pounds over a dry clay surface for a distance of sixty-six and a half inches, thus breaking the world's record for dry surface pulling. Another horse, owned by Bill Kelly, of Gardiner, pulled the same record-breaking weight, but not quite as far.

In 1968, the largest industrial drum in the world was installed at the International Paper Company in Maine.

The largest small loan firm in the nation at one time was the Beneficial Finance Corporation, in Maine.

The largest Franco-American benevolent and fraternal organization in the United States is in Lewiston, with a membership exceeding 10,000.

Maine's comprehensive real estate license examination is reputedly the most difficult one of its kind in America.

Quite possibly the oldest public cemetery in the country is Eastern Cemetery at the foot of Munjoy Hill, Portland. Two graves are those of the captains of the brigs U.S.S. *Enterprise* and the H.M.S. *Boxer*. The captains of both ships were killed off Portland Head Light during the War of 1812. The first four mayors of Portland are also buried there, as is Major Samuel Moody, whose death occurred in 1729. Many other civic and military leaders of early America rest in Eastern Cemetery.

The highest cribwork dam in the world, completed in September, 1926, was located at Rocky Brook, which flows out of Upper and Lower McNally Ponds on T 11 R 10 in Washington County. Some of its framework was still visible in the 1980s.

When the TV tower was erected in Raymond for station WGAN, it was the tallest man-made structure in the world.

In 1977, Leslie Dudley, of Bridgton, actually used the "smallest law office in the world" for his small claims cases. The seven-by-ten foot building, off Route #302, was well filled when Dudley, his portable typewriter, and a small chair were within it.

Squaw Mountain Inn, in the 1930s, had the most unusual cocktail lounge in the country, and was termed "fit for a king." It was built around a solid granite rock formation where evergreens were planted to resemble a forest. A fountain, a pool, and Maine scenes on mural decorations heightened the effect.

The only waste water treatment plant in the nation, one which is designed to take care of tannery, cannery, and domestic wastes, is in South Paris. It has won two awards of excellence from professional engineers.

Portland is the only city in the nation that has a municipal organ, the Kotzschmar Memorial Organ, sponsored for concerts by the municipality. It weighs fifty tons, has 6,518 pipes, and was donated by Cyrus Curtis in 1912.

It seems strange to mention a burial for a window, yet a large, circular, stained-glass window was buried in the basement of a demolished church, covered with board, and the hole filled with dirt. It had been contributed by four children of Daniel and Jan

M. Ferguson, of Alfred. When the church was razed, on September 29, 1932, the widow of one of the four children originally involved, suggested the idea of the burial.

Witches in Maine were not an uncommon belief. The best known legend is that of Col. Jonathan Buck, an official executioner and the founder of Bucksport. The story might be called "The Case of the Missing Leg." Although rarely found on islands, one Maine witch was assumed to be on Burnt Island. Men were not generally accused of witchery, but the city of Bangor had one such entry. All in all, Maine witches were not destructive; but according to all legends, they could be enormously annoying!

The last remaining hand-cranked magneto phones in the country are in Bryant Pond, population under 1,000. In 1980, the family-owned operation was filmed for a "Real People" TV segment for NBC. The sixty-three-year-old president of the company and the owner, Elden Hathaway, had as assistants Genneth Berryment and Althea Hathaway, an eighteen-year veteran in the service. The company has about 400 customers and 200 lines, with a complete staff of ten full or part-time operators. They connect lines, oblige with a recipe now and then, or give trivia information. In addition, they ring in the fire alarm. In 1981, the company was sold to the Oxford County Telephone Company, and the retention of hand-cranked phones was temporarily threatened.

The honorary harbormaster at Rockport is certainly unique. His name is Andre and he is a seal. He has shrewd, humorous eyes; roguish whiskers which give him the air of an "old salt;" is friendly; and is the epitome of "hams" when it comes to performing for his close friend and trainer, Harry Goodridge. Andre is actually one of the family, even mounting the steps to enter his keeper's home.

Andre was fourteen years old in 1974 and won national concern and publicity when he went AWOL from his Rockport quarters and was found in Boston Harbor, entertaining and amusing bystanders. An aquarian operator once said that Andre could not live because of various ailments: flu, bites, chaffs, and, above all, a tapeworm. But a devoted veterinarian cured each ailment one by one, and Andre was soon his clever self.

He played a part in the movie film *Man Looks to the Sea,* and performs daily throughout the summer in Rockport Harbor. He spent winters in the Boston Aquarium until the last of the 1970s, at first swimming both ways by himself, arriving after varying lengths of time. While en route, most eyes between Boston and

Rockport were on watch to report that he had safely reached this or that point of his trip. Later, he has been flown down, but returns by himself come spring.

Recently, because of new governmental regulations and other restrictions, he was allowed to go free all winter but dutifully returned to his cage and his trainer in the spring. However, during the winter of 1980–81, he came into disfavor for overturning small boats when he leapt into them for a nap, or else bothered the fishermen by being too friendly. The outcome was that Andre spent the winter of 1981–82 in the Mystic Marine Life Aquarium, in Mystic, Connecticut, a 400-mile swim for his return to Maine in the spring.

Andre had a moment of distinction in October, 1980, when he acted as ring-bearer at the wedding of his trainer's daughter, Toni Goodridge Lermond. He dove, upon cue, and brought up from the depths a small purse containing the wedding rings. His approval of the affair was indicated by a "joyful slapping of the flippers" plus "a third helping of fish." Andre is loved by all who have any heart for animals, and is one of the most distinguished citizens of Maine at the present time. Many a tear will fall when Andre goes to Davy Jones' Locker.

Most regretfully, many interesting and talented Maine people had to be omitted from this book, and many a Maine invention or worthwhile national or international contribution has had to be set aside. Each town has its share of past or present greatness. Each will undoubtedly continue to produce such personalities as "The Stebbins Boys of Bucksport Point," so highly popular in radio during the 1930s; or places like the Jed Prouty Tavern, 1798, which hosted such figures as Presidents Jackson, Harrison, and Van Buren, and still served the public in 1969.

So, too, do all of the counties of Maine provide material of national and international import. As an example, consider Washington County, the "Sunrise County."

1. It is the most northeastern county in the country.
2. It has the nation's leading blueberry output.
3. It has the reversing falls which break violently toward the land when the tide comes in and toward the sea when it ebbs.
4. It has, at Perry, a red granite marker indicating the 45th parallel of latitude, halfway mark between the equator and the North Pole.

5. It has a series of twelve three-foot-high red granite milestones between Robbinston and Calais, erected by Squire James Pike, to clock his pacing horse. The markers are completely accurate although the course was laid out when Lincoln was elected president.
6. Its St. Croix Island is believed to have been the site of the first Christmas spent by white men in the country, 1604.
7. It has the most easterly point of land in the United States.
8. It has the most easterly city in the nation.
9. It has the Moosehorn National Wildlife Refuge of 22,565 acres of woods, fields, streams, ponds, fresh and salt water, and over 190 bird species as well as plentiful fish life.

In conclusion, Maine lives in the past, Maine depends upon the past, and Maine glorifies its past. Yet, in this "Sunrise State," the beginning of each new day is very apt to bring forth another useful invention, another cultural prize-winner, another unique event or attraction, another "first," "best," or "only" that could be of interest or benefit to the nation and/or the world. It is this ever-present possibility, evidenced from its infancy, that warrants a salute to Maine.